Commitment to Excellence

Transforming Teaching and Teacher Education in Inner-City and Urban Settings

THEMES OF URBAN AND INNER-CITY EDUCATION
Series Editors:
Fred Yeo, Southeast Missouri State University
Barry Kanpol, St. Joseph's University

Charting New Terrains of Chicana(o)/Latina(o) Education
Carlos Tejeda, Corinne Martínez, and Zeus Leonardo (eds.)

Commitment to Excellence:
Transforming Teaching and Teacher Education in Inner-City and Urban Settings
Linda A. Catelli and Ann C. Diver-Stamnes (eds.)

Teacher Education and Urban Education:
The Move from the Traditional to the Pragmatic
Barry Kanpol (ed.)

forthcoming

Essays on Urban Education:
Critical Consciousness, Collaboration and the Self
Chapman University Social Justice Consortium

The Politics of Inclusion:
Preparing Education Majors for Urban Realities
Barry Kanpol

Commitment to Excellence

Transforming Teaching and Teacher Education in Inner-City and Urban Settings

Edited by
Linda A. Catelli
Dowling College

Ann C. Diver-Stamnes
Humboldt State University

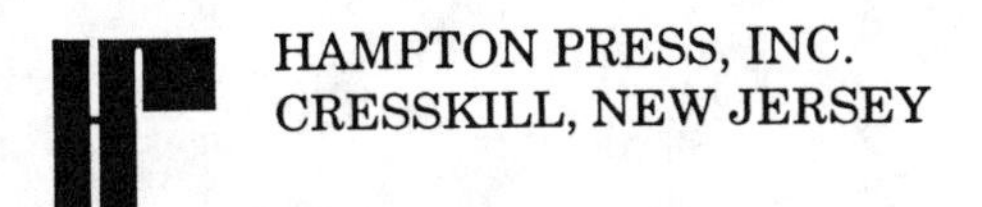
HAMPTON PRESS, INC.
CRESSKILL, NEW JERSEY

Printed in the United States of America

Library of Congress Cataloging-in-Publication Data

Commitment to excellence : transforming teaching and teacher education in inner-city and urban settings/ edited by Linda A. Catelli, Ann C. Diver-Stamnes.

p. cm. -- (Themes of urban and inner-city education)

Includes bibliographical references and index.

ISBN 1-57273-405-1 (c : alk. paper) -- ISBN 1-57273-406-X (p : alk paper)

1. Education, Urban--United States. 2. Teachers--Training of--United States. I. Catelli, Linda Anne. II. Diver-Stamnes, Ann C. III. Series.

LC5131 .C59 2002

370'.91732--dc21 2001059408

Hampton Press, Inc.
23 Broadway
Cresskill, NJ 07626

Contents

PART II: THE PRESENT–A NEW ERA

PART III: THE FUTURE–A JOURNEY OF IDEAS, INSIGHTS, AND MODELS

Introduction

Linda A. Catelli
Ann C. Diver-Stamnes

This book represents a working commitment by individuals and institutions to improve the education of urban children and adolescents and to radically transform the preparation of those individuals who will teach in either inner-city or urban school settings in the United States. The authors are educators and researchers in school and college/university programs in New York City and surrounding areas, as well as one from California. Their experiences range from years devoted to improving urban and inner-city education to extensive involvement in the complexities of the lives of inner-city and urban children and their teachers. What connects the authors is their sense of purpose and commitment to obtain a greater and deeper understanding of teaching and to propose actions that will significantly direct teaching and learning in the next two decades.

During times of dramatic systemic change, collaboration, and partnerships in education, many educators are struggling to draw from the past that which is relevant and to operate in the present in new and meaningful ways in the belief that these efforts will make a difference for those who will live most of their lives in the 21st century. This is a time of significant transformation of institutions of higher learning and teacher education programs. States and their boards are aggressively revising teacher certification regulations to ensure the public of excellence. Failing schools are being restructured, and programs in teacher education that are either underperforming or stagnant are at risk of disappearing. Education degree programs that are not meeting the new market requirements are being replaced with programs based on new concepts, such as digital degree programs that often have delivery systems housed in technologically transformed institutions of higher education.

It is within this context that educators and researchers are attempting to explore teaching and learning from diverse perspectives in order to provide their constituents with deeper meaning and understanding. This is a time in which phrases and ideas such as transformative learning, constructivism, strategic alliances, best practices, standards-based learning, learning organizations, and entrepreneurial universities are prevalent in speeches and writings by educational leaders. It is a time of transition in which schools of education as organizational entities are critiquing their own past histories and planning assertively for their futures.

As we assess current trends in education and begin to examine more closely this generation of urban youngsters and the individuals who will teach them, we note that both groups appear to have different operating assumptions than those held by past generations. They may indeed have different expectations and beliefs about their lives. Although we can see that new methods and conceptual frameworks are necessary to accommodate these changes, we also believe that it is important to assess past practices for the wisdom they may contain. Thus, the theme of past, present, and future continues to run through our analysis and leads us to the major questions we have posed as the premise for this book. What has worked in the past in urban and inner-city education, and why were these methods effective? What is currently being constructed to solve problems and to meet new challenges? What insights and visions will guide us to a meaningful future?

The book is arranged in three parts and organized around the aforementioned theme of the past, present, and future. The authors of Part I present longitudinal projects or shorter endeavors that have been successful in the past in educating youngsters and teachers in either inner-city or urban schools and communities. Their work represents models that may be replicated in other urban settings. Drawing upon their years of experience, the authors of the chapters contained in Part I go beyond a simple description of what they do by including discussions of the successes and pitfalls they have experienced. They provide the reader with lessons learned while examining what is needed during a period of transition and renewal in American education. Their projects collectively contribute to a research base for urban as well as inner-city teaching and learning.

Part II includes writings that represent the present, a somewhat new era in teacher education, and includes works written by educators and administrators from two colleges in New York: Dowling College and Lehman College. Each institution is reconceptualizing its education programs for preparing individuals interested in teaching in inner-city or urban school settings.

The first set of authors, who wrote chapters 5 through 8, are faculty members of the Department of Elementary Education in the School of Education at Dowling College, a private institution located on Long Island 50 miles from New York City. The faculty's linkage to teaching and learning in the inner city has come about as a result of an interesting series of events explained in the first chapter, written by the former dean of the School of Education and her associates. The authors focus on critical and current topics affecting teaching and learning in urban/inner-city school settings, such as teaching standards-based science education in urban classrooms, understanding and developing mathematical thinking in urban children, and developing competence for teaching cultural diversity through literature and social studies in elementary education. They use their years of teaching experience to transform the content of their chapters into usable field modules and instructional classroom learning experiences for preparing individuals to teach. The authors speak directly to teacher educators, teachers, and preservice teacher candidates who seek to excel in teaching in urban and inner-city schools. What is unique about this endeavor is that faculty members within the same department have cooperated to write these chapters which then are serving as a catalyst for initiating change in their own teacher education program. This kind of creative collaboration seems quite timely and appropriate.

Chapters 9, 10, and 11 in Part II were written by members of the Early Childhood and Elementary Education Department and Secondary Education Department from Lehman College of the City University of New York. The authors present works that capture a new era in education at the City University of New York (CUNY). Their writings represent newer paradigms of both public education and teacher education for urban and inner-city schools. Chapter 9 focuses on research on literacy instruction with young children ages 3 to 8 and on children's literacy experiences at home and the impact of these experiences on their success in the classroom. A longitudinal study of three Dominican children is briefly presented as well as a number of developmentally appropriate instructional practices. Chapter 10 goes further in depth in examining best practices in second-language learners in urban settings.

An analysis of student profiles, related research, and selected approaches to teaching are presented by the author. The author's intent is to illuminate what teachers should know and be able to do to facilitate academic success for second-language learners. Chapter 11 is a case study of a first-year urban teacher who attempted to implement a holistic, child-centered theory of teaching and learning in a highly bureaucratic inner-city school. The author captures the essence of the experience and provides insights for understanding a beginning teacher's struggle to implement a theory of child-centered practice in a setting that is characterized by standardization, curriculum-centered methodologies, and bureaucratic procedures. Together the works by these three authors provide selected research and knowledge for educating preservice and inservice teachers in other urban settings.

Part III includes two authors whose chapters serve to clarify current and future issues in urban and inner-city education and suggest ways of creating brighter futures for teaching and learning in inner-city and urban schools.

This book is designed to contribute to the literature on teaching and learning and to influence teacher educators, preservice and inservice teachers, researchers, and project directors of the new schools and centers of education. In their commitment to excellence and desire to reconceptualize professional education, the authors of the book have formed an alliance to provide others with a blend of practical, empirical, and theoretical information for transforming teaching and teacher education in the inner cities and urban centers of the United States in the 21st century. It represents a blend of idealism and practicality for improving the education of inner-city and urban youngsters by transforming the preparation of the people who will ultimately teach them.

PART I

The Past—When a Look Back Is a Step Forward

One

Walton/Lehman Pre-Teaching Academy: A Model for Growing Your Own Teachers for Urban Settings

Anne L. Rothstein
Phyllis Opochinsky
Linda Roemer Whetzel

INTRODUCTION AND OVERVIEW OF THE PROGRAM

The Walton High School/Lehman College Pre-Teaching Academy, located in the Bronx, New York, is a longitudinal partnership started in 1984 that focuses on introducing high school and middle school students to teaching as a career option. The Pre-Teaching Academy and its program, still operating today, encompass grades 7-12 with students electing to enter the program as an educational option. The partnership is a collaboration between and among the Bronx High school district, Bronx Community School District 10, and Lehman College of the City University of New York (CUNY). The connections among these institutions have, over the past decade, promoted careers in education and recruited students into teaching careers. There have been over 600 student-interns in the Pre-Teaching Academy program since 1984: 95% of them have graduated within four years and have enrolled in post-secondary education. Of the approximately 400 students that have completed college (about 200 are still enrolled), almost 25% are currently in teaching careers. Half of these individuals are teaching in New York City schools, some in hard-to-place schools and districts. The Walton/Lehman Pre-Teaching Academy's program has been identified by the Recruiting New Teachers, Inc. (RNT) as a model program, and it has been validated by the New York State Education Department.

Students in the Academy earn between six and twelve college credits by successfully completing both required and elective courses offered onsite at Lehman College (e.g. Introduction to Education, Speech, English Composition, Introduction to Computers, Math, etc.). The Introduction to Education course, taken by all interns, uses a 400 page pre-teaching manual written by student interns, mentor teachers, and Lehman College faculty. In addition, all qualified Academy graduates are guaranteed admission into Lehman College. Student progress is assessed in part through the journal that all students must maintain, as well as grades, teaching evaluations, and questionnaires completed by the student interns and their mentors. Entries are collected regularly by the project coordinator, who reads all journals, and excerpts are then featured, with permission, in the Academy's bimonthly newsletter, *ChalkTalk*. Students must also complete four semesters of a teaching internship experience in which they assume greater classroom responsibilities each year.

At the time the program was initiated in 1984, partners were concerned about the high rate of academic failure among African American and Latino youth, especially in poor urban communities. In New York City, where over 80% of public school students were members of minority groups, less than 50% of high school students graduated from high school in four years. We wanted the Pre-Teaching Academy to provide students with the knowledge, confidence, and skills they need to succeed academically, both in high school and in college. Also at the time, we were most concerned that almost 90% of all teachers in the United States were European American; and that in the Bronx—where over 90% of elementary and secondary students were children from African American, Latino, or Asian families—only 12% of their teachers were from these ethnic groups. Currently, it is 15%, but it is projected that this discrepancy will increase in the next decade as our largest cities become majority-minority. We know that today over 22% of the teachers in Bronx schools are not fully licensed, many teaching in bilingual classrooms. Thus, the program was created and continues to exist to meet the high need in New York City and New York State for qualified teachers, especially teachers from diverse racial/ethnic backgrounds. It is hoped then that by "growing" our own teachers we can ameliorate the discrepancies and alleviate current problems.

This chapter describes in detail a model venture started in the Bronx in 1984 to rectify a serious problem facing New York City and other inner cities: the preparation of a corps of qualified and effective minority teachers to teach students in inner-city settings. It is the authors' intent in writing this chapter to have project directors, school and college administrators, faculty leaders, and grant writers use the information presented as a guide and springboard for growing their own teachers for urban settings. The Walton/Lehman Pre-Teaching Academy is one of the longest running, inner-city partnership projects in the country with the best track record in terms of student success and grant funding. We are delighted to share the information with others.

HISTORY AND DEVELOPMENT OF THE PROGRAM

The Walton/Lehman Pre-Teaching Academy, initially a collaboration between Lehman College and Walton High School, was created to fill the anticipated need for well-qualified and prepared teachers for urban settings. As stated previously, at the time the Academy was conceptualized in 1984, the percentage of teachers who were members of minority groups was less than 12%, with over 90% of the school-age population in the Bronx members of minority groups. Also, education was, and still is, the number one employer in the Bronx. Thus, we were—and are—preparing youngsters whose families had high rates of unemployment (many single parent families on welfare) for jobs and careers needed in their own communities.

The goal of the program is to give qualified minority teenagers first-hand experience with teaching, provide them with the support and training necessary for success as both students and teachers, and motivate them to enter the teaching profession.

The Walton/Lehman Pre-Teaching Academy Program truly belongs to the Walton High School teachers and pre-teaching interns who have shaped the program since its inception. Initially, representatives of Lehman College (Dean and Associate Dean of Education) and the Bronx High School Superintendent discussed the concept of career-themed high schools in the Bronx to be developed in collaboration with the college. It was reasoned that because education and allied health were the two primary employers in the Bronx, these were the themes that should be initially developed. The two schools selected were Walton High School for education and DeWitt Clinton High School for allied health. Both schools were within walking distance of Lehman College and so were ideal partners for these ventures. In the case of Walton, the deans, superintendent, principal, and assistant principals who were members of the school cabinet met to discuss the concept. It was agreed that the theme would be presented at a full meeting of the school and that teachers and staff would be given the opportunity to ask questions and voice their opinions.

At the time of program conceptualization, teacher morale in New York City was at an all-time low. Thus, it is not surprising that the staff and teachers declined to support the creation of a High School for Teaching, but rather supported the notion of a Pre-Teaching Academy that would model the other academies at the high school, such as business and performing arts.

A small group of teachers, school administrators, and college representatives met with representatives from the New York City Board of Education over a period of several weeks to plan for the design and implementation of what has become the Walton/Lehman Pre-Teaching Academy. During the first year of operation, teachers, college representatives, and pre-teaching interns met at Saturday workshops that addressed issues of teaching and learning and formulated the content for the initial pre-teaching manual as well as the operational structure for the program. The position of pre-teaching coordinator was established.

Changes to the program over time have been gradual and as needed to strengthen the program. They have been initiated either by the college or high school personnel. Recent plans have been in response to the changing climate for funding of pre-college teacher recruitment and preservice teacher programs. Many past changes have taken place in response to support by external funding, but some activities have been institutionalized. For example, the college-level course, Introduction to Education, was initiated with funding from the New York Alliance for Public Education but has continued with funding from other grants and support by the College. Summer internships for pre-teaching juniors were initiated in conjunction with funding for mathematics and science programs for elementary and middle school students and the National College Athletic Association's Summer Youth Sports Program. While students were on campus for their summer internship, they completed a college course in the afternoon. The program of college courses for high school students has been institutionalized through the College and the City University of New York via funding for College Now which provides for testing of high school juniors and developmental or college credit courses based on test scores.

The program mission, goals, objectives, and outcomes have been consistent over the past fifteen years. The mission/vision of the program is best expressed by the statement in the introduction of the pre-teaching Manual shown on the next page.

In addition to its effects on teenagers, the program also has an impact on participating teacher-mentors, on the high school in general, and on the students in the classes where the pre-teachers are assigned. The program's objectives in each of these areas are presented in Table

We believe that teaching is one of the most challenging and rewarding professions in the world.
We believe that teaching must be intelligent, caring and creative.
We believe that those teachers who achieve excellence have an emotional investment in their students, looking past the performance to the person.
We believe that the ideal teacher
doesn't merely feed information, but makes you think
asks probing questions and encourages open discussion
allows you to take risks and make mistakes, and
creates independent learners, not passive ones.
We believe that teachers should help you take responsibility for your own life, and then for the lives of others.
We believe that teachers should "grow you up" and then let you go, give you roots and wings.

Phyllis Opochinsky
Linda Roemer Whetzel

1.1 and the criteria for progressing from one level to another are presented in Table 1.2. In regard to the levels, students at level 1 must qualify as members of Future Educators of America (FEA). This is a national organization that offers workshops for students and parents on college admission, financial aid, and teaching careers. Also, it provides information and ongoing support to its local chapters.

Table 1.1. Program Objectives

Pre-Teachers (Student Interns)	• promote positive attitudes towards teaching • improve self-confidence and self-presentation skills • provide first-hand experience of teaching • improve academic skills • ensure college readiness • provide accelerated education and exposure to college
Teachers	• increase morale and motivation • increase collegial communication and disseminate teaching methods
Students in Classes Where Pre-Teachers Are Assigned	• interact with positive peer role models • receive increased individual attention • encourage interest in teaching profession

Table 1.2. Criteria for Student Progress Through Program Levels

Criteria for student membership in Future Educators of America (FEA) Chapter	• Enrollment in a target middle or high school, or college • Interest in learning about teaching careers • Attendance at two FEA Chapter meetings • Parent and participant signed contract and permissions • Positive attendance, behavior, and grade profile
Additional criteria for selection of students to engage in cross-age tutoring	• Within one year of grade level in reading and math • Parent and participant signed contract and permissions • Membership in good standing in Future Educators of America Chapter
Criteria for student selection to middle school/high school level	• Within one year of grade level in reading and math • Parent and participant signed contract and permissions • Enrollment in target middle or high school • Membership in Future Educators of America Chapter • Positive attendance, behavior, and grade profile • Enrolled in grades 8-10
Criteria for student selection to internship level	• Grades of at least 80% in Regents-level classes • Completion of application form with essay • Interview • On grade or above in reading • Excellent attendance and behavior • Parent and participant signed contract and permissions • Enjoyment of learning and desire to help others as indicated in required essay • Current teaching/learning portfolio • At least junior standing or waiver from liaison • Interest in developing teaching-related skills • Successful completion of pro-team curriculum • Membership in Future Educators of America Chapter • Successful completion of 9th and 10th grade pre-teaching sequence or waiver • Recommendation from two teachers and one counselor

The Academy's program offers junior and senior students two mandated college level courses: Introduction to Education, a three-credit course taught by the program coordinator who uses as the text for the course *The Walton Pre-Teaching Manual*, now in its third edition, written by interns and teachers in the program; and Speech 100, a three-credit communication course. Students are also encouraged to enroll in other college level courses based on their grades in high school courses that are prerequisite to the college courses. Recently, the Walton Pre-Teaching students have been involved in the College Now Program, which uses the results of New York State Regents examinations and SAT and PSAT tests to qualify junior and senior students for college credit courses. Also, the personnel affiliated with the program offer developmental courses for those who require additional assistance. This has resulted in a greater number of students qualifying for college credit classes.

The central component of the program is a four-semester internship under the mentorship of Walton teachers. Over the course of the four semesters, students are encouraged to serve under four different teachers, although some students work with only three or even two different teachers. During the summers, when feasible, a selected group of students ($N = 20$) work on the Lehman campus as teacher aides for the Summer Sports Camp and for the mathematics and science programs.

The program has recently designed and implemented a new sequence of activities beginning in 7th grade (see Appendix A for descriptions of the program's activities). The four cohorts from two middle and two high schools participate in cross-age tutoring, homework help, Future Educator of America Clubs, and a four-semester sequence during 9th and 10th grade that will lead to the internship in their junior and senior year. The sequence of courses; the parent, student, college, and high school contract; and the pre-teaching intern observation form are all included in Appendix B at the end of the chapter. Both appendices are offered as resources for those urban educators and administrators interested in starting a similar Academy.

The internship has always been the central focus of the Academy's program. Another important component has been the program's workshops in which teachers, student-interns, and some college faculty participate. The college credit course was added after the program started when it was recognized that interns needed to have an increased understanding of the broad scope of careers in education and also needed a more formal introduction to lesson planning and delivery. College faculty have participated in the Saturday workshops and have served as guest lecturers in the Introduction to Education course.

Early in the program, we recognized that it was not sufficient for students to work only with high school students, and so we added the summer internship activity mentioned previously through which students were assigned to work with teachers in Lehman College's funded summer mathematics and science programs for 4th through 8th graders, as well as in the summer sports camp sponsored by NCAA. Students who worked as summer interns were also scheduled to take an Introductory Speech course in the afternoons.

The College Now component was added to permit qualified interns to take college credit courses (beyond the six offered as part of the program). Many students qualify to enroll in freshman College English, Introduction to Computers, College Mathematics, and other freshman-level college courses. Most students earn six credits but some take as many as twelve prior to college entry. The highest number of credits earned by a pre-teaching student prior to college entry was eighteen, permitting her to enter college as an upper freshman. This student also earned a Paul Douglas Scholarship, has now completed her M.S. in education (special education), has been accepted for an M.S. in science education, and plans to pursue doctoral work in educational psychology.

Lehman's work in this area has led to formalizing a Lehman-based College Now Program, funded by CUNY's Central Office. This program, based on a Kingsborough Community College Model, is in each of the New York City boroughs. In this plan, each of the public colleges in the Bronx (two community colleges and one senior college) adopts six to ten of the Bronx High Schools and works with them to encourage students to take the PSAT and SAT examinations and to do well on the New York State Regents. Those who earn qualifying scores may enroll in college credit courses. The new aspect added through our funding by CUNY is directed at those students who fail the placement tests. These students are encouraged to enroll in developmental workshops team-taught by a high school teacher and a college faculty member. During 1998-99, Lehman noted a 70% pass rate for those students enrolled in developmental workshops.

The workshops with the interns comprise the professional development opportunities for teachers. These workshops take place on Saturday mornings and after school during the academic year. Teachers from the participating high school can also receive tuition waivers against grant funds to take liberal arts and sciences or education courses to further develop or hone their skills.

Staff development has also been used to assist teachers and project personnel to identify needed changes to improve academic achievement and high school retention and completion rates. A modified Q-sort process was used to assist consensus building. In this process, each member of a small group (N = 10) lists ten strategies, methods, or programs that could increase the number of high school students prepared for and enrolled in college. Each group sorts their cards (strategies) into groups of similar concepts. The group uses the cards in each set to generate a sentence that encompasses the concept expressed. In a similar fashion, the groups combine their major ideas into one set of concepts with recommendations for students, teachers, the school, and the college.

FUNDING THE PROGRAM AND FUNDING TIPS

The Walton Pre-Teaching Academy is only one of several grant funded programs with Bronx students, schools, and teachers that the Lehman College's Center for School/College Collaboratives has conducted since 1984. We have been fortunate to be successful in our efforts to secure funding for the program. A summary of funding is presented in Table 1.3.

Over the past fifteen years, several lessons have been learned that have increased funding effectiveness. The key element is understanding that a proposal is a marketing tool and that the writers must sell the idea to the funder, convincing the funder that the project meets the requirements for funding and that the writers are the most qualified people, institution, department, or team to get the job done. To do this effectively, it is helpful to view the project from the perspective of potential funders. We read each of the funders' guidelines and then put ourselves in their shoes as we look at the elements of our program. For the best results, we try to see what elements of the program would be of greatest interest to the funder. It is entirely possible that the program will be appropriate for submission to more than one funder, and it is ethical to submit to more than one funder at the same time, although it is not acceptable to accept more than one grant for the same activities.

Table 1.3. Funding History of the Walton/Lehman Pre-Teaching Program

Date	Funding Source	Amount
1984-1985	New York City Board of Education (NYSED)	$75,000
1988-1993	New York Alliance for the Public Schools	$30,000
1987-1990	New York State Student Support Program	$135,560
1990-1993	Little Red School House (USDE)	$313,596
1990-1993	Fund for Innovation in Education (USDE)	$547,221
1992-1996	Aaron Diamond Foundation	$357,486
1998-2000	UTAP	$38,003
1999-2002	Title II Teacher Recruitment Grant (USDE)	$1,200,000
Totals		$2,696,866

Another important tip is to follow the funding guidelines to the letter. In the case of federal grants, the guidelines always include the criteria reviewers will use to score your proposal with the associated point values. If your proposal is unsuccessful, you should request reviewer comments and certainly revise your work for the next round or for submission to another funder.

Each grant writer has a different approach to creating proposals. We like to create tables that (a) juxtapose goals, objectives, activities, and evaluation; (b) list and describe the major activities; (c) show roles and responsibilities of staff; and (d) present sequence and timing of activities.

FROM PROVEN MODELS TO A MODEL PROGRAM: WHAT'S CRITICAL FOR A SUCCESSFUL TRANSFER TO OTHER SITES?

The Walton/Lehman Pre-Teaching Academy has at its core an internship model. This is the essential element of the Academy's program and critical for its transfer to other urban settings. Throughout the program, students—whether in middle school or high school—are engaged in teaching internships in classrooms. Over the three to six years in the program, interns progress from reading to younger children, tutoring, and helping with homework to teaching parts of lessons, creating and grading tests, and teaching entire lessons. These activities, the sequence, and the student-intern's progression through and across the internship activities, along with the Academy's staff development component and workshops for teachers and interns are all critical features of the Academy's program.

The Pre-Teaching Academy also shares critical features with such other models as educational pipeline, school-to-career, mentoring, and professional development. The Academy's internship model combined with the features from these other models have led to success for the more than 800 students who have participated in the program since 1984. More than 30% of the 400 or so students who have completed college and have entered careers are in teaching, and most are teaching in New York City. Cited below is a brief explanation of the models and the features we have used in our program.

Educational pipeline models are based on alignment and articulation of curriculum across the critical transitions within the educational system. Students in the Pre-Teaching Academy are engaged in preliminary activities during middle school, including cross-age tutoring, membership in a Future Educators of America (FEA), specialized course work at their home school or at the linked high school, and attendance at an annual celebration of teaching event. High school students have their own FEA chapter; specialized course work; college preparatory work; college credit courses at their home school and on the college campus; and an extensive, four semester, five day per week internship. Junior and senior high school interns also serve as mentors and teachers for the middle school students and for younger high school students during Saturday and Summer Academy programs on the college campus.

Students who participate in school-to-career models make the connection between knowledge and its applications to their lives as family members, citizens, and workers. Assessment is ongoing and conducted in all three areas. To achieve this, schools begin to use applied or contextual teaching and learning to emphasize higher level thinking and knowledge transfer, as well as developing student skill in collecting, analyzing, and synthesizing information and data from multiple sources and viewpoints.

School-to-career models also engage teachers and administrators in such curriculum planning that focuses on standards and outcomes, the combination of classroom learning with work-based learning, the phasing out of tracking, the increase of career options, and encouragement of a stronger integration of secondary and post-secondary education for high school students.

Though not initially conceived as such, it became clear that the intern-cooperating teacher relationship was also a mentoring relationship and as such is an example of a *mentoring* model. Further, we generally think of mentoring as a relationship between an experienced and an inexperienced person in which the mentor provides guidance, advice, support, and feedback. In the Pre-Teaching Academy, however, this traditional relationship is not always the case, and teachers benefit as much from their interns as the interns do from the teachers. The interns develop a sense of the teacher's role and the knowledge and skills needed to be effective through interaction with the teacher within the framework of a classroom. The interns not only learn from the cooperating teachers, but they also become keen observers and critics of teaching and learning in all situations. The relationships developed within shared classrooms frequently continue well beyond graduation from high school and college.

Within the professional development model, we discovered that in addition to the professional development that occurs through scheduled workshops and curriculum development sessions that cooperating teachers (with interns) attend, the program has yielded some unexpected sources of teacher development. Most surprising, the interns' forays into teaching have played an important role in the professional development of their cooperating teachers. We often refer to this as our flower-bee phenomenon.

In the ideal case, interns are placed with four different teachers during their two-year internship and about half the interns also are assigned to work in summer or academic-year student programs at the college. Thus, students learn different strategies, methods, and approaches from each teacher. They then take these "new" approaches with them to their next internship assignment. More often than not, when new cooperating teachers observe their interns using a different approach, they ask about it and then begin using it. The most gratifying instance of this was in a mathematics class in which the teacher did not believe in and would not try teaching math in cooperative groups. The intern, who had learned about using groups in a social studies internship, used the technique in a mathematics lesson. When the teacher saw it actually work, she was convinced and has been using this as an additional approach ever since.

In many ways, the real benefit and motivation of having an intern for the cooperating teacher are that interns become keen observers and evaluators of their own teaching. Teachers report that they feel they are "on stage" when the interns are with them and that they must "be an excellent role model" and demonstrate good teaching practice. Thus, they are more conscious of and conscientious about their planning and teaching.

With regard to recent reform efforts and national research conducted by the Recruiting New Teachers, Inc. (RNT), the elements of the Pre-Teaching Academy model have been shown to be the critical ones that lead to success. The RNT, in a national survey conducted in 1992, set out to identify pre-collegiate teacher education programs, evaluate programs based on a submitted questionnaire, conduct site visits to programs deemed exemplary, develop a categorization scheme for pre-collegiate programs, and determine the nine primary elements and/or conditions of successful programs. They chose the Walton/Lehman Pre-Teaching Academy and several others as model programs based on the degree to which the nine elements were achieved.

The conditions or elements identified as critical to successful programs are connectedness, apprenticeship style activities, adequate support for staff, clear entrance requirements with high expectations, sufficient resources, resources for college matriculation, modeling an evolving concept of teaching, rigorous evaluation, and long-term commitment at all levels. Table 1.4 briefly explains each of these elements. The elements should guide the development of similar programs.

WHERE WE ARE NOW AND WHERE WE ARE GOING

For the past year, the Pre-Teaching Academy Program has been participating in a project with the Recruiting New Teachers, Inc. to design a toolkit and materials for other high schools interested in

Table 1.4. Elements Critical to Successful Pre-Teaching Academy Programs

Element	Description
Connectedness	Integration of academic subject areas, students and teachers, middle school, high school and college, institutions, parents and schools, community based organizations, teachers of different levels and subjects leading to a strong pathway to careers in teaching and professional practice and renewal for all participants.
Apprenticeship style activities	Early and continuous exposure to the "real" work of teaching. Connecting with students is accomplished through inclusion of tutoring, practice teaching, and community service internships. These activities provide authentic and contextual learning and more importantly expose students to one of the prime reasons individuals choose to teach: to help children and to make a difference.
Adequate support for staff	There must be full-time or release-time staff to oversee the program and teachers who participate as intern mentors/cooperating teachers. They must be given time for professional development and program networking. In our case, professional development workshops include pre-teaching interns, teachers, and college pre-service teachers and faculty.
High expectations for students	Initially, teachers at Walton did not believe that their students could do this. Within a year of initiating the program, however, teachers became believers as pre-teaching interns earned their respect and admiration in the classroom and behind the desk as colleagues. Their high expectations can be seen in the responsibility they give to students as they progress during their four semester internship.
Clear admission requirements and participation criteria	This is important in conveying high expectations, but students must be helped to meet the program requirements by taking them from where they are to where they need to be.

Table 1.4. Elements Critical to Successful Pre-Teaching Academy Programs (cont.d)

Element	Description
Sufficient resources	Stipends, scholarships, and loan forgiveness programs are necessary, especially for students who would otherwise have to work part-time. A dedicated counselor for the program who works with students on college admission and identification of sources of financial aid should be a high priority.
Modeling an evolving concept of teaching	Programs and cooperating teachers should expose pre-teachers to best practices by providing a range of models of teaching strategies: team teaching, collaborative learning, contextual learning, use of technology, learning styles.
Rigorous evaluation	Programs require rigorous and systematic formative and summative evaluation and the institutional support needed to effectively follow up program alumni.
Long-term commitment	In order to see program participants through to entry into the teaching profession, program staff and funders must have a long vision to allow pre-collegiate programs to produce measurable results.

Source: Recruiting New Teachers (1996)

implementing similar academies. The materials are focused on what is referred to as contextual learning and teaching (CLT). The definition of CLT is based on series of papers commissioned through a grant to Ohio State University and Bowling Green State University and available online at *http://www.bgsu.edu/ctl/navigation/resource.html.*

Contextual teaching enables learning in which students employ their academic understandings and abilities in a variety of in-school and out-of-school contexts to solve simulated or real-world problems, both alone and in various dyad and group structures.

For the pre-teaching students, CLT is a three-phase process comprised of learning, doing, and evaluating performance. In program electives (a four-semester course sequence outlined in Appendix A), students learn to apply information, concepts, and theories to real-life contexts. For example, in a child development class, students learn about developmental stages or behaviors and go on to do a case study of a child.

Students study the purpose of lesson planning, learn how to write a lesson plan, and then prepare one to use in teaching peers. After learning new information (e.g., developmental stages, the definition of assertive discipline) and using it (e.g., observing a child and writing a case-study, explaining a discipline plan and putting it into action), students evaluate their performance through feedback from teachers and peers and/or self-reflective journal entries.

We prefer activities in which teachers' contextualized teaching strategies help students make connections with the real world. Learning through and in these kinds of activities is problem-based, has more than one context, fosters self-regulated learning, takes into account students' diverse life contexts, uses interdependent learning groups, and employs authentic assessment.

Also, we are currently examining national and state standards for teaching and learning. In recent years, curriculum planning at the Academy has been driven by the significant changes that were imposed by New York State. In order to qualify for a preliminary teaching certificate, students must earn a high school diploma, a baccalaureate degree, and, beginning shortly, a master's degree. Thus, we have to ensure that all students can achieve these goals. Though student achievement and graduation rates of students in our program have been high in the past, the standards for teaching and learning have forced us to rethink how we will ensure that students meet the higher standards and outcomes. Students who entered the Pre-Teaching Academy in 1999 will be in the high school graduating class of 2003. Thus, in order to achieve a Regents high school diploma, they will be required to pass (with grades of 65 or higher) Regents examinations in five areas: English, mathematics, global studies, U.S. history, and science. Students who earn grades of 55-64 in some of the Regents will be awarded a local diploma. Students who do not pass these standardized statewide exams will not qualify for a high school diploma.

In order to address these factors, we propose to grow our own minority teachers by providing students access to and preparation for careers in teaching as early as middle school so that they can complete the rigorous study needed to become effective students and then teachers. The need, however, is not only one of numbers, but also one of different kinds of teachers. Teachers for tomorrow's schools must be cognizant of the different strategies that can facilitate learning and engaging students by using interdisciplinary, cooperative learning; peer tutoring; hands-on experiential approaches; and by focusing on teaching and learning styles. They must also be prepared for the new learning standards in English, mathematics, science, social studies, and technology, and they must ultimately be prepared to meet the new New York State Teacher Certification Requirements. The Walton/Lehman Pre-Teaching Academy is currently planning for these new challenges.

LESSONS LEARNED

Over the past fifteen years, we have learned many lessons, and we have identified a number of factors or events that have led to successful achievement of the goals of the Walton/Lehman Pre-Teaching Academy. As we reflect on the years, we asked ourselves, if we were to start again, what would we do differently, knowing what we know now? Our answer translates into key factors we believe are essential to the success of the program. These include:

- an onsite coordinator who receives program time to oversee the implementation and development of the program and who serves as the liaison to the college;
- development of pathways (corridors) from feeder middle schools to the high school and from the high school to the college, through site visits, teacher/faculty exchange, workshops for teachers and students, joint planning for alignment, and articulation of curriculum;
- provision for service and support for students at critical junctures as they make the transitions from one level of schooling to the next, which is important so that all students are able meet the new learning standards, pass the required high school tests, and enter college prepared to do college-level work;
- expose students to the joys and satisfaction of teaching as early as possible, recognizing that when students teach and tutor others they improve their own learning and understanding;
- assess program's impact on student interns, student-intern families (parents and siblings), students in classes with interns, teachers who serve as mentors, other teachers in the school, school climate, and administrators through regular assessment methods, surveys, and interviews;
- create a follow-up system to maintain contact with program graduates;
- create an observation scale that teachers can use to evaluate and provide feedback to interns;
- obtain extensive baseline data on the school climate, students, pre-teaching interns, and teachers before the program implementation;
- work with the central Board of Education and unions to assure their participation in, contribution to, and support of the program from the very beginning;
- pay more attention to the impact of the program on the school and on the faculty and staff of both the school and

college student pre-teaching interns as an adjunct to professional development; and
- set down procedures as the program grows and develops.

Finally, we hope that we have adequately provoked interest among other urban educators to start such an Academy in their own setting and thus reap the inherent and tangible rewards we have observed in the fifteen years of the Walton/Lehman Pre-Teaching Academy.

APPENDIX A
RESOURCES AND MATERIALS OF THE WALTON/LEHMAN PRE-TEACHING ACADEMY

PROGRAM ACTIVITY DESCRIPTIONS: BRIEF OVERVIEW OF ACTIVITIES

Future Educators of America Chapters

Future Educators of America is a national organization that provides information and support for local chapters. A chapter is formed in each corridor school and at the college. The FEA sponsors trips and workshops for students and parents on college admission, financial aid, and teaching careers.

Cross-age Tutoring

This local replication of the National Valued Youth Program places middle school students in positions of academic responsibility as tutors to elementary school youngsters. Tutors are in classrooms with their students four days per week and take a class at their home school on the fifth day. Tutors are paid a minimum wage stipend for their work, reinforcing the worth of the students' time and efforts. All students are required to keep a journal and to use it to reflect on and evaluate their tutoring experience. Valued Youth Program students consistently report that they feel better about themselves and their prospects. Valued Youth tutors also improve their grades and stay in school. Another benefit of the program is its impact on families outside and in conjunction with the schools: improved communication between schools and families, lessened financial burden, and renewed family pride. Family involvement is an integrated part of the program. Teachers attend a training session to prepare them to implement this program.

Middle School Program

Students in grades 7 and 8 are given responsibility for working with individuals and with small groups of students, working in after-school tutoring programs, assisting teachers in laboratory sessions, and observing school personnel in middle and high schools in different subject classes. They are taught to use simple observation of teaching instruments. They are required to begin to assemble a teaching/learning portfolio. Beginning in 9th grade, they take an elective class each year. The course is designed to assist students to gain self-awareness and to formulate and pursue personal and professional goals. Teachers attend a training session to prepare them to implement this program.

Pre-Teaching Internship

Students in 11th and 12th grades further experience what works and what doesn't through classroom observation of their mentors and their own forays into teaching. Interns witness first-hand the application of theory in practice. Pre-teachers have a wide range of classroom responsibilities during their four semesters and two summers in the program: tutoring, instructing small groups, reviewing homework, presenting preliminary lesson materials, teaching parts of lessons, teaming with their mentors to teach entire lessons, teaching entire lessons on their own, and preparing and grading tests. Pre-teachers have even taught an entire series of lessons in classes in which in-subject substitute teachers were not available. They are registered for one credit of pre-teaching each term and receive a grade for this course that is determined by their cooperating teacher in conjunction with the program coordinator. As part of the internship, they maintain the journal begun in the pre-intern program, continue to add materials to their portfolio, and register for additional college classes (see bridge-to-college) as appropriate. (Pre-teaching students generally accrue between 3-9 college credits during their internship.) The program uses as its text a 319-page manual developed by pre-teachers and mentors. This manual covers such topics as the art of questioning, handling problem situations, using alternative learning strategies, and planning effective lessons. Teachers attend a training session to prepare them to implement this program.

After-School and Saturday Workshops

These workshops are scheduled several times a semester and cover such teaching/learning topics as creative problem-solving, discipline, communicating with adolescents, and multiculturalism. Teachers and pre-teachers, inservice teachers, college faculty, and sabbatical teachers have a chance to come together as a group and interact informally outside of the regular structures of the school.

ChalkTalk

The program newsletter, *ChalkTalk,* begun in 1989, features excerpts from student journals and teacher commentary on student performance. It is currently published in hard copy and on the program web site. The newsletter will continue, and a second publication, as yet untitled, which is to be published exclusively on the Web, will include articles relevant to teaching, references to journal articles and Internet sites of interest, information about program events, upcoming workshops, conferences, classes in which interns and mentor teachers can enroll, and scholarship and financial aid information. *ChalkTalk* and the Web-based publication will be published in the major languages of the program participants.

Saturday Academy

There is a high need for teachers who are certified in mathematics and science, are able to integrate technology into content delivery, are truly bilingual, can assist students in gaining needed literacy skills, can think critically, and are able to teach to national standards. This activity, taught by teachers from the collaborating schools, enriches student knowledge of math, science and technology, languages, literacy, critical thinking and problem solving, and national standards. Senior pre-teachers and preservice college students are engaged as tutors or assistant teachers in this program.

Summer Pre-High School Academy

Students entering high school are frequently underprepared for the independent planning and motivation required for success in high school. Many students also have deficiencies in one or more academic areas. Whereas the elementary and middle school aspects of this program are expected to greatly reduce these problems, the Summer Pre-High School Academy is to ensure that all program students begin high school ready to excel. Senior pre-teachers and preservice college students are engaged as tutors or assistant teachers in this program.

Fluency First Workshops

These workshops are part of the summer program. Students are meaningfully engaged in reading, writing, speaking, and listening in English with their peers and others and follow a natural sequence of language learning. They keep writing logs, participate in writing and reading groups, learn to actively listen to and constructively respond to others, and, most importantly, become increasingly confident users of English. Through this approach, fluency precedes clarity, and clarity precedes correctness. Senior pre-teachers and preservice college students are engaged as tutors or assistant teachers in this program.

Test Preparation Workshops

Tests are another hurdle for students who qualify to enter post-secondary education and to obtain teaching certification. These tests represent a major roadblock for many language minority students. Workshop formats that have been successful in the past are used to prepare students for a series of state and national tests (PSAT, SAT, LAST, ATS-W, CST).

College Now

Another method of introducing high schools students to college is through permitting qualified students to take college level courses while still in high school. This opportunity, already available at Lehman, has been extended to 11th and 12th graders in this program.

CONTRACT FOR PRE-TEACHING

As the parent/guardian of ____________________ I agree to:

1. Get my child up in time for school
2. Make sure that my child attends school when school is in session, including before and after holidays
3. See that my child makes time to complete homework, reports, papers, projects, etc.
4. Ask to see my child's report card
5. Confer with the coordinator, teachers, and guidance counselors as needed to ensure my child's success in school
6. Send my child to tutoring or summer school if he/she needs it to keep up with course work/ credits
7. Encourage my child to attend pre-teaching courses and workshops at Walton or Lehman College

I understand that if my child does not successfully complete his/her academic work in grades 9 and 10, he/she will NOT Pre-Teach in grades 11 and 12

____

Signature

As a student in the Pre-Teaching Academy, I agree to:

1. Handle my course work so I can graduate in four years
2. Attend school regularly and bring in notes to validate any absences
3. Attend all my classes—and get to them on time
4. Review my grades after the first marking period each semester and get tutoring for any subject in subject in which I receive "N" or "U"
5. Attend summer school if I fail courses in January or June
6. Take the Learning Teaching sequence of courses in grades 9 and 10, which may extend my school day
7. Pre-teach classes in grades 11 and 12
8. Keep a journal of all my pre-teaching experiences
9. During grade 11 or 12, take the Introduction to Education Course at either Walton or Lehman College
10. Be a role model for others, which includes treating myself, my classmates, my teachers, and my students respectfully.

I understand that if I do not successfully complete my academic work in grades 9 and 10, I will NOT be eligible to pre-teach in grades 11 and 12 OR to take the Education Course.

____

Signature

Walton School agrees to:

1. Offer a college preparatory sequence of courses that will enable the student to graduate in four years
2. Offer a sequence of Learning Teaching courses in 9th and 10th grade, including
   a. Study and Communication Skills
   b. Introduction to Computers: Learning with Technology
   c. Research and Presentation Skills
   d. Psychology
3. Notify the family should the child require additional support
4. Provide tutorial work or remedial courses if needed
5. Offer Saturday and after-school workshops to develop teaching skills
6. Offer a 3-credit course at Lehman College to eligible students in 11th or 12th grade, OR offer an after-school Education Course at Walton in 11th and 12th grades for those not eligible for the Lehman College course
7. Place students in a variety of Pre-teaching experiences in 11th and 12th grades if they have successfully completed their academic course work in 9th and 10th grades
8. Affix a Pre-teaching endorsement to the high school diploma upon the student's successful completion of the Pre-teaching course of study

____

Signature

Lehman College agrees to:

1. Offer a sequence of college courses that will enable the student to graduate in four years and prepare him/her to pass the NYSTCE and qualify for certification
2. Provide tutoring and support services as needed to program students.
3. Provide early admissions testing and college level course work or developmental workshops as needed
4. Enable Teaching Academy students to use the resources of the campus including: tutoring and library services, computer center, and APEX
5. Provide space and resources (including workshop leaders) for Saturday and after-school workshops to develop teaching skills
6. Enroll students and waive tuition and fees (as possible) for 3-credit course at Lehman College for eligible students in 11th or 12th grade, and/or offer an after-school education course at Walton in 11th and 12th grades for those not eligible for the Lehman College course

7. Provide summer and/or Saturday employment opportunities for pre-teaching students in summer camp or summer academic programs
8. Create comprehensive database to monitor and follow students
9. Collect and process survey data as needed to evaluate and improve program
10. Recruit college preservice teachers as program participants

____

Signature

COOPERATING TEACHER REPORT
WALTON HIGH SCHOOL PRE-TEACHING ACADEMY

Principal ___________
Coordinator_____________
Dear ______________________

In the interest of discovering what's working and what isn't with your Pre-Teacher, I'm asking that you take a few minutes to evaluate the students working with you and to comment on your own experience of the program. (You'll find a separate sheet for each Pre-Teacher assigned to you.) Please return the evaluation(s) to me as soon as possible so I can speak with the individual students about what they're doing.

Name of Pre-Teacher ______________________________
Class ___________________
Frequency of Attendance in the Pre-Teaching Class:
________ present every day
________ has missed a day or two
________ misses several days each week
________ hardly ever there
Has done the following: (Check whichever apply):
________ has learned students' names
________ has ONLY observed
________ has reviewed homework
________ has gone over Do-Now
________ has tutored one-on-one
________ has worked with groups
________ has presented an entire lesson
________ has checked homework and/or graded quizzes or tests
Personal interaction with entire class or with individuals
____Excellent _____Satisfactory _____Needs Improvement
____Unsatisfactory
COMMENTS:

Thank you.

APPENDIX B
OUTLINE FOR PRE-TEACHING CLASS SEQUENCE

Learning / Teaching 1

Part 1: Learning skills
- Study skills
- Note taking
- Behavior and people skills (classroom conduct, manners, character)
- Leadership and communication skills
- Speech and articulation; listening skills
- Literacy building (writing poetry, journals, critiques)

Part 2: Introduction to teaching
The second half of the class emphasizes types of lessons, learning styles, observations of teachers in the subject areas (their own classes) with guidelines and follow-up discussions. (Types of lessons, which lessons work, which lessons are most interesting, which lessons do you remember, what makes a good teacher.)

Learning / Teaching 2
Introduction to Computers: Learning with Technology
This class is taken at Lehman College as the last class of the day.

Learning / Teaching 3
Research and observation
- Primary versus secondary sources
- Note-taking for papers; format for footnotes, bibliography, etc.
- Interviewing skills
- Oral histories
- Designing questionnaires and needs assessment surveys

Compiling results and presenting them

How to use the library: card catalog, computer catalog, *Reader's Guide,* research books, *Who's Who*, microfiche, microfilm
Field trips to libraries: school, NYC branch, Fordham, mid-Manhattan and Lehman libraries.
How to use the Internet to gather information

Learning / Teaching 4
Psychology
Observation in the nursery school and local grade schools
Tutoring
Community service

Learning / Teaching 5, 6, 7, 8
Placement in a subject class
Big Brothers/Big Sisters program
Placement at local elementary schools

Note: Learning/Teaching 5, 6, 7, 8 has a seminar to pull them together.

REFERENCE

Recruiting New Teachers. (1996). *Teaching's next generation: Five years on and growing*. Belmont, MA: Author.

Two

Teachers as Leaders in Mathematics: A New York City Professional Development Project

James Bruni
Anne Campos
Ray Durney

What prompts a movement, a call to leadership, and a commitment to support long-term change? In the case of mathematics education and New York City (NYC), answers to these questions have something to do with the power of collective action, political and social dynamics, and the vision of a host of individuals dedicated to steering the course on a bumpy road to reform. However, as Larry Cuban (1998) has observed, educational reform in this century is characterized by great expectations and dashed hopes. Cuban's perspective also suggests that the circumstances for reform are particular:

- to the moment in time—the contextual dimension,
- to how individuals implement the vision for reform—the strategic dimension, and
- to how momentum is sustained to achieve long lasting results—the human dimension.

This chapter will present a case study of an urban initiative designed to transform K-12 teaching and learning in mathematics. It is our hope that the decade-long experience of the New York City Mathematics Project, a professional development program of the Institute for Literacy Studies at Lehman College/City University of New York (CUNY), will inform a wide range of practitioners: K-12 teachers, college and university faculty, those who facilitate instructional and school improvements, future educators, and policy makers.

THE CONTEXTUAL DIMENSION

The New York City Mathematics Project (NYCMP) was established in 1989 as a program of the Institute for Literacy Studies with a grant from the National Science Foundation (NSF), six years after the nation was declared "at-risk" by the National Commission on Education (1983). Among the many concerns raised by this report, it forecast a national need to better prepare citizens for the challenges of a globally driven service economy, calling for people who can solve problems, think critically, and adapt to technological change. Mathematical literacy headed the list of vital signs for national well-being. The education community interpreted these challenges as a broad mandate to improve standards for K-12 teaching and learning, particularly in the area of mathematics, where international data pointed to significant gaps in the performance of U.S. students. Statistics for urban, minority students were especially discouraging.

The National Council of Teachers of Mathematics (NCTM) rose to the call for leadership by adopting a proactive stance. College and university faculty and K-12 teachers from across the country were solicited to provide guidance and feedback to this national organization for purposes of developing and disseminating new expectations for mathematics teaching and learning. In 1989, NCTM published its *Curriculum and Evaluation Standards for School Mathematics*, which advocated for mathematics classrooms as places where problem solving, concept development, and the construction of learner-generated solutions and algorithms are given more prominence than memorizing procedures and using them to get the right answers. This view of classroom practice emphasized a pedagogy based on a constructivist theory of learning (Brooks & Brooks, 1993):

- posing problems of emerging relevance to learners,
- structuring learning around "big ideas" or primary concepts,
- seeking and valuing students' point of view,
- adapting curriculum to address students' suppositions, and,
- assessing student learning in the context of teaching.

In a constructivist framework, students and teachers are actively and reciprocally involved in their own development and growth.

NYCMP staff—mathematics education faculty, public school mathematics teachers, and a director of a university research unit engaged in the study and delivery of professional development programs in reading, writing, and mathematics—recognized the potential of a student- and teacher-centered approach to professional development. They framed their proposal to the National Science Foundation on the basis of a new model, one that would engage elementary, middle, and secondary school teachers in processes designed to prompt re-examination, experimentation, and reflection on the beliefs, knowledge, and practices implied by the recommended pedagogical form. The New York City Mathematics Project's vision for educational improvement would:

- immerse teachers in mathematical tasks,
- support teachers in the development of curricula for their classrooms congruent with NCTM standards,
- emphasize assessment of student work to help teachers understand how students learn and improve classroom practice,
- connect teachers to other professional networks and initiatives, and
- assist teachers in constructing leadership roles for themselves in their schools as well as the larger educational community.

The professional development model included a variety of approaches as described below.

A STAGED APPROACH

Recognizing that change is a personal process, that the pace of growth varies, and that the most effective strategy for initial system reform focuses on the individual at the classroom level (Fullan, 1993), this model assumes participation for a sustained period of time, typically two to three years. Program activities are designed to move participants through a multistaged process (Hall & Hord, 1987)—from the initial and intermediate stages of self-concern (awareness, knowledge, personal impact) and task-oriented concern (management, implementation of change)—to a final stage of impact-oriented concern (consequence, collaboration, student learning). As participants advance through these stages of staff development, they:

- experience first-hand changes in the learning and teaching of mathematics as recommended by NCTM Standards,
- begin to make appropriate changes in their curriculum and classroom strategies,
- develop skills to lead effective workshops and seminars, and
- become leaders—agents for change—within their classrooms and schools, as "teachers of teachers" when they eventually co-teach in the NYCMP, and as mathematics educators when they gain recognition in a wider professional community.

INTENSIVE SUMMER INSTITUTES AND SCHOOL-YEAR SEMINARS

Each summer and school year, participants attend an intensive summer institute and an inservice course held after the school day or on Saturdays. These courses focus on theoretical and practical approaches to mathematics education and present material from a constructivist, inquiry-based, problem-solving point of view. Emphasis is placed on content, methodology, NCTM standards, and alternative teaching and assessment techniques. Incentives are provided to attract both new and experienced teachers. Participants may receive tuition-waived graduate credits, stipends, or credit towards Board of Education requirements for new teachers. Courses are developed and taught by Lehman College mathematics education faculty, project directors (experienced public school mathematics teachers), and NYCMP teacher-consultants, who are released by the New York City Board of Education to support the program and to work on-site at participants' schools.

ON-SITE CONSULTING

A key feature of the model is its teachers-teaching-teachers approach, derived from another Institute for Literacy Studies program, the New York City Writing Project. Teacher-consultants not only teach NYCMP courses, they provide on-site assistance by visiting participants' schools on a regular basis, typically one day a week. The dual functions of teaching and on-site consulting support our beliefs that teachers should play an active role in their own continued growth and that learning is most dynamic in collaboration with others. The ongoing presence of a teacher-consultant at school sites helps learners—participating teachers—make immediate connections between theory and practice. Teacher-consultants provide assistance by:

- serving as mentors;
- creating a sense of community among participants;

- conducting demonstration lessons, co-teaching, and co-planning with teachers;
- guiding group discussions and reflection on current research on teaching and learning, aspects of student work, and instructional tasks during designated meeting times; and
- forging links between project directors, participants, and school and district personnel to nurture the acquisition of knowledge, for its practical applications in classrooms and schools and as a foundation for the generation of new knowledge.

ASSESSMENT AND INQUIRY

The ways in which teachers deal with daily life in urban classrooms affect their decisions about how subject matter is taught. Studies of learning suggest that teachers filter information about new ways of teaching through their prior knowledge and experience of being a student in a K-12 classroom and through cultural expectations (Stein, Smith, & Silver, 1999). The task of transforming teaching requires persistent investigation of and reflection on the values and habits that influence both current and new forms of practice. These values and habits are both personal and contextual. The NYCMP believes that assessment of learning is crucial to meaningful reform. One of the Project's most unique features is its focus on ongoing inquiry into how students perform mathematical tasks; what is produced while students engage in mathematical problem solving; and which school structures, policies, and procedures constrain or bolster productive learning environments. In seminar, Project staff guide discussions of select readings and participants' observations. On-site teacher-consultants also conduct similar sessions during designated meeting times at participants' schools.

The NYCMP professional development model is based on several assumptions about the change process and the dynamics of collective action for reform:

- the change process is a long-term endeavor,
- teachers cannot facilitate reform—of their own practice or of students' attitudes about and understanding of mathematics—unless they experience mathematics in new ways themselves, and
- professional growth is best served in a community of colleagues.

In 1989, these assumptions represented a major departure from trends at the time—district-sponsored staff development days, elective workshops and special courses, half- and full-day conferences, and how-to presentations—and are still not the norm today. How, then, has it been possible to establish an active network of teacher leaders and sustain the original vision of the co-founders?

THE STRATEGIC DIMENSION

From its modest beginnings in 1989, serving thirteen K-12 public school teachers from the Bronx, the NYCMP now operates city-wide, working with about 300 teachers annually. Though difficult to quantify, it is safe to say that the Math Project has reached close to 4,000 teachers over the past ten years through its various forums: courses, consulting, workshops, seminars, conferences, and involvement in local, state, and national leadership functions. Although these statistics offer some measure of effectiveness, they do not convey the special circumstances that have contributed to the Math Project's endurance.

Since 1989, the NYC Board of Education has been guided by three schools chancellors. The decade began with a reform-minded chancellor who was keenly interested in curriculum change, especially in the area of mathematics instruction. Within moments of his arrival, the schools chancellor announced his intentions to "make early and swift progress." He formed a working group on mathematics education, assembling local policy makers and college, university, and public school leaders. A math project director was a member of this group. The working group disseminated its recommendations for overhauling delivery of instruction in mathematics in a June 1990 report (New York City Board of Education), citing an urgent need to improve teacher professionalism.

The report pushed for specific actions:

- increasing teacher involvement in professional networks,
- encouraging teachers to take responsibility for and leadership in implementing reform, and
- expanding opportunities for teacher professional development to ensure that all students have access to high quality mathematics education.

The Board of Education named the NYCMP as one of its lead partners in enacting these recommendations.

In response to NCTM's promulgation of new standards for mathematics education, the NSF carried the banner further through targeted funding of urban initiatives that addressed the dual challenges of raising the quality of instruction and student achievement. NSF supported efforts that would involve teachers directly and result in curriculum enhancements at the local level. The intertwined movement of these two national organizations—one highlighting a process for educational reform, a constructivist framework, and the other lending support for the instruments of change, professional development, and curriculum materials—coincided with both the priorities of the NYC Board of Education and the Math Project's well-articulated local plan for enhancing teachers' professional growth.

As one of the earliest recipients of NSF funding, the Math Project initially received a two-year grant and has subsequently been funded through two additional cycles. The substantial investment of a national organization in NYCMP programs is one kind of legacy. Another kind reflects a history of collaboration that can sustain the movement and vision for implementing meaningful change.

The Math Project provides an interesting example of a university and a board of education working together to promote implementation of NCTM standards in an urban school system. One of the Math Project's central principles is that "the key to curriculum change is the classroom teacher, and that creating a leadership network of teachers in NYC public schools offers the best opportunity for significant change." This principle is most evident in the way the Project is structured and staffed and in the ways in which the Project has situated itself over time.

The NYCMP is housed at the Institute for Literacy Studies (ILS) at Lehman College, a senior college of the City University system, located in the Bronx. The College serves a majority of African American and Latino poor working-class students, many of whom have graduated from NYC public high schools. The interdependence of the College and NYC public schools exemplifies the City's public education enterprise. They shape and reinforce one another. As a senior college, Lehman offers undergraduate and graduate teacher preparation programs. Many students who enter Lehman's graduate program in mathematics education have experienced mathematics at the high school level in terms of city- and state-mandated curricula that are integrated with standardized testing. In this type of environment, which was the case in 1989 and remains so today, teachers are under pressure to "teach to the test," and students are anxious to demonstrate concomitant results. Such a singular approach to promoting educational achievement does not always equate with depth of knowledge in the subject area, on the part of those providing the instruction or on the part of those seeking understanding of it. The Project Directors understood this paradox and realized that the NYCMP could play a pivotal role in systemic reform, spanning divides between elementary, secondary, and higher education, particularly in the Project's home borough of the Bronx.

From its inception, the Math Project encouraged open dialogue among college and university faculty, project staff, and its K-12 public school colleagues, especially where the design of program content and delivery of services in school-based contexts are concerned. The highly reciprocal relationship between the delivery of its courses and on-site consulting is one of the Project's most distinctive characteristics and has proven to be a crucial source of its credibility over time. Where course work has emphasized mathematics content, NCTM standards, and student assessment, the aim of on-site consulting is to improve classroom-based practice, encourage school-based coherence in mathematics, and build school capacity to sustain improvements. As the push to raise standards and student achievement has intensified in the past ten years, the Math Project has not swerved from its mode of operation or its commitment to accommodate a range of personnel, including new and experienced teachers.

Although there have been staffing changes over the past ten years, the NYCMP has always been co-directed by a college faculty member in the Department of Mathematics Education and a former public school mathematics teacher. NYCMP full-time staff are experienced elementary, middle, or high school teachers who are released to the Project by the Board of Education. Similarly, program participants represent the entire K-12 spectrum. Though the Project serves K-12 schools throughout NYC, it has focused its efforts most intensively on schools in underserved areas, particularly in the Bronx. In addition, the Math Project has been steadfast in its willingness to assess its impact throughout its history and make adjustments accordingly.

Between 1991 and 1995, for example, external evaluators weighed carefully the Math Project's progress towards introducing a constructivist pedagogy, developing teacher leaders, and supporting school change. Their evidence supported the premise that urban teachers need time and flexibility to listen to, observe, and reflect on how mathematical knowledge is produced within their classrooms, but acknowledged that teachers often experience conflicting demands between existing curriculum and assessment mandates and a constructivist approach. The evaluators also found that whereas the NYCMP catalyzed and supported teachers' ability and commitment to participate in leadership networks inside and outside of their schools, whole school change in mathematics requires the active support of the school administration and a school community interested in substantively rethinking mathematics curriculum and instruction. Of particular note was the observation that the flexible scheduling, organization, and curricula of urban elementary schools appeared to be more conducive to implementing a constructivist approach (Belzer, Blanc, & Christman, 1995).

These findings clarified for the Math Project that without development of a unifying vision of exemplary mathematics teaching, without shared goals, without an agreed upon curriculum framework for instruction and assessment, and without collective effort on the part of staff developers, teachers, principals, and district administrators, the impact of an individual teacher's revised practice is seriously diminished. These insights led the Project, together with Lehman College, to form a partnership with all Bronx community school districts (a total of six) and the high school division, in another NSF-funded undertaking, the New York City Urban Systemic Initiative (NYCUSI). Through a competitive process, the Bronx was selected in 1994 as the second borough to initiate a collaboration for purposes of building a shared commitment to effective mathematics, science, and technology education. Over a four-year period, College faculty, NYCMP project directors, district superintendents, district curriculum specialists, principals, and teachers met regularly to advance instructional coherence in mathematics, including borough-wide implementation of nationally validated mathematics curricula. The NYCMP expanded its professional development activities to include curriculum developers and staff from national implementation centers.

In 1995, with support from the Greenwall Foundation, the Mathematics Project set out on a venture to identify, document, and honor Bronx public school teachers in grades K-8 who were successfully implementing teaching practices that exemplify the vision of the national standards for mathematics, science, and technology. A year later, the NYCMP published *Towards Deeper Understanding: Portraits of Exemplary Bronx Mathematics and Science Teachers* (Wolfe, 1996), featuring the accomplishments of thirteen dedicated mathematics and science educators. Two of these teachers are now full-time teacher-consultants with the Math Project; one is a project director for the Math Project's newest initiative, discussed below; and another holds a full-time appointment in the Lehman College graduate program in mathematics education.

By 1998, a core of exemplary teachers, close to 1,100 in 90 schools throughout the Bronx, had shifted their classroom practices towards a constructivist pedagogy and had become familiar with nationally validated, standards-based mathematics curricula. As impressive as this record may be, the Math Project realized that this core was not concentrated enough to sustain continued improvement in mathematics education for all students, nor could it adequately address the need for school-based teacher leadership in the context of tighter and emerging district-specific expectations. Clearly, formation of the Bronx cluster of the NYCUSI was instrumental to reform of mathematics teaching and learning in the Bronx, but its progress is fragile indeed in a large, diverse system addressing the needs of some of the City's most vulnerable young people. In the next ten years, the Board of Education expects to hire approximately 35,000 new teachers who will replace retiring teachers and serve an expanding student population. In addition, the educational policy climate in New York City has shifted considerably since 1989. It has moved from one of consensus on the need for reform in mathematics education and from openness to the thinking of a wide range of educators to an environment where there is less room for individual progress and where specific achievement goals are determined by grade levels.

These considerations factored prominently in the Math Project's growing awareness of an acute need to adapt its professional development model for purposes of supporting school-based leadership in mathematics on a district-by-district basis. During 1998-99, the NYCMP sought and received a five-year grant from the National Science Foundation for a new program, Teacher Leaders for Mathematics Success (TL=MS). TL=MS is a K-8 professional development program designed to sustain mathematics education reform by building the capacity of Bronx schools. In the next five years, three cohorts of twenty TL=MS school teams (80 participants per cohort) will move through three levels of development, with each emphasizing integration of standards-based models for curriculum development with processes to build TL=MS teams' mathematics content knowledge, recognition among colleagues in professional networks, and involvement in broad and particular discussions about the direction of district- and school-based instructional adaptations. Each school team includes teachers and a staff developer or an administrator. At the end of five years, we expect TL=MS school teams to serve as districts' interschool resources. We also expect that the capacity of schools and districts to continue improvements in mathematics education will be strengthened through the existence of 240 school-based Teacher Leaders and their work with an equivalent number of colleagues.

TL=MS PROGRAM COMPONENTS

Lehman College	Participating Schools	Community School Districts
Summer institutes	Leadership team meetings	Articulation meetings
Academic-year seminars	On-site consulting by TL=MS	Professional development
Saturday meetings	Leadership plan	Principals' meetings
Conference planning	Leadership activities	Conference planning

The Mathematics Project believes in teachers as agents for change and understands change in developmental terms. It continues to support development of learning communities, providing teachers with ongoing opportunities to grow. Participants still experience professional growth as a multistaged process, individually and systemically. Today, however, participants come to discover themselves as mathematics educators not only in their classrooms and through the access they gain to wider professional networks, they now experience change in concert with a group of colleagues in their schools. This latter shift marks a turning point. The Mathematics Project's current conception of the change process now integrates two contexts: the experiences and knowledge of classroom teachers and the priorities, policies, and procedures of the school. In the current configuration, teachers remain at the center, leading the way.

THE HUMAN DIMENSION

The primary aim of the New York City Mathematics Project is to reform urban education by providing ongoing professional development services to NYC public school teachers. A subsidiary aim, of no less importance, concerns the impact of this kind of support on learners, in our case teachers and students alike. Given the growing diversity of NYC student and teacher populations and the multiple contexts in which teachers work—schools, districts, communities, states—norms for teaching and learning are neither self-evident nor static. Even though today's reform goals and standards forecast high expectations, they shed scant light on the conditions most likely to support learners on the road to achievement. In our experience, the road to reform is neither easy nor swift.

From our vantage point, it takes people years to unearth deeply held beliefs, appreciate cultural and contextual complexities, develop secure conceptual foundations, and obtain professional standing and leadership. In the case of reform of mathematics education, the charge to promote a constructivist theory of learning, prompting teachers to relearn mathematics, is especially challenging. We have tried to highlight here some of the factors that have influenced and sustained the New York City Mathematics Project:

- A Constructivist Foundation: courses, seminars, and on-site consulting that promote acquisition of knowledge in terms of practical applications such as devising classroom strategies and discovering students' learning styles and as a foundation for understanding primary concepts or "big" mathematical ideas;

- Teachers-Teaching-Teachers: assistance that focuses on participants' daily struggle to teach in new ways and work in multiple contexts;
- Ever-widening Learning Communities: open points of entry to and levels of participation in the project, expansion of program activities to include developers of nationally validated mathematics curricula, and programmatic shifts to build school capacity through work with teams of teacher leaders; and
- Local Contexts: school, district, and borough-wide collaboration, ongoing dialogue among university, college, and school-based colleagues, and expansion of the program design to include school administrators and staff developers.

FINAL THOUGHTS

Beliefs about educational reform inform the vision of those who are called upon to enact change as well as the structures that are designed to facilitate it. Though the history of educational change is beyond the scope of this chapter, it is useful to note some perspectives about various theories of change. In their review of the development of technical assistance throughout the last half-century, Wahl, Cahill, and Fruchter (1998, pp. 8-10) observed four broad historical trends and the theories of change inherent to each:

1. A technology transfer approach assumes that the tools and knowledge [for change] exist but are not known at the local level and need to be transferred from external sources to the local situation.
2. A medical approach assumes that change is brought about by defining the problem and understanding its pathology so that the pathology may be treated and the problem eradicated.
3. A systems approach assumes that the parts are interdependent and that change is brought about when the parts of a system or community collaborate together on addressing the problem.
4. A capacity building approach nurtures self-reflection and critical thinking with the goals of encouraging exchange and support among peers. Change takes place when the collective action of individuals redirects customary activities and a balance of power, enabling others to apply new knowledge and skills to other problems and settings.

Analogies about the work of the New York City Mathematics Project (NYCMP) may be drawn from the foregoing typology. Our experience begs a few questions: What beliefs guide efforts to help people develop and put into practice new ways of thinking and learning? What is a teacher's role in helping students develop and understand mathematical concepts? Who needs to be involved in supporting new visions about teaching and learning in mathematics? What theory of change or theories of change are most likely to direct long lasting human development?

In 1989, the NCTM launched a revolution after the National Commission on Education identified an alarming problem: Americans are underprepared in the area of mathematics. Experts—college and university faculty and K-12 teachers—were gathered, standards were set, and assessment protocols were formulated. The National Science Foundation carried NCTM's banner further by funding the transfer of technology and systemic initiatives. Within this national movement, the NYCMP received support to implement new visions for mathematics reform. Power and incentives for reform moved from the top down and outside of local sites.

It is here that the story diverges. New York City dynamics and the beliefs of the NYCMP's leaders converged on the local stage where enactment of a capacity-building theory of change has continued for over ten years. In simple terms, the NYCMP operates from the standpoint of building local capacity. As Wahl et al. describe (1998, p. 21), this approach distributes power horizontally through the formation of networks among those with common purposes: "The network is not responsible for reaching consensus and taking action as a body . . . it exists to provide support and as a fulcrum for individual action as well as a means for disseminating change efficiently and for building a base of political action by gathering numbers of participants around a shared vision."

NYCMP leaders acted initially and persist to act today from the belief that change begins with the individual teacher in the classroom, placing the means of reform in the hands of those closest to the heart of education. The NYCMP professional development model is structured to organize communities of action among teachers, promote their access to and influence in decision-making, and offer strategies for affecting change—within their classrooms and schools and among a range of professional colleagues. The NYCMP theory of changes rests solidly on the belief that reform in mathematics education is a long-term endeavor, one that is highly dependent on the accrual of individual transformations. In our case, we aim for transformation among teachers and students alike. For us, this means providing teachers and students with the means for self-reflection, critical thinking, and experimentation.

We work with big ideas on a small scale, and we measure our results in terms of how those with whom we work expand their understanding of mathematics. At all moments, we work collectively towards change.

ACKNOWLEDGMENTS

Many people have contributed to and continue to sustain the New York City Mathematics Project. We wish especially to acknowledge Marcie Wolfe, Executive Director of the Institute for Literacy Studies at Lehman College/CUNY, Lehman College Education faculty, New York City Board of Education administrators, mathematics coordinators, teachers and superintendents, and the various funders who have supported the Project over the years.

REFERENCES

Belzer, A., Blanc, S., & Christman, J.B. (1995). *An evaluation of the New York City Mathematics Project.* Philadelphia: Research for Action.

Brooks, J.G., & Brooks, M.G. (1993). *In search of understanding: The case for constructivist classrooms.* Alexandria, VA: Association for Supervision and Curriculum Development.

Cuban, L. (1998). How schools change reforms: Redefining reform success and failure. *Teachers College Record, 99*(3), 453-477.

Fullan, M. (1993). *Change forces: Probing the depths of educational reform.* New York: The Falmer Press.

National Commission on Excellence in Education. (1983). *A nation at risk: The imperatives of educational reform.* Washington, DC: Author.

Hall, G.E., & Hord, S.M. (1987). *Change in schools: Facilitating the process.* Albany: State University of New York Press.

New York City Board of Education. (1990). *Mathematics education in New York City: What it is and what it should be.* New York: Author.

Stein, M.K., Smith, M.S., & Silver, E. (1999). The development of professional developers: Learning to assist teachers in new settings in new ways. *Harvard Educational Review, 69*(3), 243.

Wahl, E., Cahill, M., & Fruchter, N. (1998). *Building capacity: A review of technical assistance strategies.* New York: New York University Institute for Education and Social Policy.

Wolfe, M. (Ed.). (1996). *Toward deeper understanding: Portraits of exemplary Bronx mathematics and science teachers.* New York: Institute for Literacy Studies.

Three

Cognitive Development Through Literacy for Inner-City Students: A Curriculum Staff Development Project in the South Bronx

Dorothy Stracher

INTRODUCTION AND OVERVIEW OF THE PROJECT

As we enter the new millennium, a public education that encourages all children to achieve to their potential is the goal of this nation. The United States was conceived as a country that could provide its least fortunate citizens with a public education that, within a generation or two, would transform their lives and lead them onto the path toward a middle-class existence. Perhaps, in an earlier and less complicated era, such was possible.

Today, to be considered literate and to be capable of achieving in the marketplace, adults must have a minimum of a tenth grade reading level. In fact, success in school is clearly related to reading success. The percentage of American children whose reading problems prevent them from reading on grade level is so high that both political parties are proposing massive support in an attempt to garner votes while responding to the populace's prime concern.

This chapter presents the why and how of a successful literacy project that was developed specifically for an inner-city elementary school. After nearly a decade of a working relationship between the school and a college, better than 90% of the students scored on or above grade level on mandated reading tests. More specifically, the project involved the implementation of staff development activities and graduate courses for the purpose of designing a curriculum to effect cognitive development through literacy experiences for youngsters in an elementary school located in the South Bronx. The project was a joint school-college venture engaged in by the principal of the school, 30 teachers, and me in my role as a professor at Dowling College. I served as the project director and was hired as a consultant for the school district. From the mid 1980s to the mid 1990s, participants designed and engaged in phases of the project. The courses and staff development activities of the first phase of the project introduced the teachers to children's literature in the various genres and provided them with guides on how to identify, by the use of a variety of tests, each pupil's specific level in spelling, syntax, word identification, reading and comprehension, and writing. The first course also included an explanation of the knowledge base and the theoretical framework, which then served as the foundation for developing unit themes included in the curriculum. The unit themes combined reading and quality literary selections for the pupils of the project. The second course included additional staff development activities that facilitated the teachers' development of a curriculum that was appropriate to their pupils' needs, interests, and varying levels of ability. Participants designed and put into action procedures for implementing, assessing, and evaluating the curricular experiences. The courses were taught on-site at the school. Additional staff development activities included having me work with the teachers in the classroom and having selected lessons videotaped for purposes of analysis and assessment. Within the first two years, the teachers of the project developed their first "integrated curriculum" book that incorporated a universal theme around which literary selections were used for reading selections, higher-order questions, project work, and integration of other subject areas. The curriculum that was designed and implemented by the participants contributed to the following outcomes and results achieved within several years of the project:

- Better than 90% of the pupils in the school achieved on or above their grade level on the standardized reading tests administered;
- A high proportion of the youngsters passed the writing tests, and the teachers noted the achievement of the youngsters in writing;
- The pupils learned the best example of various genre and were able to identify the salient characteristics of each;

- The pupils were asked and responded to inferential questions that were linked to higher levels of thinking/reasoning;
- The teachers reported that they learned a new way to approach the learning process that focused more directly on pupil learning;
- The teachers reported that their knowledge base increased, particularly in literary selections of the various genres;
- The teachers worked effectively as a group to develop universal themes for the curriculum that were then implemented in other grade levels.

What follows is a brief description of the context and situation in which this undertaking took place and an explanation of the phases of the project. My intent is to communicate the critical features that led to the project's success so that it may be implemented or at least useful in developing similar projects in other inner-city settings.

CONTEXT AND SITUATION

The school itself, although located in a difficult inner-city neighborhood in the South Bronx, had as its principal an individual who firmly believed that all of the children could be academically successful if the teaching were appropriate. She ran a tight ship. The custodians kept the old building in spotless condition, and the P.T.A. parents signed in all visitors. The principal arranged to have the school labeled a magnet school so that, in addition to providing for children in their area, they also welcomed a greater range of local youngsters who were viewed as gifted.

The principal, in her quest for the next step for her school, enrolled in a graduate class I taught that presented strategies for encouraging literacy in the classroom. I was invited by the principal to work in the public school with the staff so that the teachers could better help their students become literate, thinking adults. The approach to the metacognitive development of elementary school children was to be centered on the synthesis of reading and writing. Initially, the program provided a graduate class for the first fifteen teachers in the school who volunteered. No one involved in the course was interested in another course that provided isolated bits of information. I spent one day a week working alongside the teachers, and, as soon as the school day ended, the graduate course began in an empty classroom. Their efforts resulted in the beginning of a pilot project that was to be evaluated at the end of the year to determine if it was meeting the original goals.

Prime among the expectations was the hope that literacy teaching in the school would be invigorated. The principal knew that her staff, who were capable and committed, had, to date, been unable to raise the reading level of the majority of their students to their grade level. The principal could not pinpoint the reasons for this failure but looked to me for answers. I eagerly accepted the task as an opportunity to test long-held theories and to implement a process that could be assessed and evaluated.

Although the teachers were being provided with a free graduate course that, eventually, led to a salary deferential, the amount of work that they were expected to complete guaranteed that the numbers of teachers who volunteered were almost within the original chosen number.

PHASE ONE AND THE THEORETICAL FRAMEWORK

The first semester of phase one began with a discussion of what the teachers wanted to accomplish during this project. The teachers recognized that their approach to their students' literacy was not adequate. Most of the teachers were using a basal series, but all of them were eager to be part of the class that promised them another way of teaching. The first course was similar to the one taken by the principal; it provided a theoretical framework and knowledge base as a foundation for developing unit themes that combined reading and fine-quality literary selections. Further courses and/or projects were dependent upon the directions that the teachers deemed purposeful.

First, the staff was provided with an overview of the theoretical framework that informs the programs, and the classes discussed the significance of each of the readings. During the earlier part of the day, I was in the classroom with the teachers where I interacted with staff and students. In this role, I was not an evaluator but a facilitator; the teachers' comfort level allowed them to start discussing and critiquing their own lessons. As time went on, when they felt secure in their new role, they taped a lesson to be presented at the graduate class. Whenever a specific teacher presented an outstanding lesson, I arranged for visitation from the other faculty.

Early in the sessions, as the faculty reviewed what they wanted for their students in literacy, they decided that they needed initially to *assess* their students. I provided whatever qualitative tests they required. First, the teachers wanted to know the depth of the children's background in literature. The youngsters, individually, from grade K through six, were asked to name two examples of various literary genres that they had read; they were also asked to indicate what was unique to each specific genre (Mindell & Stracher, 1980). At the next class, the teachers related with surprise how much their students did not know about genres. As they talked, they noted their own knowledge deficits in fine children's literature. This led to the faculty's decision to study the best examples of each of the children's literary genres and, thus, each week that first year, they concentrated on one specific literary genre. They read the originals in nursery rhymes, fairy tales, folk tales, fables, fiction, nonfiction, biographies, autobiographies, and poetry. The second semester, they met together before school, after school, and other times as they began to put together curricula for each grade. The principal freed the teachers in the pilot for half a day a week so that they could continue working on their new curricula. Because of their theoretical framework, each grade had a universal theme whose center was fine children's literature. The teachers, in time, incorporated other disciplines so that all the learning was interrelated.

The excitement that was generated by the teachers reached the rest of the staff. The children began to be more interested in reading and in writing. Their knowledge base was expanded, and their scores on standardized reading tests showed movement upward. Further, the teachers compiled a first curriculum guide called *Differentiated Curricula for the Potentially Gifted: Reading, Writing and Reasoning: A Teacher's Guide.*

The first phase of the project can only be understood if the reader is aware of the theoretical framework that gave rise to this approach. It evolved from the premise that the major responsibility of the public schools in the United States is to facilitate the growth of its students so that they will become literate, effective adults. To reach this highest reasoning level, Piaget (1992) posited that students must be involved in interacting with their environment. Translated into language that is more familiar to those of us involved in the education of the young, Piaget is suggesting that children will reach their appropriate stages of cognitive development if their teachers provide them with educational experiences, help, and support at the appropriate time. That is, the teachers must recognize at what level their students are and encourage further development. Thus, if their educational offerings are too far above the children's level, the information will be over their heads; if the experiences are too easy, children will be bored. In either scenario, further cognitive growth is compromised.

How does the teacher assess children's stages of development? One model was created by J. Stanley (1976) who developed the Johns Hopkins program for potentially gifted youngsters in mathematics and English. He asked what educators learned about youngsters when they were at the 99th percentile in standardized tests. He suggested only one piece of information: the tests were too easy. In similar fashion, educators could ask what is learned when children score very poorly on standardized tests? One possible answer is that the test is too hard. Stanley provides a framework that suggests that children must be limit tested; that is, educators need to know what stage the children are at in every aspect of the particular discipline.

Important in the early sessions was a discussion of the Bettelheim and Zalen (1982) premise, presented in their book *On Learning to Read*, that American children don't choose to learn to read because what they are offered to read is not authentic and not worth the effort. This approach is analogous to Piaget's (1992) premise that the reason youngsters want to learn is so that they can make sense of their environment.

Further, the literature clearly informs that learning must be meaningful and purposeful for the students to be able to amass a significant knowledge base. How can teachers ensure that the content they present to their students and the methodologies they employ will relate to their students and their lives? All learning must be part of the spiral curriculum; that is, it becomes broader and deeper (Bruner, 1966) throughout the lifetime of the student's educational experiences. In addition, Gardner (1985), in attempting to understand why some information once taught is retained whereas other teaching is lost almost immediately, posited that the learner must overlearn to truly know.

The work of George Henry (1974) was introduced to the group as a model of how to subsume literature and literacy within a universal theme. Specific genres were reviewed, and group readings included fine literary examples of fairy tales, folk tales, fables, myths, and so forth. Each week, each student would select some of her readings and describe, tentatively at first, how to combine the Henry model and use in the classroom. These became the basis for the lessons that were attempted on the weekday when I was in the room. Each teacher developed a universal theme and a genre that had been discussed in the seminar. At the end of each lesson, the teacher and I would talk about the strengths and needs of the lesson. Gradually, as the teachers became more comfortable in their theme presentations, classes were videotaped to be discussed in the seminar so that all the teachers could add their input. Henry (1974) provides the researcher with the understanding that synthesis, the highest reasoning stage, can be encouraged among the students by offering a concrete way of noting the differences (analysis) and similarities (synthesis) between and among fine literature that is centered around a universal theme.

According to Kohlberg and Mayer (1978), less than 50% of all adults achieve the level of abstract reasoning. Because human beings as a biological species have the capacity to reason logically, the poor showing may be indicative of the quality of their education. This would mean that the experiences offered to many of the children in their quest for reading and thus literacy are inadequate.

Many of the differing approaches to reading over the years have claimed to be the panacea. If only people would follow this particular method, the thinking goes, all reading problems of the country would be resolved. Even *The New York Times* has entered the fray by publishing the contrasting views of Hirsch (1999) and Gardner (1999), which may not be in such conflict as claimed. The former believes in teaching phonics explicitly and is concerned that other approaches may be keeping minority children from becoming literate. He mentions Keith Stanovich's (1986) research, which notes that a strong predictor of academic achievement in 11th grade is a child's score on a first grade standardized reading test.

However, as Bond and Dykstra's classic first grade study (1967) proposed, the success of children learning to read has less to do with the method than with the teachers' knowledge base and firm belief that their students could learn to read. Such a concept was reiterated by Stanovich (1986) in "The Matthew Principle" in which the investigator notes that youngsters who believe they read well keep improving in their reading; those who are viewed as being poor readers keep failing throughout their school careers. This explains why reading tests in first grade can be a predictor of academic achievement in the 11th grade. Hirsch (1999) neglected to add the importance of positive teacher attitudes and knowledge.

As Gardner noted (1999), it is important to utilize both educational visions; indeed, both must exist if children are to become truly literate. To insist that these approaches are diametrically opposed is inaccurate. Every effective program, including the one that is presented here, describes both. However, this program never allows for learning in isolation. All knowledge must be interrelated, and all learning must be meaningful and purposeful for the children so that they can internalize this new information.

Can children in public schools be guaranteed the opportunity to succeed to their potential? Can they develop formal logic at the appropriate stage? Unfortunately, achievement in elementary and secondary school seems to be directly related to the community's socioeconomic level: the higher the income, the better the students' scores; the lower the income, the poorer the results. Thus, can inner-city youngsters be provided with the same chance to reach their highest cognitive levels? The answer is a resounding yes.

All of the above were incorporated into phase one of the project. The common goal was to seek successful strategies to help the children become literate, thinking adults. The theoretical framework was arrived at by group discussions of the various theorists and research coupled with the teacher's classroom experiences with youngsters. The idea was to have all the participants share a similar view.

The next concern in phase one was how to determine the stage for each of the children in various aspects of literacy. The areas questioned were reading, writing, spelling, knowledge of literary genres, and study strategies. Because it was impossible to test all individual children in a such a short time period, the group determined that it could limit test (Stanley, 1976) five children in their class. The teachers were to select youngsters who represented the differing literacy levels in their classrooms. Thus, they chose the youngsters who seemed to be the most and the least adept readers, as well as three other children who were assumed to be somewhat typical of their groups. In this manner, all children would be limit tested once every five or six years. The youngsters were asked to read passages aloud and then to answer questions about their readings. The teachers did not do a formal miscue analysis (Goodman, 1965). Instead, they noted if the children's oral reading was stronger than their comprehension or vice versa. Once the youngsters had reached their frustration level (could not understand at least half of the questions), the examiner read the passages aloud and asked comprehension questions; some children are able to understand at a much higher level if the print translation (decoding) is removed.

Further, the teacher examined a typical example of the youngster's writing; the emphasis was on the child's ability to develop a concept, and the teacher was to note the sophistication level of the child's writing. Writing can be judged by its use of syntax. As this is developmental, people keep maturing in their ability to use complex sentences and embedding in their writings. In this manner, children who are capable of logical writing are not penalized if they cannot spell; the correlation between spelling and intelligence is zero. (Today, the common use of word processing and spell check alleviate the spelling problems somewhat.)

However, spelling tests were administered because they can be a useful window into the mind, and spelling is also developmental. The child's level was determined by using Mindell's Qualitative Functional Analysis (Mindell & Stracher, 1980). When children learn to spell words, first they overlearn the initial part of the word; the second overlearning occurs with the ending of the word. The most difficult is the recall of letters in a word's middle. Some children make errors because they cannot differentiate between spellings for the same sound (perch and lurch), whereas others do not know foreign derivations (psychology). Some children have learning disabilities that make appropriate spelling very difficult or impossible to master.

The youngsters' knowledge of the various literary genres was also tested utilizing the five selected students. First, they were asked to give two examples of each specific group: nursery rhymes, fairy tales, folk tales, fables, myths, novels, fiction, nonfiction, biographies, autobiographies, and poetry. Then, they were required to note the characteristics that made that genre unique. Next, the youngsters were asked about their knowledge of various study aids, from defining words such as illustrator and copyright date, to explaining how they practice note taking, and when they use specific books, such as *Who's Who*, and so forth.

As the fifteen teachers completed their tests, they explained the results in class with great animation. It was the first time in their careers that they had this in-depth knowledge of their students. Many of the teachers had assumed that the children's standardized reading tests were accurate measurements of their level of reading. These scores had been used to determine where in the basal readings the youngsters were to be placed. Now the teachers had a much wider view of the literacy strengths and needs of their students. They talked about those children who were much more capable of understanding what they had read if the decoding aspect were removed. While the teachers provided strategies to help the children learn how to better translate print, they decided that they would also provide tapes for those children to follow along. The teachers were also impressed by the approach to writing that viewed the children and their developmental stages.

As the teachers began to consider strategies to help increase their students' writing capabilities, they reviewed the caliber of the literature that elicited written statements from the youngsters. In all instances, the students imitated the developmental level at which they were reading. Those youngsters who had been perusing more sophisticated literature attempted to copy that writer's style; the children who had been reading a basal story that required little of them wrote in a much simpler fashion. The writing process (Calkins, 1986) was implemented by the teachers who marveled at how well the children worked together as supporters and editors of each other's works.

One of the more surprising results for the teachers was the information gleaned from the questions about the literary genre. The children could name some examples, particularly among the nursery rhymes and fairy tales, but could not identify their unique characteristics. These results caused the teachers to offer their students more examples of each genre. Because the school did not have a full-time librarian, the teachers did not have the resource person who would have made the task easier. However, the teachers and the professors worked together and included the librarians with whom they worked. Soon, the teachers were discussing the 800 different versions of the same fairy tale and what it said about the needs of society and its universality. Further, as the teachers increased their knowledge base about the various genres, they began to incorporate the readings in their classroom. Often, they invited me to join them and to add to the class. Many of the exciting classes were taped for all the members of the course to enjoy. A camaraderie developed in which all the teachers were willing and eager to share what they had accomplished. Soon teachers on the same levels were sharing their lessons and extending their concepts.

Another surprise for the teachers was the youngsters' inability to verbalize what the significance was of a table of contents, an index, and so forth. As the teachers began to consider what kind of curriculum they wanted to develop, they recognized that their students needed to have better study strategies. In addition, many of the children could not distinguish between many significant sources, such as dictionaries, encyclopedias, and atlases. The children, even the older ones, did not know the differences between an abridged and unabridged dictionary, nor the many kinds of maps to be used. The teachers in the school who attempted to function as the "specials," that is, the science person, the art person, and so forth, began to view the results and determine what they could do to help in the curricula to be established.

The teachers began to work on preliminary curricula. Those excellent lessons the participants developed that first semester were incorporated into the curricula. Henry (1974) became the model as the teachers worked together in developing universal themes around which all disciplines were incorporated. The curriculum was always developing because it never stopped becoming broader and deeper (Bruner, 1966). Thus, the first phase of the project culminated in the development and implementation of a teacher's curriculum guide, *Differentiated Curricula for the Potentially Gifted: Reading, Writing and Reasoning*, compiled by the teachers of the project.

PHASE TWO

The original fifteen teachers generated much excitement within the school. The other teachers, who had remained aloof for fear that this new approach would simply be more work with no lasting effect, began to ask to be included. As the students who had been in classes with the original fifteen moved into other classrooms and examined new ideas and readings in a more mature manner, other staff asked to be incorporated in a phase two aspect. After a discussion that included the administration, teacher leaders of the first group, and me, a second group of fifteen teachers was welcomed.

Whereas the first phase was predicated on all of the participants reasoning together until they established their theoretical framework antecedents, phase two did not repeat the "aha" aspects of the original group. The second phase meant that these fifteen would accept the already selected gurus who informed the theoretical framework. This decision did not negate the option of including other thinkers, but such extensions would have to meet the approval of both groups. Further, the first group clearly recognized that its new curriculum, although laudatory and superior to that which currently existed within the mainstream publishing field, was just a first attempt that required enormous editing and extending.

The second year thus began with an additional group of fifteen teachers. Several of the original fifteen continued on in the class to act as mentors to the new teachers. That which had taken the first group months to achieve (selecting those educational thinkers who would compose the models for the theoretical framework) was presented for a brief review to the new group. Leaders who had been part of the original group in each of the grades shepherded the new students through the testing process, which then became mandated for all classes and students in the school. A review of the various genres also was built upon that which the first group had already accomplished. A compilation of the fine literature initially selected was available for the second group to peruse and to review with their grade leaders who had worked through these genres the previous year.

Within the first couple of months, the staff was working together within their grade levels. I still spent one day a week working in the classrooms alongside the teachers in implementing the new curriculum. We continued to videotape any new lesson that was particularly exemplary and then presented it to the new group so that they could note the strengths and needs that still required addressing.

The original members were quite helpful in defining what they viewed as the most important information that they gained from the first year. Prime among their comments was the literacy growth that they viewed in themselves. They stressed to their colleagues, who were just beginning, that they were more effective teachers because they knew more. They indicated that teachers could only teach what they knew; they clarified that even the quality of their questions was better because of their extensive knowledge base. In this manner, the second group of teachers was ready to extend the units quite early. As the teachers added to the units, they field tested it in their own classrooms; those aspects that they viewed as being significant and deserving of being incorporated within the grade's unit were provided to the rest of the classes on that level. As the teachers used the new materials, they discussed which aspects were most beneficial and which they thought needed further extensions. In this manner, the teachers worked together for the two semesters that sustained the graduate courses.

Thereafter, I still spent time at the school, although no longer on a weekly basis but frequently enough to be a hands-on observer as the staff continued to field test the units.

The teachers continued the literacy testing of five students in their classes each year. By the second and third year, the staff saw significant differences in the students' responses, particularly in their understanding of the unique characteristics of specific genres. Further, as the youngsters read literature that was of a superior quality, their writing showed a maturity and sophistication that belied their ages.

Three years after the publication of the first curriculum guide, the school was ready to print its second and more comprehensive guide, *A Literature Based Integrated Curriculum—Grades Pre K-6: Reading,*

Writing and Reasoning. A Teacher's Guide. It was an elaboration of what the original group of fifteen teachers began; it was still viewed by all the staff as a work in progress. In that sense, phase two is always occurring.

In reviewing the years that I spent as a consultant at the school, I identified certain major realizations. The first of these, certainly, is that the time I spent at the school is always to be viewed as preliminary. In learning, there is always another stage to achieve. What the staff and I clearly understood is that the question "When is one finished learning?" can only be responded to as "Never." Each year, the curricula need to be reviewed and extended so that they reflect that which is currently meaningful and purposeful for the class and the teacher.

CRITICAL ASPECTS OF THE PHASES

In reflecting on the phases and extracting those aspects that led to the success of the project, three areas of concentrated work come to mind: (1) the teacher's literary background; (2) the teacher's skills background in terms of her knowledge of learning specific to the area and her ability to raise the student's level of literacy; and (3) the teacher's knowledge of specific strategies for teaching reading, writing, studying, spelling, coupled with her ability to individualize the instruction. All of the areas supported by the staff development activities of the project came to fruition in the units of the curriculum guide developed by the teachers.

Literary Background

As the above sections indicate, during the first and second phases of the project, the teachers concentrated on (1) developing an extensive knowledge base; (2) becoming familiar with the great minds in education who preceded them; (3) learning how to assess youngsters and to limit test in every aspect of literacy; and (4) recognizing that the quality of writing is determined by the quality of reading. Included therein were many examples of fine children's literature and its background. This led to a deeper cultural understanding of the story's plot and the period in which it was created. For help, the teachers had as resource materials both Huck's *Children's Literature* (1979) and Sutherland and Arbuthnot's *Children and Books* (1977). The books are divided into various genres and different age groups, and the teachers could peruse sections of these books to select the best in children's literature.

For example, in reading alternate versions of the same fairy tale, the teachers were fascinated by how the society's changing roles were reflected in the various versions. They examined different ethnic approaches so that their presentations to their students centered on the similar needs of all people throughout the world. Robert Darnton's (1984) and Jack Zipes' (1991) historical perspectives of fairy tales added greatly to their knowledge base. Further, the teachers determined that they would present both expository and fictional writings within the same unit so that the students could analyze and synthesize the different writing patterns.

A specific example of the utilization of fine literature was the use of Rudyard Kipling's (1974) *Just So Stories* in a fourth grade class. After reading "How the Elephant Got Its Tail," the class felt that they could explain various physiognomies of animals by using their South Bronx milieu. Instead of the Kipling concept, the children suggested that an elephant coming to visit the South Bronx would be most interested in visiting the subway and seeing a particular line that serviced the neighborhood. The children had the elephant tramp down the stairs to the subway and stick his nose into the train. Unfortunately, the train door closed, and the poor elephant's nose was stuck. The elephant pulled and pulled. Finally, he released his nose, but it had been so misshapen that it became the trunk with which we are all now familiar.

Skills Background

The teachers, as they evolved, understood that learning requires both extending their own knowledge base, increasing their pedagogical-skills ability and the level of literacy of the youngsters they teach, all of which needed to be included within the units as integral aspects. Unfortunately, in the history of the teaching of reading and, especially, literacy, educational policy makers seem to veer from one extreme to the other. The units incorporate both authentic language and literacy skills. That both are critical was never more evident than when the newspapers carried the story of the plummeting reading scores in California within the last decade. California, similar to New York, is another state that also has within its public school population a large minority representation. Some years ago, California selected whole language as the only method to teach reading; however, they instituted this system without any of the supportive services necessary to guarantee success. Then, some years later, the reading tests indicated that California public school children were reading way below that which was expected. To know the history of the field is to understand that learning is multifaceted, and no one method can be taught without any other, just as no single discipline be taught in isolation of all the others.

Even writing, viewed by some as a skill and by others as a marker of metacognitive growth, is dependent upon all other abilities. "People who cannot put strings of sentences together in good order cannot think. An educational system that does not teach the technology of writing is preventing thought" (Mitchell, 1979, p. 46). Vocabulary is another aspect that can be isolated but not successfully. Real vocabulary development is dependent upon the multimeaning of words, not a one-sentence memorized definition. Words are learned in context; again, the good reader is the person with an extensive vocabulary knowledge. Spelling is also developmental, as is syntactical growth. Each skill is itself interdependent upon every other; to be truly literate is to be skillful.

Strategies

Incorporated within the unit were strategies to benefit each of the students. What they needed was clearly identified in the assessment procedures. The teachers needed to be very knowledgeable about the variety of strategies that are available for all of the various aspects of literacy, reading, writing, studying, spelling, and so forth. Each of the strategies explained in the literature is successful with some students, some are helpful for most, but none work for everybody. The unit chapters included strategies that seemed to offer support for the students but always with the caveat that every strategy must be refashioned in some manner for each unique student. This philosophy has been fashioned over a lifetime of teaching. First, it was evident from watching the teachers in the inner-city school work with the children, and second, it was reinforced by observing how students with learning disabilities finally achieved to their academic potential (Stracher, 1992). If students can be provided with appropriate strategies that permit them to function to the level of their peers, they may also, in many instances, reach the top percentiles of their class.

UNIT EXAMPLES

The best way to provide the reader with an understanding of what was accomplished is to present examples of the curriculum that the staff, with support, developed. Please remember that the description of an exemplar unit of the curriculum presented here represented several years' work, and to this day is still a work in progress. The emphasis is always on the process of becoming; thus, the units included in the curriculum reflect the progress of the school at one point. Learners are always looking for the next step.

The fourth grade unit is offered as a typical example of the stage at which the staff had progressed to that point. The unit was formally integrated into the school's curriculum, at which time some of the youngsters had had four years of this approach to literacy, dependent upon who their classroom teachers had been. All of the children, other than recent transfers, had at least two years of integrated units. Thus, the concepts of literature being meaningful and purposeful, of the interrelatedness of knowledge, of analysis and synthesis were all familiar to the youngsters.

Fourth grade is also selected because it is the year when many struggling readers are initially identified. It is now that Stanovich's (1986) Matthew Effect comes into full play; by fourth grade, the children are no longer expected to be learning to read but reading to learn. At this stage, children who have had difficulty with print translation are suddenly condemned to read only that which they can decode. That may explain why poor readers have such a paucity of information as high school seniors. This fourth grade unit is for all the fourth graders; their decoding abilities may vary, but their knowledge input will be fairly consistent.

The universal theme for this grade is "People Persevere and Achieve in Spite of Numerous Obstacles." The three subheadings are "People Challenge Themselves," "People Take Risks," and "People Coexist with Nature."

Each reading has a list of (1) the vocabulary words needed to know, (2) analysis and synthesis questions, and (3) suggested and related activities. For example, after the children have read two poems, Langston Hughes "Dreams" (1964) and a poem about Columbus under the subheading "People Challenge Themselves," and answered specific analysis questions, the students are asked if they thought Columbus followed Hughes' advice and why. Another is a science activity stemming from the Columbus poem. The youngsters are asked to study different types of winds (gale wind is mentioned in the poem). Further suggestions are to study the Beaufort Scale of wind speeds and to make wind instruments (wind vane, windsock, anemometer). Another option is to study what causes winds and for experiments using winds to be incorporated into the unit.

Under the subheading "People Challenge Themselves," the youngsters read a biography of Dr. Elizabeth Blackwell (Clapp, 1974). One of the analysis questions asks what Elizabeth Blackwell's aunt's comment that it's a pity she wasn't born a boy tells the reader about England in the 1820s. Under Social Studies, the children are asked to draw a timeline and research some of the more significant events that occurred within her lifetime (e.g., slavery, the Mexican War, etc.). Under Science, the youngsters are asked to research the diseases that are controlled today but were virulent in Dr. Blackwell's time. A visit to a health clinic is suggested so that the youngsters can observe the procedures that are followed to avoid disease today, such as inoculations, hygiene, and proper nutrition.

Under the subheading "People Take Risks," the youngsters read a biography of Pocahontas (Fritz, 1987). One of the analysis questions asks the children to identify what was the "Starving Time," to note where starvation exists today, to define malnutrition, and to respond to the question of how starvation and malnutrition can be overcome. Under Social Studies, the youngsters are asked to research the Indian tribes that have lived in New York State, to identify the towns and cities in their area that have Indian names, and to write the mayor and/or town council requesting information about the Indians who lived there. Under Music and Dance, the curriculum suggests listening to recordings of Indian music and visiting a local Indian reservation to watch the Indian dances.

After reading about Prometheus (D'Aulaires, 1962), one of the analysis questions asks the youngsters to list the characteristics of a myth and to explain why ancient people developed them. A synthesis question asks the students to compare Pocahontas and Prometheus and explain how they are different (analysis) and similar (synthesis). In Related Activities, under Language Arts, the youngsters are asked to research the affixes, suffixes, and roots in the English language that have their derivation from the Greeks. The children are also asked to keep an ongoing record of newspapers and magazines that use the names of Greek gods and goddesses and myths.

After reading *My Brother Sam is Dead* (Collier, 1985), under Related Activities in Social Studies, the children are asked to use and make maps showing the setting of the story and the places mentioned and to trace Tim and his father's route from Connecticut to New York. They are also to write to the Connecticut State Legislature to ask for any brochures and/or information about life in that state during the Revolutionary War. In addition, they study the United States Constitution and the reasons for its need and then write a class Constitution defining the rights of students.

After reading a biography of Harriet Tubman (Bains, 1982), the children are asked, under synthesis questions, to compare Harriet's life at age eight to theirs. They analyze who in the novel *My Brother Sam is Dead* might have agreed and/or disagreed with Harriet's view of liberty and death, compare Harriet Tubman and Elizabeth Blackwell as to their individual qualities and the ones that they shared, and compare the differences and similarities between Harriet's fearless nature and Pocahontas. Under Social Studies, the children are asked to research and read biographies and autobiographies of other African Americans in the fields of science, math, history, literature, arts, and so forth, and to note how each individual persevered, overcame obstacles, and achieved. In Science, the suggestion is to study the stars, such as Polaris, the North Star, and the constellations. They can contact the Hall of Science about their Star Lab for children and use gummed stars to illustrate the constellations. The children may turn the ceiling of the classroom into the night sky with stars or research the use of stars by early navigators to chart direction. Under Music, the children are to tape freedom songs, such as "Follow the Drinking Gourd." Under Language Arts, the children are expected to develop an equality code for the classroom that lists responsibilities to help all classmates achieve to their maximum potential.

Under the subheading "People Coexist with Nature," the youngsters read both the poem "Johnny Appleseed," (Rosemary & Stephen Benet, 1933) and the folktale (Anderson, 1974). The children, under Social Studies, place Johnny Appleseed's life on a timeline that also includes the significant historical events during that period. Under Science, the youngsters plant apple seeds and learn about seed classification and germination. They study types of apples, their uses, and nutritional value, and the effects on humans of the insecticides used on apples. In Language Arts, they create a modern New York folk hero or heroine, describe the problem that this person is helping to resolve, and relate one pertinent adventure. The writers must also indicate how the New York area itself (the setting) influences the story.

Another one of the readings is the fairy tale of *Cinderella* in both the Perrault (1954) and Grimm (1976) versions. Among the activities, the children are asked to contrast the two versions and to write their own updated account; they are also asked to compare life in France and Germany at the time that the two Cinderellas were written, how they were different and/or similar.

In reading a biography about the life of Rachel Carson, the youngsters are asked, under synthesis questions, how Johnny Appleseed's dream for his society was different from and similar to the one Rachel Carson made. When she described *The Silent Spring*, Rachel Carson had powerful enemies, as did Prometheus, when he tried to help man. Children can explore ways in which their enemies were similar and different. Under Science, the children research information about harmful pollutants in the atmosphere; then, they write to their state environmental agency posing the problems and asking what steps are being taken to ameliorate this issue. The youngsters discuss with classmates the steps they can take to improve the quality of their environment. In Social Studies, they study the original American Indian environmental policies and today's policies. In Art, the children engage in a poster campaign to encourage classmates to work for a safe, clean environment. They distribute "environmental buttons" to all the people who promise to abide by the rules the class has developed.

All the readings and suggestions in *A Literature Based Integrated Curriculum—Grades Pre K-6* provide meaningful and purposeful learning experiences for the youngsters for whom they were developed. Within this context, the students' skills needs are incorporated. The teachers select those activities that they deem most important for their youngsters. All of the learning, as the above suggests, is interrelated; all the disciplines function within the rubric of fine literature to which the children can relate. The teachers have the skills knowledge. They have limit tested their youngsters. The staff has itself first mastered the chosen readings and incorporated the Henry model for metacognitive development.

LESSONS LEARNED AND A LOOK AT THE PRESENT

Writing this chapter was a welcome retrospective, to view again the project that raised the literacy level of children in an inner-city elementary school. It was also an opportunity to re-evaluate what, how, and why we did what we did. This led to the identification of those aspects that can be implemented in similar urban projects and to the important lessons that were learned in conducting the project. Also, it gave me the opportunity to view the project in light of the situation or conditions that exist today in teacher education and in most inner-city schools.

Inner-city conditions have changed since the project was completed. If anything, the need to provide special curricula so these youngsters will become literate, reasoning adults is even greater, as is the requisite support for the teachers of these children. Recent reforms appear to have given up on inner-city schools and concentrate instead on competition in the shape of charter schools and vouchers. To understand the damage that such fragmentation accomplishes is to recall what one New York school district that expends enormous sums per child in educational costs responded when the request for permission to begin a charter school occurred.

The school district demanded that the state veto this request. Their rationale was that if permission were given for the charter school, all youngsters who select that option would take their yearly education allotment with them. The school district felt strongly that it needed the money in its public schools to continue to provide quality education. How much more critical are per-student dollars in the inner city? What will happen if even that paltry amount (compared to the sums expended in certain school districts) is cut further because of charter schools and vouchers?

Further, as each state around the country mandates higher standards for all its teachers, we look at the current plight in the field. Within New York State, in particular, there are 10,500 teachers who are teaching in areas in which they are not licensed, and not surprisingly, 10,000 of them are located in New York City. Obviously, the need for qualified, licensed teachers for New York City schools as well as for other the inner-city schools around the nation is enormous. As part of the upgrading of the professional caliber of elementary and secondary school teachers in New York State, all staff will be required to clock 175 hours of professional studies within a five-year period. Teacher inclusion in similar projects that target cognitive development through literacy would certainly more than satisfy this new state requirement. Not only would they be benefiting their students, but they will be meeting their own professional development requirements and, one hopes, decreasing the astronomical number of teachers in the inner city who are not licensed or qualified to teach the subjects for which they are currently responsible.

A school district that is forever raising its sights is also one that has a strong, dedicated leader who can generate the change necessary. Unfortunately, in this arena also, politics, not educational theory, determines who will be the superintendent for inner-city schools. Should the head of the educational system disagree with the mayor or other politico, that person is removed, and another superintendent who will be more willing to meet the political demands is employed. Whereas this may make for good politics, it is an abomination for a system that is charged with educating inner-city children to their potential.

Today in the United States, two million people are currently incarcerated. Throughout the world, the number of prisoners is eight million; we have one quarter of that world total. A high proportion of people in jails and prisons in the United States are individuals who cannot read at an appropriate level; in an increasingly technological society, people who do not have an adequate literacy level are condemned to remain at the lowest rungs of the economic ladder. Any attempt to provide adequately for their families is limited because they do not have the requisite minimal skills to be employed for a living wage. Raised in poverty, condemned to an education that neither helps them meet their potential nor become literate, they can become victims of drug pushers and other hardened criminals. They are the population from which the greatest number of our prisoners derive, and they are primarily from inner cities. Thus, a comprehensive effort should be made by teachers, parents, administrators, politicians, and law makers to ensure that all youngsters in the inner cities have adequate opportunities and financial support to become literate, thinking adults. This should the nation's priority in this new millennium.

If we were to start the project today, certainly we would design a plan of action in accord with present conditions, and we would incorporate within the project that which is available to us in the areas of cognitive development, educational research and theory, and children's literature. Since the original curriculum was written, many better choices of relevant children's literature and reading programs (e.g., Success For All) are available from book publishers. (See Appendix A for suggested current works and materials.) However, the staff development process and critical aspects of the project identified in this chapter are generic and would remain the same for a very simple reason. They worked.

Over the course of my involvement in this project, I learned:

1. It is absolutely critical that the principal of the school be involved on day one and throughout the phases of the project. The principal must be an effective leader who understands all the steps necessary to achieve the goals of the project.

2. The project is owned and developed by the teachers. The project was sustained over a decade and institutionalized because of this, and it was sustained because of the teachers' commitment to helping students learn.
3. There must be a specific time and place that the teachers can work on the curriculum. In the original project, every Monday afternoon was set aside at the school to conduct the work and hold graduate courses that were planned for and by the teachers. The choice of the school itself as the place to work was propitious; this was the laboratory where the experimental project was conducted, and, therefore, it should also be the place where the group works. Without a consistent time and place, things tend to fall apart.
4. Participants must come to realize and then operate on the notion that a curriculum is always in the process of changing or becoming. Because all learners remain somewhere on a spiral curriculum throughout a lifetime, teachers must perceive the work as ongoing and facilitating not only student learning but their own professional development as well.
5. Parents must take an active role in the process and be adequately prepared to team and collaborate with teachers. Without a home component, substantial student achievement is questionable.

Probably the most important addition or idea I would include today to ensure continuity of the work would be to develop from the outset a strong connection to the business world. To expect that any inner-city school will have adequate sums for all aspects of the project is unrealistic. However, every modern business, particularly those located in metropolitan hubs, requires that their employees be literate, thinking adults. To guarantee that outcome, businesses could be approached to donate or lend the needed materials. What better advertisement for major booksellers than to be the providers of the selected books? What advertising coups are possible by technology firms that provide inner cities with the needed computers and other relevant technology?

Finally, this complex society can only function if its educational system provides it with literate, rational adults. That is the goal for all public schools throughout the country. Such an outcome is already a reality for many middle-class communities. The challenge is to provide inner-city youngsters with the same rights so that they too may achieve to their potential. This project offered the children in one inner-city school the opportunity to become literate, thinking people. The entire school community worked together in a partnership to further the aims of education. Administration was sensitive to the needs of its faculty and provided the time for the teachers to develop meaningful and purposeful curriculum. As a professor of education and director of the project, I was committed to working alongside staff. My role was to provide the knowledge base; the how-to of limit testing; a review of fine children's literature; and a system for assessing, programming, and evaluating. In the same way that the curriculum continues to be broader and deeper in one school, so can all the schools throughout the country emulate this project. First, the educational community needs to join hands and make the system responsive to the needs of its children in their right to become literate, thinking adults.

The initial result of the project, after its first year, was that other teachers in the school wanted to share this heightened sense of learning in their classrooms also. The following year, another group of teachers joined, thus extending the graduate course information. Within three years of the original curriculum presentation, the teachers, with my guidance, presented another, more extensive curriculum guide titled *A Literature Based Integrated Curriculum Grades Pre K-6: Reading, Writing and Reasoning: A Teacher's Guide*. With each year, the teachers were encouraged to extend the curricula and to make it their own. Within a decade, better than 90% of the students in the school scored at or above grade level in the standardized reading tests. The evidence also demonstrated that:

- A high proportion of the youngsters passed the writing tests, and the teachers noted the achievement of the youngsters in their writing;
- Pupils learned the best example of various genres and were able to identify the salient characteristics of each;
- Pupils were asked and responded to inferential questions that were linked to higher levels of thinking/reasoning;
- Teachers reported that they learned a new way to approach the learning process that focused more directly on pupil learning;
- Teachers reported that their knowledge base increased, particularly in literary selections of the various genres;
- Teachers worked effectively as a group to develop universal themes for the curriculum that were then implemented in other grade levels.

What this project clearly establishes is that if we unite committed administrators, teachers, and college faculty, literacy for all our students is within our grasp.

APPENDIX A
CURRENT WORKS AND MATERIALS

Some years have passed since this unique literacy approach was successfully implemented in one inner-city elementary school. Today, several new elementary programs have been created that offer reading proficiency to children in poor urban settings. Those that currently appear most promising according to the research literature are documented in the following publication:

> Charles A. Dana Center, University of Texas at Austin, *Hope for Urban Education: A Study of Nine High-Performing, High-Poverty, Urban Elementary Schools.* (Washington, DC: U.S. Department of Education, Planning and Evaluation Service, 1999).

All of these schools used federal Title I dollars to create school-wide programs. The characteristics that these schools shared with the original study reported in this chapter are the minimum requirement for any effective reading program. They all had committed administrators and teachers who were knowledgeable, parents who were actively involved, and a firm belief that the children could and would learn. The programs themselves that the schools used differed somewhat. For example, the James Ward Elementary School in Chicago, Illinois, had the following key programs: *Lighthouse After-School Program, Community Learning Center, 21st Century Empowerment Zone, Links to Literacy, Hug-a-Book, Chicago Science Academy,* and *Annenburg Foundation Grant.*

The Goodale Elementary School in Detroit, Michigan, used the following key programs: *Sylvan Reading Program, Peer Mediation, Efficacy Program, After-School Tutoring Program,* and the Lora B. Peck Elementary School in Houston, Texas, had as its key programs *Project GRAD: Success for All, Move-it Math, Consistency Management Discipline Plan, Communities in Schools, Family Support Team, Head Start, Bilingual Program* (pre-kindergarten through fifth grade), *Voyager After-School Program, Project Reconnect Parent Center,* and *Home-School Connection.*

Another recent program that appears to make a difference in the literacy success of elementary students is *Success for All* (Balkcom & Himmelfarb, 1993. ED364641 August 1993 Success for All. Education Research Consumer Guide, Number 5. Office of Education Research and Improvement (ED), Washington, DC. Office of Research.)

Success for All began as a partnership between the Baltimore City Public Schools and the Center for Research on Elementary and Middle Schools (CREM) that was housed at The Johns Hopkins University. It began in Baltimore in 1987-88 and has been fully implemented in 50 schools in fifteen states.

The premise of this program is also that every child can learn and that early support prevents later problems. The children are expected to achieve grade-level reading by the end of third grade. Its school reform programs are all-inclusive and address the family's ability to help their children by providing the appropriate, food, shelter, and medical care.

The preschool and kindergarten activities concentrate on language development and a positive sense of self. The early reading program is very phonic in approach. From grade two through five, the reading materials are more extensive. Youngsters who are identified early as having reading difficulties are provided with individual tutoring that can extend from grades one through three. The research literature clearly establishes that one-on-one tutoring, with well-trained teachers, is most effective. (The next program to be discussed, Reading Recovery, insists on just such a ratio: one-to-one.) Further, each *Success for All* program has a full-time facilitator who works with the teachers, all of whom have been trained prior to entering the classroom. Although the program is viewed as successful, 1991 program data indicated that almost 40% of third graders were reading somewhere from a month to a year below grade level.

Reading Recovery was initiated by Marie M. Clay in New Zealand in the 1980s to prevent reading problems before they began (*http://www.ed.gov/databases/ERIC-Digests/ed364641.html* ED352601 December 1992. Reading Recovery. Education Research Consumer Guide Number 3. See Thomas, 1992). The bottom 20% of readers in a first grade class are placed in a highly structured program where, on a daily basis, they receive one-on-one tutoring from a trained teacher (not an aide) for 30 minutes for up to 20 weeks. Although the original results are impressive, longitudinal studies indicate that Reading Recovery youngsters who continue on in classrooms without the parent-child-school connection or selected appropriate readings lose their reading edge. In addition, when the training of a Reading Recovery teacher was reduced, so were the results (Pinnell, 1994)

Another aspect of successful literacy training is certainly the effective teaching of writing (ED250694 84 Qualities of Effective Writing Programs. ERIC Digest. See Holbrook, 1984). The characteristics that define successful writing programs are similar to those that have been noted previously in effective reading presentations. Among these are in-service programs, total school commitment, strong administrative support, and time spent in perfecting reading. Successful programs have students writing anywhere from 45 to 90 minutes daily. Much of the original success came from the Bay Area Writing Project that is now known as the *National Writing Project*. This was the first emphasis on writing as a process and not simply a product. The features include composing, syntax, sequence, small group experiences, and writing. (This new approach to writing follows the research of such people as Donald Graves, Lucy Calkins, Jane Hansen, Nancy Atwell, etc. The underlying concept is that writing is a process that reflects the reasoning level of the individual who presents the written work.) The *National Writing Project* offers teachers workshops where they can improve their own writing skills. When they become proficient, they serve as consultants for schools and inservice programs. This program, as all the others mentioned, depends upon total administrative involvement, well-trained teachers, parent involvement, constant feedback, and belief that children can succeed. The program described in this chapter assumes that its approach to literacy will lead to cognitive development. The latter development will, in time, foster adults who are capable of higher-level reasoning. Although there were glimmerings of youngsters who seemed comfortable with both analysis and synthesis, there is not yet a longitudinal study that verifies the significance of this approach. In fact, none of the new programs mentioned in Appendix A has a long enough history to determine which, if any, not only ensure that the students will be able to decode but will also be literate enough to be abstract thinkers.

Whatever approach is selected, excellent sources in determining which trade books to offer youngsters are Charlotte Huck's (1979) *Children's Literature in the Elementary School* and May Arbuthnot's (1976) *Arbuthnot Anthology of Children's Literature*. Both list and offer a synopsis of much fine children's literature presented by age appropriateness, genre, and category. In addition, every children's library and/or librarian can provide the names of Caldecott and Newbury winners, both of which offer the best in current children's literature.

Minimally, all excellent literacy programs guarantee committed and well-trained administrators and teachers, parental and community involvement, a belief that all children can learn and the reading of fine children's literature together with the writing process. The program presented in this chapter also insists upon all readings integrated within a universal theme that incorporates all the academic and creative activities. The premise is that it is this approach that guarantees real cognitive growth and higher level reasoning. Only time will tell which particular program offers the best approach; the probability is that there will be several that will prove to be significant because of the uniqueness of each individual.

What all these programs do seem to promise, however, is that the right to literacy must be guaranteed as part of the democratic heritage and that we in the educational community must lead in providing it.

REFERENCES

Anderson, L. (1974). *The story of Johnny Appleseed*. Campaign, IL: Garrard Publishing Company.

Arbuthnot, M. H. (1976). *The Arbuthnot anthology of children's literature*. Glenview, IL: Scott, Foresman.

Bains, R. (1982). *Harriet Tubman—The road to freedom*. Mahway, NJ: Troll Associates.

Balkcom, S., & Himmelfarb, H. (1993). *Success for all*. Education Research Consumer Guide (No. 5). Washington, DC: Office of Education Research and Improvement (ED). Office of Research. (ERIC Document Reproduction Service No. ED 364641).

Benet, R., & Benet, S. V. (1987). *A book of Americans*. New York: Henry Holt & Co,

Bettelheim, B., & Zalen, K. (1982). *On learning to read*. New York: Knopf.

Bond, G. L., & Dykstra, R. (1967). The cooperative research program in first grade reading instruction. *Reading Research Quarterly, 2*, 5-142.

Bruner, J. (1966). *Toward a theory of instruction*. Cambridge: Harvard University Press.

Calkins, L. (1986). *The art of teaching writing*. Portsmouth, NH: Heinemann.

Charles A. Dana Center, University of Texas at Austin. (1999). *Hope for urban education: A study of nine high-performing, high-poverty, urban elementary schools*. Washington, DC: U.S. Department of Education, Planning and Evaluation Service.

Clapp, P. (1974). *Dr. Elizabeth, the story of the first woman doctor*. New York: Lothrop, Lee & Shepard.

Collier, J. L. (1985). *My brother Sam is dead*. New York: Four Winds Press.

Darnton, R. (1984). *The great cat massacre and other episodes in French cultural history*. New York: Basic Books.

D'Aulaires' book of Greek myths. (1962). New York: Dell Publishers.

Fritz, J. (1987). *The double life of Pocahontas*. New York: Puffin Books.

Gardner, H. (1985). *Frames of mind*. New York: Basic Books.

Gardner, H. (1999, September 11). Toward thinking on essential questions. *New York Times*, pp. B9, B11.

Goodman, K. S. (1965). A linguistic study of cues and miscues in reading. *Elementary English, 42*, 639-645.

Grimm's complete fairy tales. (1976). New York: Pantheon.

Henry, G. (1974). *Teaching reading as concept development*. Newark, DE: International Reading Association.

Hirsch, E.D., Jr. (1999, September 11). Finding the answer in drills and rigor. *New York Times*, pp. B9, B11.

Holbrook, H.T. (1984). *Qualities of effective writing programs*. ERIC Digest. (ERIC Document Reproduction Service No. ED 250694)

Huck, C. S. (1979). *Children's literature in the elementary school* (3rd ed.). New York: Holt, Rinehart and Winston.

Hughes, L. (1964). Dreams. In *New negro poets*. Bloomington: Indiana University Press.

Kipling, R. (1974). *Just so stories*. New York: Signet Classics New American Library.

Kohlberg, L., & Mayer, R. (1978). Development as an aim of education. In *Harvard Educational Review* (reprint No. 13). Cambridge: Harvard University Press.

Mindell, P., & Stracher, D. (1980). Assessing reading and writing of the gifted: The warp and woof of the language program. *The Gifted Child Quarterly, 2*, 14-20.

Mitchell, R. (1979). *Less than words can say*. Boston: Little Brown.

Perrault, C. (1982). *Perrault's complete fairy tales* (A. E. Johnson, Trans.). New York: Dodd Mead.

Piaget, J. (1992). *The origins of intelligence in children*. New York: International University Press.

Pinnell, G. S. (1994). Comparing instructional models for the literacy education of high risk first graders. *Reading Research Quarterly, 29*(1), 8-39.

Stanley, J. (1976). The case of extreme acceleration of intellectually brilliant youth. *The Gifted Child Quarterly, 20*, 1.

Stanovich, K. E. (1986). Matthew effects in reading: Some consequences of individual differences in the acquisition of literacy. *Reading Research Quarterly, 21*, 360-407.

Stracher, D.A. (Ed.). (1989). *A literature based integrated curriculum—grades preK-6*. New York: Board of Education.

Stracher, D. A. (1992, Fall). Providing strategies for learning disabled college students: Continuous assessment in reading, writing and reasoning. *Research and Teaching in Developmental Education*.

Sutherland, Z., & Arbuthnot, M. H. (1977). *Children and books* (5th ed.). Glenview, IL: Scott, Foresman.

Thomas, R. L. (1992). *Reading recovery*. Education Research Consumer Guide (No. 3). (ERIC Document Reproduction Service No. ED 352601)

Zipes, J. (1991). (Ed.). *Spells of enchantment: The wondrous fairy tales of western culture*. New York: Viking.

Four

Project SCOPE I and II: Holistic School-College/University Partnership Projects for Instituting Change and Improvement in K-18 Education

Linda A. Catelli

In the past twelve years, the academic sector of society has witnessed the emergence of new visions and creative model approaches for reforming education and professional education in the United States.[1] For the past 21 years, the partnership movement in education in the United States has linked schools and colleges/universities for a variety of purposes, and it has restructured these institutions in significant ways. Now, well into a fourth phase of the movement, leaders of school-university/college partnerships are increasingly directing their efforts toward reconceptualizing the U.S. education system and redefining the profession of teaching.[2] During this phase, we are witnessing:

---

[1]For reform models, see U.S. Department of Education (1998, 1999a) and Northwest Regional Educational Laboratory (1998).

[2]See Albert (1991), Catelli (1997), and Haycock, Hart, and Irvine (1992), for an explanation of the phases.

- state education departments recommending and funding closer working relationships between schools and teacher education institutions (e.g., New York State Regents Task Force on Teaching, July, 1998);
- the U.S. Department of Education providing grant opportunities for improving teacher quality and teacher preparation via partnership arrangements between schools and universities (U.S. Department of Education, 1998, 1999a, 1999b);
- public university systems such as the California State University and the City University of New York calling for a vision of a K-16 education system with special attention to increasing the quality of their teacher education programs with linkages to K-12 schooling (California State University [CSU] Presidents' Group, 1996; The CSU Institute for Education Reform, 1996; and Schmidt, Badillo, Brady, MacDonald, Ohrenstein, Roberts, & Schwartz, 1999);
- the establishment of over 2,322 formal school-college collaborative arrangements reported in a national survey sponsored by the American Association for Higher Education (Wilbur & Lambert, 1995) and research on such collaborative-type arrangements (e.g., Slater, 1996); and
- the creation of over 300 formal Professional Development Schools (PDSs), a *teaching-hospital notion* originally conceptualized by the Holmes Group (1986, 1990, 1995), along with an emerging body of research on such schools.[3]

In this chapter, a holistic school-university/college partnership model is presented with its accompanying conceptualization, initial change strategy, and its integrative approach for changing and improving K-12 education and teacher education. The original model, successfully implemented for eighteen years in a program entitled Project SCOPE [I], was a partnership I began in 1980 between school teachers in the New York City area and professors and education students of the City University of New York at Queens College. Aspects of that project still operate today. In 1998, the model was expanded and adapted to another academic setting and location in New York at Dowling College under the title of Project SCOPE II—School-College Operation in Partnership Education. One of the goals of a SCOPE project is to transport the major features and critical elements that make a holistic partnership work.

A holistic school-university partnership has twelve major features, three of which are considered critical elements or defining

[3]See Byrd and McIntyre (1999), Kochan (1999), and Darling-Hammond (1994).

features of the partnership. The first element is its *smallness*, that is, its size in terms of the relatively small number of participants that constitute a unit or a team. The second element is the *organic* relationship that is created among the participants and between the partnering institutions. The third element is the partnership's *integrative* and *coordinative* approach to educational change and improvement. These three elements combined with nine other features are the main elements of a successful holistic school-university partnership. For purposes of this chapter, I am interested in proposing a holistic perspective on school-university partnerships for urban and inner-city settings. Further, I am interested in promoting a vision of a coordinated and integrative K to 18 education system in the 21st century.

The chapter is arranged in four sections. In the first section, I briefly explain the theory and conceptual framework for a holistic school-university partnership and its use as a viable model-approach for integrating and changing K-12 schooling and professional education (13-18). The second section provides an initial change strategy that was designed to achieve the partnership's goal for revising and expanding the professional roles of the school practitioners in the New York City Project. The third section presents a summary of the twelve major features of a holistic partnership model that can be transported to other academic sites. In the fourth section, I make brief mention of the accomplishments of the two Project SCOPE partnerships. The accomplishments of Project SCOPE I and II are presented as supporting evidence of the partnerships' productivity and effectiveness. Finally, at the end of the fourth section, I offer reflective comments on the lessons learned in conducting both projects. Much of the information in the chapter is drawn from my 33 years of partnership work with school practitioners, a synthesis of the research on education, and my past writings on Project SCOPE I and II.

THEORY AND CONCEPTUAL FRAMEWORK FOR A HOLISTIC PARTNERSHIP

Since its inception over 20 years ago, Project SCOPE I has been a conceptually based, holistic, evolving partnership that seeks to change, integrate, and improve professional education and K-12 schooling. As a holistic enterprise, its theory fosters a notion that an organic whole has a reality independent and greater than the sum of its parts. The partnership's parts—its programs, people, and institutional levels—function in an interdependent manner toward a common goal and for the benefit of the whole.

In a holistic partnership, the relationship between and among people and programs is for the most part organic rather than symbiotic.

In a symbiotic relationship, there are two equal parties, a school and university, who work together to satisfy their mutual self-interests (Catelli, 1990b, 1997; Clark, 1988; Goodlad, 1988, 1990, 1994; Schlechty & Whitford, 1988). Each party remains in the relationship or arrangement until the desired goal is achieved. Once the goal is achieved, the relationship ends, and the partnership ceases. Often such school-university arrangements are temporary and lack the stability necessary to bring about lasting or comprehensive change and improvement. These types of arrangements or relationships could be compared to collaborations, such as when a song writer and lyricist collaborate on a musical piece for a period of time. In an organic relationship, the two parties and their programs operate in a more lasting, integral, and intimate fashion. The two institutions assume joint ownership of selected programs and responsibility for commonly agreed-upon agenda goals and their associated problems. Their relationship is ongoing, and their work is directed at the improvement of an entire education system.

The idea of organic relationships was best promoted by Fritjof Capra in *The Web of Life* (1977), Arie DeGeus in *The Living Company* (1977), and Philip Schlechty and Betty Lou Whitford in a chapter written by them in 1988 entitled 'Shared Problems and Shared Vision: Organic Collaboration." Schlechty and Whitford state:

> In organic relationships the parts fulfill unique functions, sometimes in a semi-autonomous fashion, but the purpose of these functions is to serve the body of the whole. Indeed, each part has a major investment in the survival of the whole because ill health of the body has potentially devastating effects on each of the separate parts. Thus, unlike symbiotic relationships, which emphasize mutual self-interests, organic relationships stress the common good above all else. (pp. 191-192)

An organic relationship between a school and university is one of the critical elements of a holistic partnership. All members of the partnership conduct their work interdependently for the common good and health of the partnership's educational system. This is the perspective upon which activities, practices, and policies are designed and from which a professional culture is developed.

Members of a holistic partnership may, at times, engage in a collaborative type of arrangement, one that is perhaps more symbiotic in nature. For example, members of a holistic partnership may decide to collaborate with a neighboring school district, contracting with an outside agency to provide staff development training for the teachers of both districts to acquire new skills for teaching reading. Subsequently, they will share the cost, space, knowledge, and personnel for the venture. Their relationship and contractual arrangement with personnel from the other school district are, in this case, short-term and symbiotic. However, if this arrangement occurs, it does so within the organic structure of the partnership.

Holistic school-university partnerships are special cases of the existing partnership models.[4] In such a partnership, a university and school come together for the expressed purpose of establishing a new type of *educational laboratory*, one that is directed at comprehensive change, innovation, improvement, and reform. The partners' work is focused on operating a laboratory of the future: a setting in which people create newer forms of education for improving student learning in a more coordinative system of education. Functional connectedness among the levels of education and teacher education is essential; experimentation and innovation are key; and planned integration and coordination of programs, personnel, and content are paramount.[5]

Many of the concepts for a holistic partnership originated from my earlier work in the 1960s and 1970s at the Agnes Russell Laboratory School at Teachers College, Columbia University. There, in my studies and interactions with such educators as Kay Vandergrift, Jane Hannigan, Bruce Joyce, and Robert Schaefer (then dean of Teachers College and author of the seminal work *School as a Center of Inquiry*), newer forms of teaching and teacher education were tested. Also, new organizational structures for schools were designed (Joyce, 1969; Joyce & Weil, 1972a, 1972b). The work of Robert Schaefer (1967) and Elizabeth C. Wilson (1972) on centers of inquiry; Jonas Soltis (1968, 1978), Ronald Hyman (1971, 1974), and Israel Scheffler (1960, 1965, 1966) in educational philosophy; Ann Gentile (1972) in psychology; and William G. Anderson (1971, 1974) and B.O. Smith (1960, 1962, 1963) on the analysis of teaching all shaped much of the conceptual underpinnings for my partnership work.

In 1980, the concepts and ideas were operationalized in a partnership project I founded at Queens College of the City University of New York (CUNY) entitled Project SCOPE [I]. The partnership involved two college professors, education students, and teachers in the subject areas of health and physical education. The teachers were from schools in New York City and the surrounding suburban areas of Westchester and Long Island. The partnership focused on the separate education domains of the school's curriculum and staff development program, and the College's preservice and inservice teacher education programs. The goal was to integrate these domains to effect change and improvement in education.

---

[4]For an overview of partnership models, see Jones and Maloy (1988); Maeroff (1983); U.S. Department of Education (1984); Whiting, Whitty, Furlong, Miles, and Barton (1996); and Wilbur and Lambert (1995).

[5]See Bellah, Madsen, Sullivan, Swidler, and Tipton (1990, pp. 275-307) for an in-depth explanation of functional connectedness.

The conceptual framework for the holistic partnership project is illustrated in Figure 4.1. Figure 4.1 identifies the three educational domains (A, B, C) that form a *dynamic triad* inclusive of programs, content, students, and teachers. The conceptual framework was founded on three assumptions from which all project activities were designed. The three assumptions are:

1. that closer linkages among and eventual fusion of the major domains will result in improving education at all levels and creating a new coordinated K-18 education system;
2. that the quality and effectiveness of a university's teacher education program is ultimately dependent on its meaningful connection to schools, educational practice, and student learning; and
3. that the development of teaching as a profession and its knowledge base is best served by a more participatory and organic relationship among school and university personnel.

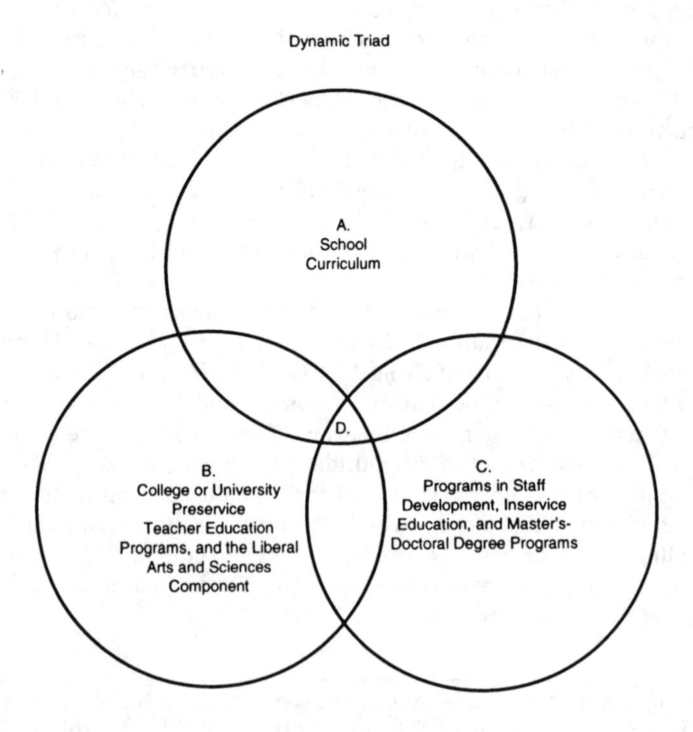

Figure 4.1. Conceptual framework for a holistic school-university/college partnership

These three assumptions were and are the main agenda goals for a holistic partnership project. They operate as the guiding principles for all partnership activities and action research studies impacting one or more of the domains.

Over time, domains B and C of the conceptual framework were expanded, in theory, to include the faculties of the liberal arts and sciences for the preparation of preservice teacher candidates and for the professional development of inservice teachers via master's and doctoral programs. Although this was never achieved at CUNY, it became part of SCOPE's conceptual framework in the early 1990s (Catelli, 1993). Such institutional barriers as a nonresponsive faculty reward system, rigid department lines, and a negative perception of teacher education held by a small percentage of the College's faculties all prevented this from occurring. However, it is now clear to the larger education community that the liberal arts and sciences faculties of a college or university must join the team of teacher educators and school teachers to adequately prepare teachers. The Carnegie Foundation for the Advancement of Teaching under the directorship of Lee Shulman has begun to conduct research on collaborative models between faculties of liberal arts and sciences and faculties of education. Also, many master's level teacher education programs have recently incorporated course work on the new national K-12 pupil learning standards. In this phase of education reform/renewal, we are witnessing teacher education being conceptually reshaped and linked to K-12 pupil learning.

As a *triad*, the conceptual framework for a holistic partnership promotes the idea that each domain relies on the others to accomplish the agenda goals. For example:

1. if instituting major changes in a school's curriculum (e.g., standards-based education) necessitates the implementation of new pedagogical approaches or skills (e.g., constructivism), then the training of such skills for the practitioners responsible for the curriculum relies on the school's staff development program for its accomplishment;
2. if student teachers who will be assigned to the school are expected to demonstrate the new pedagogical skills, then this requires that the university's teacher education program include in its course content and experiences adequate preparation of such new skills; and
3. if cooperating teachers at the school are expected to facilitate the student teacher's performance of the skills, then the acquisition of supervisory knowledge for the development and assessment of such skills requires the university and school to provide adequate inservice training or professional development for the cooperating teachers.

The main idea I am promoting is that for fundamental change and comprehensive improvement to occur each domain is dependent upon the others. Whether new education practices are initiated by research findings, a revised school curriculum based on pupil needs, or the creative ideas and practical wisdom of school practitioners and professors, all parties must be involved in a integrative, innovative, and coordinated fashion for its success and implementation. Similarly, all parties must be involved to facilitate student learning and produce new knowledge for the profession of teaching.

Central to SCOPE's holistic theory and ideals is area D of the conceptual framework. Area D represents the point at which the programs, personnel, content, and resources come together on common ground for the improvement of professional education and K-12 education. It is the area in which integrative activities, courses, and research studies involving pre- and inservice education students, teachers, and professors are conducted and coordinated. It serves as the partnership's catalyst for change and its laboratory for experimentation and innovation (see Wilson, 1972). Area D is the heart of a holistic partnership. It is semi-autonomous in its structure, governance, and policies.

As an evolving and spiraling process, a holistic partnership moves slowly toward increasing the size of area D while improving and revitalizing professional education and school curriculum. This is the area that places educators from schools and the university in a new configuration where their roles and relationships are defined differently. Such new professional roles for teachers as action-researcher, student-teacher supervisor or mentor, university course instructor, change agent, institution-builder, curriculum developer, proposal writer, conference speaker, and author of professional articles are intertwined, and often jointly participated in by members of the partnership (e.g., Catelli, 1995; Catelli, DeCurtis, Nix, Johnston, McLaughlin, Mongiello, & Moskowitz, 1995; Catelli, Johnston, Nix, Stack-Lennon, Turner, & Escobar, 1994; Catelli & Nix, 1992). In a holistic partnership, education professors engage in the interconnected roles of partnership director, staff developer, and research coordinator. The skills for each role are developed over time in what may be referred to as a professional development plan or change strategy (see Figure 4.2). The new professional roles for professors and teachers and the activities associated with each of the roles are critical to achieving the ultimate goals of the partnership.

Let me give you an example that I have used often in past writings that best illustrates the ideas presented above. The school teachers who served as student-teacher supervisors in the original partnership project in New York City conducted an action-research study that involved the use of goal-setting procedures and videotaped analysis

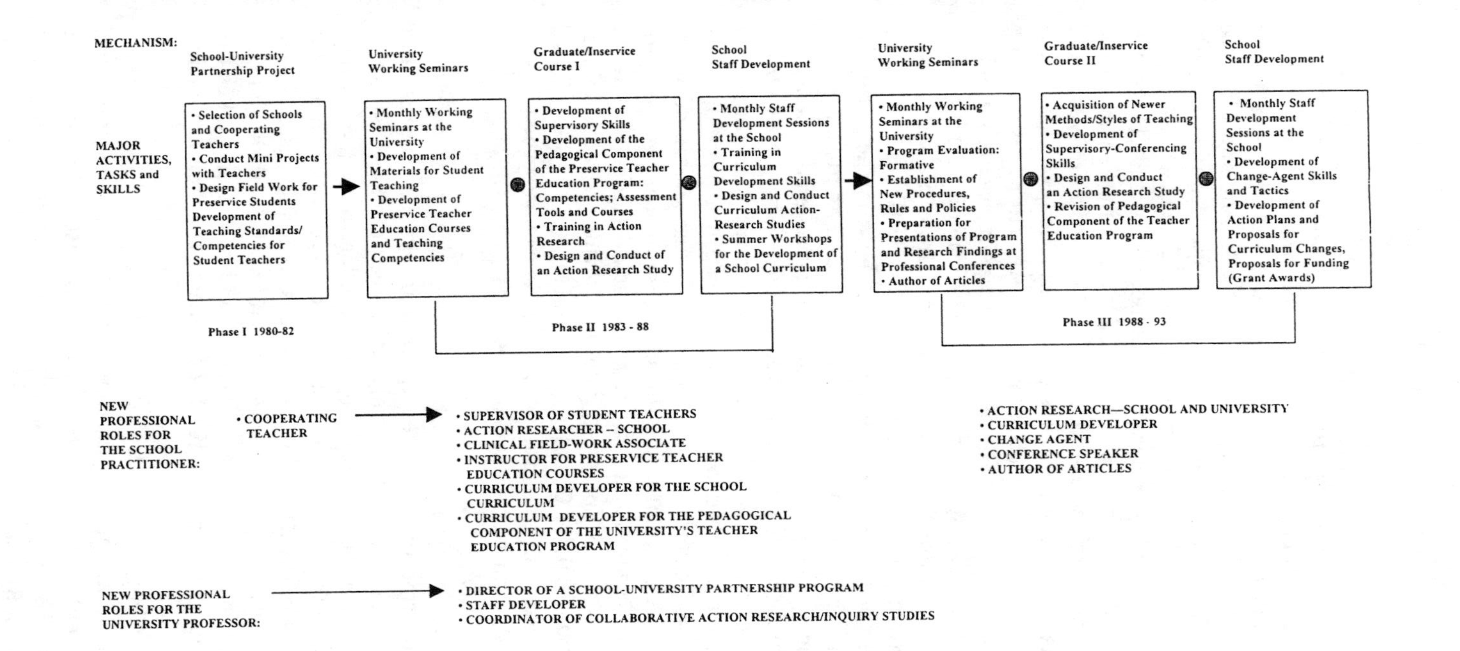

Figure 4.2. A model strategy for changing the professional roles of school practitioners in a holistic school-college/university partnership program
Project Scope I. Professional development component

to improve their supervisory practices and the instructional performances of their student teachers. The study was initiated by the SCOPE members based on our desire to ensure that students who complete the program would be able to conduct efficient and effective lessons for pupils. All school practitioners participating in the study trained for their role as action-researchers in a graduate inservice course specifically designed for the partnership's members. During the course and the semester that followed, the practitioners and I implemented the traditional phases of an action-research study. Data were analyzed, and changes were made in the partnership's programs. The inservice course and action study enabled the partnership's teachers to develop observational skills. Also, it enabled them to engage in research/inquiry, evaluation, and action planning directed at educational improvement (Catelli, 1995). The data and information obtained from the study were used for the following purposes: to improve SCOPE's supervisory procedures, to revise pedagogical competencies and learning activities for preservice student teachers, to alter the content and requirements of courses taken prior to student teaching, and to improve K-12 learning experiences for pupils in SCOPE-affiliated schools. True to SCOPE's holistic nature, the action study and course served to change and integrate the preservice and inservice professional development domains, which in turn positively impacted school curriculum and pupil learning experiences. After completing the study, the school practitioners and I presented the research findings at professional conferences (e.g., Catelli, DeCurtis, Johnston, Nix, Mongiello, Moskowitz, & McLaughlin, 1993; Catelli & Nix, 1994; Catelli & Johnston, 1994). Also, the practitioners participated in the publication of articles about the work in professional journals and conference proceedings (e.g., Catelli & Nix, 1992; Catelli et al., 1995).

Thus, the idea of area D of a holistic partnership is to artfully design partnership projects and research that integrate, change, and improve all three domains, simultaneously or in a coordinated fashion. It is the area in which to prepare educators and students to serve in new professional roles that are deemed more conducive to the needs of education and society in the 21st century. The goal is to increase the size of area D so that it encompasses and integrates more of the three domain areas. It is to institutionalize the partnership(s) in a way that makes the emergence of a new coordinated K-18 education-teacher education system visible.

It is interesting to note that the California State University System (CSU) in 1996 announced its commitment to a K-18 education system (CSU Presidents' Group, 1996; The CSU Institute for Education Reform, 1996). In the mission statement prepared by the CSU Presidents' Group (1996), the presidents of the various units committed their Universities to the notion of a K-18 education system with ongoing renewal of all segments, sharing resources and personnel. More particularly, they committed the CSU system to strengthening K-12 education and publicly announced it as its key strategic priority. Similarly, in a report entitled *The City University of New York: An Institution Adrift*, commissioned by the mayor and governor of New York in 1999, a recommendation for a more coordinated K-16 public education system with an emphasis on teacher education was made by members of the task force (Schmidt et al., 1999). It should be fascinating to observe both of these public systems as they move toward operationalizing a concept of a K-18 education inclusive of teacher education. Also, it will be interesting to see if private institutions, especially those that are more entrepreneurial, follow suit by infusing such an idea in their mission statements and strategic plans. Whatever route institutions take, it is important to reiterate that the intent of area D is to foster innovation, functional connectiveness, continuous experimentation, and research for purposes of student learning and educational improvement. The work of individuals in area D is directed at the purpose of a creating a new education system for a district, region, or state.

Members who operate in such a structure do so concurrently on both a macro (institutional) and micro (classroom) levcl. Their managerial styles and governance structures slowly change from hierarchical to organic. Ultimately, the partnership through area D becomes institutionalized. The relationship between the institutions takes on a type of ongoing coherence that ensures programmatic quality, teaching and learning effectiveness, and professional and institutional accountability. The larger question is how does one begin or at least what are the initial steps that will move those who adhere to such a vision closer to the desired state? In the next section, I offer an initial strategy to foster change based upon my partnership work.

AN INITIAL CHANGE STRATEGY

An initial change strategy for a holistic partnership should be built around altering the professional roles of educators. The tactics of the strategy must be directed at achieving the partnership goals, derived from a concept of teaching and learning and responsive to the needs of the partnership's constituents. The tactics should be designed to occur in phases. Some of the phases are planned for, and others may simply evolve. The overall strategy that provoked change and instituted new professional roles for members of the original partnership was implemented over a thirteen-year period of time (1980 to 1993). An overview of the phases of the strategy is seen in Figure 4.2.

Phases of An Initial Change Strategy

In the first phase, a title for the partnership and logo (Project SCOPE) was created to serve as the partnership's tool for public relations. Such mechanisms as pre- and inservice courses, graduate seminars, and staff development days at a school were targeted for conducting the partnership's activities. The major activities of phase one included the selection of cooperating teachers and their schools, the design of mini action projects and field-work experiences for preservice students (e.g., Catelli, 1985), and the development of teaching competencies for the teacher education program (Catelli, Foglia, Lettera, Loret, Lovins, Pardew, & Schwartz, 1980). Most of the activities were designed by the cooperating teachers and me in my role as director of the partnership. The idea was to increase the teachers' involvement and to establish with each teacher a healthy working relationship.

The cooperating teachers in phase one assumed more responsibilities and began to step out of their traditional roles. As the director of the project, I spent a large amount of time (three to four days a week) developing trusting relationships with the teachers in their respective schools. In one of the schools, the College's administrators had a special collaborative arrangement with the New York City Board of Education (see Trubowitz, Duncan, Fibkins, & Longo, 1984; Trubowitz & Longo, 1997). I was at that school for one day a week and was given three-credits of released time from my department responsibilities to work with teachers. Also, I was responsible for making contributions to the larger collaborative project between Queens College/CUNY and the New York City Board of Education (see Catelli, 1989). My department was reimbursed for my work with funds from the College's Center for the Improvement of Education.

In the second phase, the cooperating teachers were exposed to holistic partnership ideals and then educated to serve in new professional roles. Phase two included preparation for the teachers to change their role from cooperating teacher to (1) supervisor of student teachers, (2) action researcher, (3) clinical field-work associate, (4) instructor of preservice education courses and (5) curriculum developer of both the school curriculum and the College's teacher education curriculum. All of the activities of phase two were supported, in part, by my department, the College's School of Education, and its Center for the Improvement of Education. The work of phase two resulted in such tangible outcomes as five action research studies, a middle school's curriculum in a subject area (Catelli, 1990a), and a number of revised competencies for the preservice teacher education program.[6] Formal

[6]See Catelli et al. (1987) for revised competencies and the Appendix for outcomes and accomplishments.

contracts were agreed to by the teachers in this phase. In 1987, Queens College/CUNY hired and paid the partnering teachers for their work with education students, assigning to each teacher the official title of adjunct instructor. From my understanding, we were one of a few institutions in the nation to do so within a partnership arrangement. The structural mechanisms created to achieve the role changes included:

- monthly working seminars at the College,
- a graduate/in-service course for credit for Project SCOPE personnel,
- a school's staff development program, and
- summer workshops for the development of school curriculum.

In 1987, the wall between the two cultures, school teachers and college professors, began to collapse. The teachers who had once complained about higher education's poor preparation of teacher candidates had become adjunct faculty members of the City University of New York. They were now the professors.

The third phase included training for the teachers in the additional roles of (1) change agent, (2) conference speaker, and (3) author of published articles. The same mechanisms as in the first phase were utilized. However, not all of the teachers participated in the training for these roles. Time and money constraints, a lack of administrative support from their school administrators, and a lack of interest on the part of some of the teachers prevented all members from participating.

For the professor, the traditional role and responsibilities assigned to a teacher educator also changed dramatically. The professor's role became that of a director of a partnership program, staff developer, coordinator of action-research/inquiry studies, advocate for the partnering teachers, and chief officer responsible for securing the partnership's survival.

A System of Operation

Beyond the phases that expand the traditional role of the teacher and professor, a holistic partnership must have in place a system of operation that ensures that change and progress toward the agenda goals take place. In order to foster the productive and effective operation of SCOPE I's partnership, the members met on a regular basis. Once a month, they engaged in a working seminar at the College to review and revise pedagogical competencies of the program and to discuss problems with students. The members were also expected to periodically evaluate the overall effectiveness of the partnership. Every fifth semester, the school practitioners as a group enrolled in a special inservice graduate course specifically designed for them to update their skills and knowledge in the areas of supervision, teacher education, pupil learning, and research. In addition, the course served as a vehicle for conducting SCOPE's action research studies. Also, summer workshops and staff development days at one school for four of the SCOPE members served as the avenue for instituting change and improvement in any one or more of the educational domains. Staff development at that school occurred one afternoon, once a month for the academic year. An evaluation of all aspects of the partnership was achieved via written reports, interviews, videotaped performances of students and supervising teachers, and a variety of assessment tools. All of the materials and data remain on file for Project SCOPE I. The implementation of curriculum revisions generated by a SCOPE research study were made via the combined efforts of the participants (teachers, administrators, graduate and undergraduate students, and the director). This system of operation allows for the infusion of new content, more recent educational practices, and relevant research findings.

In 1989, the partnership in conjunction with other department programs was reviewed by outside evaluators hired by the College. The reviewers favorably described the partnership as having "exceptional merit" (Beyrer, Montoye, & Placek, 1990, p. 5). The partnership's success was largely attributed to the partnering school practitioners' work and the continued financial support we received from the then-chair of the department Margaret Franco (1989 to 1996).

From 1980 on, the school teachers of the partnership participated in restructuring education courses, assessment tools, and pedagogical competencies of the teacher education program (see Catelli et al., 1987). They had joint ownership and shared decision-making of the pedagogical component of the teacher education program. There were six education courses included in the partnership program. Most of the courses were offered at the College, and one was collaboratively taught by the director and teachers at a SCOPE-affiliated school.

Figure 4.2 is a summary of the strategy employed for changing the professional roles. Figure 4.3 presents (1) a listing of the mechanisms, (2) the new and expanded professional roles of the teachers and professor-director, and (3) the yearly financial costs for accomplishing the work. Also included in Figure 4.3 are examples of the benefits commented on by the eighteen school teachers who participated in Project SCOPE I. Eight of the eighteen teachers who began the project remained with it throughout its years at CUNY. All eighteen teachers, who represented fifteen schools, served as pioneers in a different type of laboratory setting where they engaged in new activities and professional roles in newer structures that then became the template for a holistic K-18 school-university partnership. They prepared over 350 preservice teacher education students using the holistic approach. In 1990 and 1991, the director, the partnership project, and its membership received

SCHOOL-COLLEGE/UNIVERSITY PARTNERSHIP MECHANISMS

- UNIVERSITY GRADUATE AND INSERVICE TEACHER EDUCATION COURSES FOR PARTNERSHIP MEMBERS
- STAFF DEVELOPMENT PROGRAMS IN THE SCHOOLS
- MONTHLY WORKING SEMINARS FOR PARTNERSHIP MEMBERS AT THE UNIVERSITY
- SUMMER WORKSHOPS FOR PARTNERSHIP MEMBERS AT THE SCHOOL/UNIVERSITY

YEARLY FINANCIAL COST - PROJECT SCOPE I

A. COST TO THE UNIVERSITY/DEPARTMENT — Academic Year

Supervisors of Student Teachers hired as Adjunct Instructors by the University (1 credit per student teacher for one-hour sessions/ competency assessment once a week for a 15-week semester).
$700 per credit/per student for 30 student teachers a year ($700 x 30)........$21,000

Instructors of Preservice-Teacher Education Courses
- Orientation to Teaching - Course is Team-Taught by the Partnership's School Teachers and Director at a Project SCOPE-Affiliated School (3 cr.)........$4,200
- Methods of Teaching and Field Experiences - Course Taught by Teachers (4cr.)........$5,600

$30,800

B. COST TO THE SCHOOL
Support for Partnering Teachers to Speak at Professional Conferences........$1,500 (per teacher)
Professor-Director hired to Conduct Staff Development as a School........$1,600
(Monthly sessions are paid by the School or the Professor receives three-credits of released time for the partnership's Staff Development Sessions).
Professor-Director hired to Conduct Summer Workshops........$3,000

$6,100

C. COST TO THE SCHOOL PRACTITIONER
Enrollment in a three-credit Graduate/Inservice Project SCOPE Course every five semesters. (Three credits of tuition exemption is given to the practitioner for his or her work as a Cooperating Teacher and Field Associate.)........$0

NEW PROFESSIONAL ROLES FOR SCHOOL PRACTITIONERS IN THE PARTNERSHIP

- UNIVERSITY STUDENT-TEACHER SUPERVISOR AND ADJUNCT INSTRUCTOR
- CLINICAL FIELD-WORK ASSOCIATE
- UNIVERSITY COURSE INSTRUCTOR PRESERVICE TEACHER EDUCATION COURSES COMPONENT (ADJUNCT INSTRUCTOR STATUS)
- ACTION RESEARCHER
- CURRICULUM DEVELOPER
- CHANGE AGENT
- CONFERENCE SPEAKER
- AUTHOR OF ARTICLES

SELECTED BENEFITS AS VOICED BY THE PARTNERSHIP'S TEACHERS

Participation in the partnership and our new professional roles has
- provided a sense of ownership in the University's Teacher Education Program that has given us a "true" sense of empowerment;
- become a source of professional renewal and rejuvenation;
- increased self-esteem and professional pride;
- expanded our knowledge base in teaching and enhanced our professional abilities to examine teaching and learning in a more detailed and reflective way;
- provided opportunities to keep up-to-date with new content and methods of teaching;
- expanded our repertoire of professional skills;
- provided opportunities for reducing the teacher-to-pupil ratio with the teacher education students participating in class instruction;
- helped to articulate and refine our practical knowledge;
- provided a meaningful opportunity to give back to our chosen profession and and the next generation of teachers;
- improved our own teaching performances which has led to improved learning experiences for our pupils.

FIGURE 4.3
OVERVIEW OF THE PARTNERSHIP'S MECHANISMS, NEW PROFESSIONAL ROLES, FINANCIAL COSTS AND VOICED BENEFITS BY SCHOOL PRACTITIONERS - PROJECT SCOPE I

Figure 4.3. Overview of the partnership's mechanisms, new professional roles, financial costs and voiced benefits by school practitioners—Project SCOPE I.

recognition and honors for pioneering work in school-college collaboration from the American Association of Higher Education (AAHE, 1990), and the City University of New York's Faculty Achievement Award Program (CUNY, 1991).

TRANSPORTABLE FEATURES OF A HOLISTIC SCHOOL-UNIVERSITY PARTNERSHIP

There are twelve major features including three critical elements or defining features that make a holistic partnership work and function productively. They are the operating principles of a holistic partnership that may be transported to other academic sites. The twelve features presented below are the areas that should be used to conduct research in and on a holistic partnership. They are the areas in which to provide others with evidence of the partnership's productivity and effectiveness. The twelve features have been extracted and abstracted from my 33 years of research and work with school teachers in formal partnerships, beginning with the Agnes Russell Laboratory School at Teachers College, Columbia University (1969-74), then at Queens College of the City University of New York (1975-76; 1980-98) and lastly at Dowling College on Long Island in New York.

Teachers and Professors Are the Heart of the Enterprise

1. Holistic partnerships are started with teachers and professors. Although, administrators may set the stage, they should remain in the background as facilitators in the earlier days of the partnership. Verbal contracts are initially agreed upon by teachers with either a university professor or a school teacher as the initiator. Administrators become involved when written contracts and proposals for the partnership are created. Ideally, it should be all parties collaborating from the very beginning with equal status. However, this rarely works because of time constraints and conflicting schedules on the part of all members and because of the cultural differences that often hamper communication. As a process, it is a more integrated and spiraling one, from the bottom up and top down. However, it is important to be mindful that school and university administrators often do not remain in their positions for long periods of time.[7] Their career ladders or frustrations with the job often do not permit

[7]This was especially so in the urban school settings with which I was affiliated with Project SCOPE I.

them to remain in their positions at institutions. Teachers, on the other hand, usually remain in their positions at schools longer than administrators. Therefore, it makes sense to initiate holistic partnership relationships with teachers. Teachers and professors are the heart of the enterprise.

Written Contracts, Trust, and Honesty Are the Essentials

2. Charles Reed, Chancellor of the California State University System, and Sir John S. Daniel, Vice-Chancellor of the Open University, said it best when at the 1999 national conference of the American Association for Higher Education they presented their joint project in teacher education. Sir John Daniel made the comment that having written contracts that spell out as much of the details of the venture as possible as well as making time to develop trusting relationships among the participants were the important lessons they had learned in the early phases of their joint venture (Daniel, 1999).

   Most assuredly, the two most valuable characteristics that need to be demonstrated by partnering individuals at all levels and throughout all phases of a partnership are trust and honesty. Trust and honesty are to be valued and embraced in every interinstitutional transaction, in each written contract, and in every personal interaction between and among members of the partnership. If trust and honesty are violated, they are extremely difficult to regain and will set the partnership back a number of steps, even years. They impact personal and professional credibility and institutional integrity.

Organic Relationships Are the Defining Element

3. The element that defines a holistic partnership is its organic nature. The partnership's theory, practice, and policies foster an organic-integrative relationship among professionals and institutions rather than a symbiotic one. This was explained at length in a previous section of the chapter. Although John Goodlad in his 1994 book entitled *Educational Renewal: Better Teachers, Better Schools* had commented that a partnership's success is often tied to its affecting symbiosis, he subsequently acknowledged in that same work that moving it toward fusion and an organic state is ultimately desirable (pp. 103-104). However, in a more recent article for *Change*, Goodlad (1999) emphasized and promoted the need for partnering institutions to have symbiotic partnerships with

agendas and strategies that focus directly on mutual self-interest, stating that "... the price of satisfying self-interest is that of satisfying the interests of others" (p. 31). There was no mention by Goodlad in the article of moving a school-university partnership in teacher education to an organic state. It should be restated and emphasized that holistic partnerships are special cases of a partnership model. They are laboratories of the future, newer catalyst structures for educational research and development. Their agendas and strategies revolve around the goals of innovation and research as well as comprehensive improvement and education reform/renewal. The work of their members is directed at student learning and ultimately at creating a new coordinated and integrative K-18 education system for a school, district, region, or state. Thus, they require long-lasting organic-type of interinstitutional relationships with symbiotic ones occurring to support more temporary or immediate needs.

Small Is Better

4. In a holistic partnership, another critical element is its smallness, that is, the number of people that make up each team in the partnership. It is the main ingredient for success, and it is what makes the organic partnership between people work. The partnership consists of a series of teams comprised of no more than eighteen teachers and one professor. Each team is responsible for eighteen teacher candidates a semester. Thirty-six students are supervised by the team each academic year for their student teaching, field or internship experience. I have found that when the number of school-based supervising teachers and preservice students is above eighteen for the semester, the partnership's productivity and level of effectiveness decreases. Often, communication between members was hampered, and each member's ability to solve daily problems of teaching and learning diminished significantly.

   There may be any number of teams representing the same subject areas within and across school districts. In fact, the across-district arrangement is most desirable for a partnership's research agenda. It provides members with a varied sample of school sites and educational contexts to conduct research studies from which findings may then be generalized. The increased number of professors that are needed in this plan come from a pool of faculty from the liberal arts and sciences, or from a consortium in which the college may participate, or they may come from a pool of educators who have retired from their systems.

The relatively small number of members that constitute a team allows for the much needed professional intimacy among and between the members. It allows members to collaborate for class instruction, peer coaching, and curriculum development. More importantly, the small number of participants on a team usually provides the partnering members with more opportunities to communicate with one another, which is absolutely critical to conducting the daily operations of the partnership effectively. Also, it allows members to immediately solve problems that arise within the team. This is especially important in urban and inner-city settings where teachers and students confront enormous social, educational, and economic problems on a daily basis. The team's membership, which includes student teachers, a professor, and supervising teachers, reduces the teacher-to-pupil ratio in the classroom, thus allowing for more individualized instruction to occur. This was cited by the teachers of Project SCOPE I as a key benefit of the holistic approach (Catelli, 1992).

The team strives to become a community of people with other teams within and across schools. The team is a smaller unit for change within the larger catalyst unit of the partnership (Figure 4.1, area D). Also, given the partnership's integrative nature, the team must remain small in its membership. Teachers are preparing for and then serving in different professional roles with varied functions at different points in time; that is, they are teaching education courses, supervising student teachers, serving as mentors, assisting in clinical field experiences, conducting action research studies, and engaging in collaborative inquiry. In essence, they are instituting integrative change and improvement focused on student learning at both the K-12 and university levels in a coordinated fashion. More importantly, they are responsible for and responsive to the all-inclusive needs of their pupils. To do all of this effectively over long periods of time and to keep everyone who is on board motivated and growing professionally, the teams must remain small in size. Smallness is key to the success of a holistic partnership in an inner-city, urban, or suburban setting. Size counts and does matter, as we have found in the research conducted on class size.[8] It is a significant factor in

[8]See Molar (1999) for a recent and comprehensive review of research on class size.

learning and teaching, and it is a critical feature of a holistic partnership. The holistic approach substantially reduces the pupil-to-teacher ratio in the classroom, and it increases opportunities for student learning and achievement.

Professional Roles Both Change and Expand

5. The strategy and mechanisms for carrying out initial change in a holistic partnership are built around altering and expanding individuals' professional roles. The roles are directed at achieving the partnership's goals in phases. They are derived from clear and coherent concepts of teaching-learning, teacher education, and education reform. Project SCOPE I's concepts of education were originally designed by the school teachers and professors in a competency-based teacher education document approved by the New York State Education Department in 1980 (Catelli, Foglia et al., 1980), and then later revised by participating teachers who implemented and adapted the pedagogical competencies (Catelli et al., 1987).

   The professional roles and teaching concepts should be based on an analysis of current literature in education, (i.e., the teacher's role as facilitator), and on recent research conducted in the setting(s) in which the partnership resides. They should represent the future in education (i.e., teacher-researcher) and relate to the present needs of the communities in which the partnership resides. Also, the roles and the partnership's articulated concepts of teaching and learning must be drawn from the partnering teachers' practical understanding of youngsters who are living in the communities. This is especially important in that it is the teachers who are primarily responsible for guiding and shaping the education of student teachers.

   To prepare students to teach in urban settings, I found the work of such experts as Martin Haberman (1988), Lois Weiner (1993), and a book entitled *Celebrating Diverse Voices* edited by Frank Pignatelli and Susanna Pflaum (1993) to be particularly useful. However, in the initial years of the partnership, I drew more heavily upon the working knowledge of those teachers in the partnership who had taught in various sections of New York City for the earlier portions of their careers. Their ideas as well as those of the partnering teachers from suburban schools shaped many of the concepts related to teaching and teacher education. Also, I drew upon my years of professional work in New York City and my personal experiences, having grown up and attended college in the Bronx.

Roles Need to Be Rotated Among Team Members

6. In order to sustain the participation of the members of the partnership, the professional roles should be rotated among members of the team. For example, the teaching of an education course can be rotated among the eighteen teachers and the professor, or the course can be taught by a team of two or more teachers and the professor. With this plan, it is most important that members experience professional growth in their new roles in order to sustain their interest, enthusiasm, and quality involvement. Talented and creative people usually need change. If they have that change within the system, they will not go elsewhere. There must also be inherent and external rewards for the participating members as well as genuine recognition and respect from administrators. Recently, the American Association for Higher Education in collaboration with four universities published the results of their work on exploring and revising roles and rewards for faculty who engage in K-12 partnership work (Gips & Stoel, 1999). The report, entitled *Making a Place in the Faculty Rewards System for Work with K-12*, identifies a number of strategies others might use to advance their strategies for rewarding faculty.

Teams Must Be Diverse By Design

7. Each team should consist of a mixture of veteran and newer teachers; older and younger teachers; elementary, middle, and secondary school teachers; and male and female teachers. Also, the membership, if possible, should be made up of teachers representing urban or inner-city school settings as well as teachers who reside in a neighboring suburban-school settings. This was the case in Project SCOPE I at CUNY, and it was key to its success. In that project, the team's diverse membership provided the partnership with differing perspectives that not only enriched group discussions but also favorably impacted the partnership's action research studies (e.g., multisite and grade level). Evidence of this appeared in the members' curriculum work, the competencies they designed for the student teachers, and the field work they conducted with teacher candidates in both urban-suburban settings (Catelli et al., 1987; Catelli et al., 1994; Catelli, 1995).

I should caution readers that the diverse backgrounds of members will at times provoke intense and heated debates about how education should be conducted across the K-12 grade levels and about the advantages and disadvantages of teaching in an urban or suburban setting. These are highly desirable outcomes. In Project SCOPE I, it was important for the teachers to compare their current and past experiences. Many pedagogical insights were gained because of it that in turn altered some of the teachers' instructional practices with their pupils and teacher candidates.

In addition, the diverse membership made possible the mentoring of newer teachers of the team by veteran teachers. Also, it made the research conducted by the members more varied (e.g., urban and suburban; elementary, middle, and secondary levels). The message here is that diversity by design favorably impacts the quality of the partnership's educational programs, its research, and its innovative products.

The Partnership Is an Ongoing Enterprise

8. A holistic partnership is ongoing. Members should constantly strive to remove barriers between the K-18 education levels as they embrace a vision of an education system that is more comprehensive and integrative. Also, it is an ongoing enterprise in that the partnership's system of operation allows for systematically infusing new content, teaching strategies, and relevant research findings. Through the partnership's action research, improvements are instituted and monitored based on the particular needs and strategic goals of the partnership. This is an inherent benefit of a holistic partnership's system of operation. Educational research, change, and innovation are integrated and then infused in each institution's daily operation and culture. Eventually, they become part of an individual's teaching practice and professional fabric. In this system, change has a better chance of translating into progress.

Collaborative Action Research/Inquiry as the Partnership's Tool for Change and Improvement

9. Collaborative action research/inquiry is an integral part of a holistic partnership. As a research methodology, action research is the partnership's tool for initiating change and

documenting the impacts, changes, innovations, and improvements that occur. It is fundamentally employed as a methodological strategy for improving educational practice and for the production of relevant, practical, and useful knowledge. As viewed by prominent leaders as well as other educators, action research is seen as a viable school-college collaborative approach to education reform and improvement (Argyris, Putnam, & Smith, 1985; Catelli, Padovano, & Costello, 2000; Grundy, 1987; Hollingsworth, 1997; Holly, 1991; Oja & Smullyan, 1989).

Within the context of a holistic partnership, action research takes on dimensional qualities of collaborative inquiry.[9] The research/inquiry is focused on the work of the participants within and on the partnership in relation to partnership's goals. The heart of the inquiry enterprise for the partnership resides in the fact that it is collaborative, critical, and evaluative, and that it is directed at action in an integrated and coordinated manner. Thus, collaborative action research/inquiry is the conceptual frame for the research that is conducted in a holistic partnership.

Project SCOPE I produced five collaborative action research/inquiry studies.[10] The information and findings generated by the studies, to give a few examples, were used to alter teachers' instructional practices, which in turn impacted pupil learning time; improve supervisory procedures of the partnership's teacher-supervisors, which then initiated changes in selected courses of the teacher education program; provide direction for units of instruction for an affiliated school's curriculum, which concurrently revised the pedagogical competencies of the preservice program; and to provide members with data to persuade school administrators to change scheduling practices, thus impacting school curriculum (Catelli, 1995, 2000; Catelli & Costello, 1998; Catelli, Mongiello, Moskowitz, & Jordan, 1993).

Project SCOPE II produced two action studies in elementary education. The studies focused on establishing baseline data for the teacher education program. Any partnership that does not collect such data or have such evidence of its work and eventual effectiveness will die in this round of education reform and renewal. Although such

---

[9]For an in-depth explanation of research as collaboration inquiry within a partnership, see Catelli (1995), Catelli and Costello (1998), and Sirotnik (1988).

[10]See the Appendix for a listing of the studies.

comprehensive partnerships are considered long-term endeavors to change a system and therefore should not be evaluated prematurely, it is, however, important for the participants to collect relevant data and document the impacts, changes, and outcomes that occur during the initial phase.

The collaborative research/inquiry in which partnership members engage are action studies that integrate and impact two or more educational domains, that is, preservice education, staff development, and school curriculum. The goal is to design all studies from this integrative perspective or at least to align the results with the major components of the strategic model seen in Figure 4.4. In essence, the action studies serve as a vehicle for obtaining information, reflecting, and taking action focused directly on the partnership's needs in the aforementioned domains. It is a powerful tool that enables the members to systematically evaluate their agenda goals and operationalize the partnership's themes of innovation and experimentation. The results of the studies are of interest first to the partnership's members and secondarily to a larger education community.

In addition, and in later phases, it is important to conduct research on assessment, student learning, and teaching. This type of research is subject to different rules and regulations than that of action research. Its results are more generalizable and transportable. The collaborative action research/inquiry that is conducted in a holistic partnership program supports research on student learning and teaching. It is action research/inquiry conducted within and on the partnership; that is, it serves the participants and the partnership's needs and goals in an integrative-holistic fashion, and it studies the partnership itself. This is critical if the goals of improved teaching and student learning are to be realized and coordinated between the school and college level.

Smaller Ideas Are Set in a Larger Plan: An Overall Strategic Partnership Model for Instituting Change and Improvement

10. Presented in Figure 4.4 is a diagrammatic representation of phase one of an Overall Strategic Model of a Holistic School-College/University Partnership to effect change and improvement in student learning and teacher education. To achieve its goals, a holistic partnership must have a strategy that conceptually identifies and functionally links the areas of the partnership. There are seven major components of the

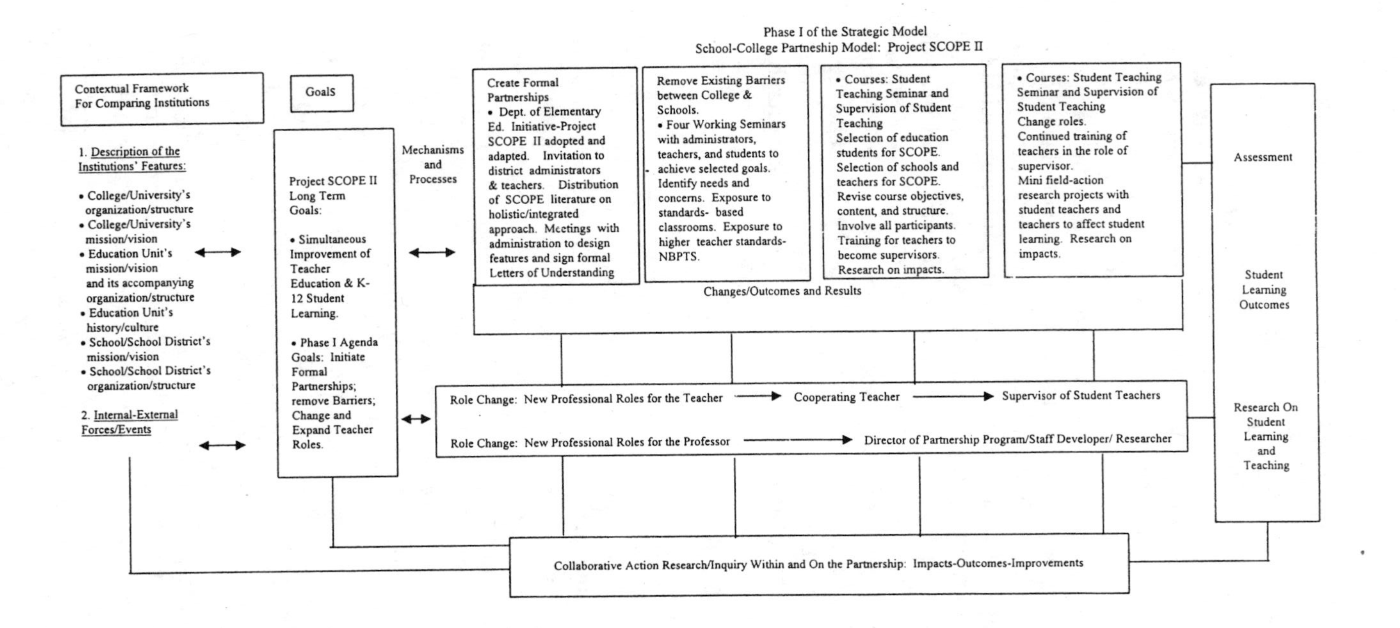

Figure 4.4. Overall strategic model of a holistic school-college/university partnership to effect change and improvement in learning and teacher education

model: (1) contextual framework for comparing institutions; (2) goals; (3) mechanisms and processes; (4) research; (5) changes/outcomes, impacts, and improvements; (6) assessment; and (7) student learning outcomes and performance. Each major component has key features or areas associated with it. For example, the component entitled *contextual framework* for comparing institutions includes such areas as organizational structure, mission, and vision. These areas interact with one another. They are the areas that are strategically changed or aligned to foster continuous improvement in an integrative and coordinated fashion. This model fosters a dynamic, strategic approach to effect, monitor, and assess comprehensive change and continuous improvement in K-12 student learning and professional education (13-18). It is a conceptual tool for managing the change process and a tool for comparing institutions and their partnership approaches (Catelli & Costello, 2000). The components of the model can be used by other institutions in researching their formal, interinstitutional partnerships.

Leadership Is Key

11. Leadership by a number of people at the macro (administrative) and micro (classroom) level is key to initiating a holistic partnership. The leadership team—college or university president(s), school superintendents, principals, project director, lead partnering teachers, and professors—must be able to live with a certain amount of ambiguity and uncertainty. Most administrators with whom I have conversed know this or learn quickly that they have to operate with a degree of uncertainty and ambiguity. The task is to be able to do it. In my conversations with administrators, many have said that having a good sense of humor certainly helps to offset the uncertainty, and it definitely helps to relieve the internal tensions that often occur between faculty and administrators. It also relieves the pressures that come from external forces (i.e., state mandates, etc.), which are usually ongoing in institutions.

    For a holistic partnership to begin and continue over time, the leaders have to be or become conceptually oriented individuals; that is, they must be able to integrate academic concepts and financial matters with varied dimensions of an array of issues and problems that often arise. Subsequently, they must be ready to take action in an integrative fashion. They must recognize that their decisions impact both the college and school(s). Also, they must know when to delegate power in order to change hierarchical structures and rigid managerial styles to those structures and styles that are more organic, holistic, and participatory.

Ultimately, president(s), deans, superintendents, and principals of a holistic partnership are responsible for removing existing adverse conditions that prevent the partnership from providing its members with a safe place to work (Figure 4.1, area D), a place where members can go to learn, create, innovate, experiment, and be free from any political-academic consequence. Throughout all my years of partnership work, which includes eight college presidents, seven deans, and over fifteen superintendents and principals, I have never been so convinced of the notion that for colleges or universities, a president sets the tone and determines the culture of an institution. Hence, it is the president and superintendent who together are ultimately responsible for the health of the partnership. As special cases of the partnership category, holistic school-college/university partnerships require chief executive officers who have a clear understanding of the principles and benefits of such new structures. The partnership requires chief officers who have the capacity to arrange with their faculties the physical and psychological environment to institutionalize partnerships and initiate the initial stages of a new education system.

Partnerships Are a Matter of Time, Money, Motive, and Maturity

12. Those who initially direct holistic partnerships need the time to develop trusting relationships with participating members. Participating members must become convinced that the director's actions form a pattern that clearly reveals his or her positive motive for conducting the partnership. The director must dispel any notion that the college wants to either use the school for its own research agenda or use it just as a place to assign student teachers with superficial involvement from the teachers. Time is also the feature that almost everyone involved in either partnership work or educational change cites as most important in starting and then sustaining a successful partnership (Fullan with Stiegelbauer, 1991, p. 34; Joyce, Calhoun, & Hopkins, 1999, pp. 11, 34-35, 55; and Kochan, 1999). Time is needed for members to (1) internalize the goals of the partnership, (2) meet to adequately discuss policy issues and problems regarding students, (3) experiment with ideas, (4) conduct

collaborative research/inquiry, (5) produce innovative products directed at the goals, (6) solve problems, and (7) prepare for new roles. It is a labor-intensive venture. To do it effectively, the director needs to have support from the administration and the teachers' union as well as sufficient funds to restructure the way partnering teachers and professors spend their time. The amount of the funds needed in the initial stages is relatively small and can come from a combination of internal-external sources (i.e., department and college funds, grant awards, etc.). However, for a holistic partnership to be fully functioning with all of its change features operating effectively, it needs school and college administrators to allocate sufficient funds.

Lastly, partnership directors need to be professionally and personally mature. They must demonstrate through their actions a professional attitude that represents a high level of maturity. Patience, judgment, foresight, and professional wisdom are important characteristics. The intense interactions and conflicts that often occur among and between people who come from different institutional cultures are so complex at times that having patience and using judgment are essential traits for the director to have in order to sustain the partnership.

ACCOMPLISHMENTS OF HOLISTIC PARTNERSHIPS AND LESSONS LEARNED

Over the eighteen years of Project SCOPE I at Queens College/CUNY (1980-98), the partnership received national and international recognition. In 1990, the project and its director were one of 56 from around the nation recognized and honored by the American Association for Higher Education for pioneering efforts in school-college collaboration (AAHE, 1990). In 1991, the project's director received the City University of New York Faculty Achievement Award for creative achievement and work in school-college collaboration (CUNY, 1991). In 1996, because of the partnership's accomplishments, the director, representing the membership, was selected by a committee of referees from the University of London to serve on an international panel of experts to represent an American perspective at a conference for exploring futures in teacher education (Catelli, 1997). In 1997, in recognition of innovative and successful work in school-university partnerships, the membership and director were invited by the University of London's Institute of Education and the Teacher Training Agency of England to serve as international coordinators and hosts for an Enhancement Program for the University's graduate students in math and science.

Within the eighteen years of Project SCOPE I, the professors, teacher education students of the project, and the eighteen school practitioners, who represented fifteen schools in the New York City area, produced more than 25 collaborative works. The school practitioners prepared over 350 preservice students, three-fourths of whom have been tenured in teaching positions. They have spoken at regional, national, and international conferences (e.g., Catelli & Johnston, 1994; Catelli & Nix, 1992; Catelli, DeCurtis, Johnston et al., 1993; Catelli, Johnston, Nix, Stack-Lennon, Turner, & Escobar, 1994); they have authored published articles (e.g. Catelli et al., 1995; Catelli, Franco, & Mongiello, 1996); they have taught education courses; they have conducted five collaborative action-research studies (e.g., Catelli & Mongiello, 1994; Catelli & Moskowitz, 1994; Catelli & Nix, 1994; Catelli, Johnston, & Franco, 1996); and they have presented papers at conferences with their teacher candidates and graduate education students (e.g., Catelli, Nix, & Papapetrou, 1996). Their accomplishments, which are identified in the Appendix of this chapter, are evidence of that partnership's productivity, effectiveness, and success.

In June of 1998, Project SCOPE II (*S*chool-*C*ollege *O*peration in *P*artnership *E*ducation) began at Dowling College with formal letters of agreement with two school districts. The partnership involved 21 cooperating-classroom teachers representing six elementary schools, and 21 student teachers who had volunteered for the project for the first semester. The second semester enrolled fifteen more student teachers. Serving as a template for a holistic approach to change, the transportable features and materials of Project SCOPE I were adopted by the faculty of Elementary Education and then adapted to a different academic setting. The expanded version of the project included a focus on subjects appropriate to elementary education and elementary teacher education. The activities of the first year of the partnership emphasized (1) changing and expanding the role of the cooperating teachers and that of the professor-director, (2) effecting changes in courses and seminars, and (3) collecting baseline data for the partnership's action research studies and teacher education program.

In June of 1999, a second letter of agreement/understanding was signed by school and college administrators. The second year of the project focused on action research and the analyses of selected data from the first year of the partnership. The second year engaged, on a volunteer basis, the participation of the partnership's cooperating teachers and graduate education students in an action research course. Thirty-five graduate education students agreed to join Project SCOPE II to become Dowling College's first action researchers to conduct action research on phase one of the project (Catelli & Carlino, 2000, 2001; Catelli & Dowling's First Action Researchers, 2001). Much of the partnership work was supported by released-time credits awarded to me as director-professor of the project.

Not unlike other higher education institutions, Dowling College is currently undergoing a dramatic transformation to meet the needs and demands of education in the 21st century. Project SCOPE II, in its second year, had focused primarily on the action research component of its strategic model. During the years 1998 to 2001, the participants of the partnership initiated a number of changes that produced tangible outcomes. Whether some or all of the changes will last depends on a number of factors associated with the institution's transformation, such as its new or renewed mission and institutional identity, and so forth. However, it is fair to say that the work that has been completed by the participating members of Project SCOPE II since 1998 has impacted the academic learning experiences of a small population of individuals in the preservice and inservice teacher education programs. Examples of Project SCOPE II's accomplishments during Phase One are identified in the Appendix.

Lessons Learned

It is hoped that this chapter contributes to a greater understanding of the initial stages of an integrated-holistic partnership model to bring about substantial change and harmony in content, structure, and personnel for a new education system. As director of both partnership projects, the more important lessons I have learned over 30 years of living this idea may be reduced to a series of personal thoughts and reflections on my conversations with others who have assisted me in making sense of the experience. It is my set of rules and message to those who value this vision and want to direct or initiate such a venture.

1. There are times when you may have to check your ego at the door or go with hat in hand to chief executives or classroom teachers in the initial stages. It is essential not to let your ego get in the way of doing something you know will ultimately benefit students.
2. Some people feel that if they blow your candle out, theirs is brighter. Be patient with such individuals; however, if there is something you need to say to someone who acts in that manner, say it and move on.
3. Never hold a grudge. It does not move anything forward. Never let an institution define you, and never put your sense of self-worth, health, or family at risk.
4. Symbiosis is good to a point, but you have to make reasonable strides toward an organic state for a holistic partnership to become a reality.
5. What is and what should be are often miles apart. Do not agonize over it. Inch your way toward what you think should be, keeping lines of communication open with others.

6. When you see that a relationship with a school or individual is not working, just bow out and end it gracefully.
7. Over the 33 years of my professional career, I have met with four types of people in education: those who are opportunists, people who will exploit a system for their own good; those who are good opportunists, individuals who will take advantage of situation to benefit all; those who are careerist, faculty members who do only that which will further their careers; and those who are principled, individuals who will take risks and accept consequences for their convictions. Align yourself with those individuals who are principled and those whom I call good opportunists.
8. I have found that whenever something new, a project or venture, is presented, 25% of the faculty will cheer and be enthusiastic, 25% will try to sabotage it, and 50% will sway with the politics of the day. If you are unsure of someone's intent or motive, ask them to elaborate on current matters; if they cannot or will not, then you will know what position they take.
9. You are not perfect; you will make mistakes and sometimes errors in judgment. Try to get over it as quickly as possible. You cannot do this kind of work alone. Find the right house for the work and the right people with whom to work. Look for institutional integrity, administrative integrity, and personal integrity. If there is at least one of the three, continue the effort.
10. When you confront either a difficult situation or crisis, call upon those you respect to provide advice on issues of process. Draw upon their experience and wisdom. They can save you a lot of heartache and frustration. I have learned this through my work in Project SCOPE I and in a relatively short time with Project SCOPE II.

In order for this type of partnership to begin, evolve, and progress, institutional conditions (cultural, financial, organizational, etc.) have to be receptive. Initial change must translate into progress, and any condition perceived as adverse needs to be eliminated or minimized. As mentioned previously, leadership by a number of people at the macro and micro levels is critical to achieving the goals at the initial stage. A holistic school-college/university partnership over time must be institutionalized and eventually transformed to a more integrated and coordinated K-18 education system for a district, region, or state. This is what was envisioned, this is what I value, and this is the direction as a professional I have pursued from my earlier days to date. There are currently a number of partnership models including professional development school (PDS) models that may serve somewhat similar and different goals (e.g., Byrd & McIntyre, 1999, and Whiting et al., 1996). This model is one of a number of alternatives. However, based on my years of research and partnership experience, successes and failures included, I believe that the younger teachers and students of today, especially those in urban and inner-city school settings, are ready for this type of innovation and integrative form of education. The benefits are many, as I have attempted to demonstrate in the chapter.

Finally, in this phase of education reform and institutional transformation, it has been extremely satisfying for me to observe what was attempted in the 1960s by such leaders as Schaefer (1967), Joyce (1967, 1969, 1972), Wilson (1967, 1972), and Goodlad (Goodlad & Sirotnik, 1988) arrive now at a point where the U.S. Department of Education is actively supporting teacher education reform efforts on a large scale, turning rhetoric into reality. In September of 1999, the U.S. Department of Education sponsored a Summit on Teacher Quality for college and university presidents to explore their leadership role for improving teacher preparation. In January of 2000, a National Conference on Teacher Quality in Washington, DC, was attended by over 800 university personnel, partnering K-12 educators, school district administrators, policy-makers, and representatives from teacher unions. At the conference, over 30 successful models in teacher education were presented, many involving school-university partnerships. Subsequently, in the summer of 2000, the U.S. Department of Education brought teams of higher education leaders and their K-12 partners together in regional institutes to design plans to improve teacher education.[11]

Undoubtedly, the time has come when school-university partnerships are valued and when many of the educators who began earlier partnerships are recognized as pioneers. They know what works, why it works, and under what conditions it works. Finally, it is most rewarding for me to have witnessed within my career a vision of a K-18 system of education and research promoted by education leaders in the 1960s and 1970s fast becoming a reality.

[11]See the U.S. Department of Education's Teacher Quality Website on-line: http://ed.gov/teacherquality/teach.html and http://ed.gov/teacherquality/prepare.html.

APPENDIX
ACCOMPLISHMENTS OF PROJECT SCOPE I AND PROJECT SCOPE II

Project SCOPE I

Below are selected accomplishments and tangible outcomes produced by the members of Project SCOPE I during the years of 1980 to 1998 at Queens College of the City University of New York.

- Five action research studies for the improvement of teacher education and school curricula.
  Researchers—Catelli, L. A., Anslow-Chakrian, N., Johnston, D., Jordan, J., Nix, W., McLaughlin, P., Mongiello, B., & Moskowitz, K. *The Use and Effects of Goal-Setting Procedures and Videotaped Analysis on Instructional Performances of Student Teachers at SCOPE School Settings*. An action-research study involving the use of goal-setting procedures and videotaped analysis to improve instructional performances of student teachers and supervisory procedures at four Project SCOPE schools (see Catelli, 1995; Catelli & Nix, 1992, 1994; Catelli et al., 1993).
  Researchers—Catelli, L.A., Johnston, D., Jordan, J., Nix, W., McLaughlin, P., Mongiello, B., Moskowitz, K., & McLaughlin, P. *Descriptive Analysis of Conferencing Behaviors of Project SCOPE's Student-Teacher Supervisors*. An action-research study involving the use of the *Kindsvatter and Wilen Conference Category System* (Kindsvatter & Wilen, 1982) to code and analyze Project SCOPE supervisors' videotaped conferences with student teachers (see Catelli, 1995; Catelli & Johnston, 1994).
  Researchers—Catelli, L. A., Mongiello, K., & Moskowitz, K. *A Longitudinal Study of Individual and Group Change in the Health-Related Fitness Performances of an Urban Middle School Student Population*. The study involves an analysis of data collected over a four-year period of time to determine individual and group change in the health and fitness levels of an urban middle school student population (see Catelli, 2000; Catelli & Mongiello, 1994; Catelli et al., 1993).
  Catelli, L. A., Jordan, J., Mongiello, B. & Moskowitz, K. *A Survey of Preferred Goals for a Comprehensive Middle School Curriculum*. A survey-questionnaire requesting parents, teachers, students, and administrators to rank goal statements and reveal their perceptions of a quality curriculum for an urban middle school population (see Catelli, 1990a; Catelli & Moskowitz, 1994; Catelli et al., 1993).

Catelli, L. A., and Shurgin, S. *A Survey of Learning Preferences at the Louis Armstrong School*. A four-page survey questionnaire was designed and administered to students in classes at a SCOPE-affiliated school. The information obtained from the study was used to adjust and design classroom instructional techniques and to identify learning preferences of an urban middle school population (see Catelli et al., 1993).

- Fourteen collaborative paper and program presentations at state, national and international conferences by professors, school practitioners, and teacher education students of Project SCOPE. Examples:
  Catelli, L. A., Franco, M., & Johnston, D. (1996). *Teachers and Professors as Action Researchers in a School-University Partnership Program . . . Can It Work?* Paper presented at the 1996 annual convention of the NYSAHPERD. Long Island, NY, November, 22, 1996.
  Catelli, L. A., Johnson, D., & Franco, M. (1996). *What Do Teachers Say in a Student-Teacher Conference? A School-University Action Research Study*. Paper presented at the 1996 annual convention of the NYSAHPERD. Long Island, NY, November 22, 1996.
  Catelli, L. A., Nix, W., & Papapetrou P. (1996). *Teachers As Action Researchers in a School-University Partnership: What Do They Do and What Is It For?* Paper presented at the Annual Meeting of the American Educational Research Association. New York, April 10, 1996.
  Catelli, L. A., Johnston, D., Nix, W., Stack-Lennon, M., Turner, W., & Escobar, S. (1994). *Changing the School's Practitioner's Role in Student Teaching and Teacher Education: A School-College Partnership Endeavor*. Program presented at the EDA-AAHPERD Annual Convention. Philadelphia, PA, March 11, 1994.
  Catelli, L.A., & Nix, W. (1994). *The Use and Effects of Goal-Setting Procedures and Videotaped Analysis on the Instructional Performances of Student Teachers at SCOPE School Settings*. Research paper presented at the 1994 EDA-AAHPHERD Annual Convention. Philadelphia, PA, March 10, 1994.
  Catelli, L. A., & Moskowitz K. (1994). *A Survey of Preferred Goals of Parents, Students, Teachers and Administrators*. Research paper presented at the 1994 EDA-AAHPHERD Annual Convention. Philadelphia, PA, March 10, 1994.

Catelli, L. A., DeCurtis, P., Johnson, D., Nix, W., Mongiello, B., Moskowitz, K., & McLaughlin, P. (1993). *A Holistic School-University Partnership Model for Reforming Education for the 21st Century: New Professional Roles*. Program presentation at the 1993 National Convention of the AAHPERD. Washington, DC, March 26, 1993.

- Twelve published articles in professional journals, proceedings, etc. (e.g., Catelli, 1990b, 1992, 1995, 1997; Catelli & Franco, 1998; Catelli, Franco, & Mongiello, 1996; Catelli, DeCurtis, Nix et al. 1995; Catelli & Nix, 1992).
- Two research symposia on school-university action research at regional conferences.
  Catelli, L. A., Johnston, D., Mongiello, B., Moskowitz, K., & Nix, W. (1994). Symposium—*School/University Action Research: Practitioners and Professors of Project SCOPE*. Research symposium and presented papers at the 1994 EDA-AAHPERD Annual Convention. Philadelphia, PA, March 10, 1994.
  Catelli, L. A., Mongiello, B., & Moskowitz, K. (1992). Symposium—*Collaborative Research to Effect Change in a Urban Middle School*. Research symposium and papers presented at the 1992 EDA-AAHPHERD Annual Convention. Baltimore, MD, February 21, 1992.
- The development of the Pedagogical Component of *The Preservice Teacher Education Program*, including four education courses, teaching competencies, materials, assessment, and evaluation tools (Catelli et al., 1987); and two graduate inservice courses for Project SCOPE participants.
- The development of a curriculum program for a SCOPE-affiliated middle school (Catelli, 1990a), and two articles about the curriculum published by two major New York City newspapers.
- The preparation of over 350 preservice teacher education students using Project SCOPE's holistic approach, 75% of whom have graduated and subsequently received tenure in teaching positions in the New York City area.
- National recognition for the project, its members, and director (AAHE, 1990; CUNY, 1991).
- Partnership assessed as having "exceptional merit" by outside reviewers (Beyrer, Montoye, & Placek, 1990, p. 5).
- The preparation and participation of Project SCOPE's school teachers in new professional roles for the 21st century (e.g., action researcher, change agent, student-teacher supervisor, university course instructor, and curriculum developer; Catelli, DeCurtis, Nix et al., 1995).
- International coordinators and hosts—Invited to serve as international coordinators and hosts of an Enhancement

Program for graduate students in math and science sponsored by the University of London and the Teacher Training Agency of England April 7-11, 1997. Project SCOPE coordinators and their host schools: L. A. Catelli, M. Franco, CUNY; W. Nix, The Townsend Harris High School at Queens College; J. Jordan, The Louis Armstrong Middle School.

- The development of a *Process Model for Linking Learning Standards, Assessment, Instruction, and Curriculum Change* (Catelli, Franco, & Mongiello, 1996); and
- Provision of services to 15 schools and 5,000 students.

Project SCOPE II

Project SCOPE II began at Dowling College in June of 1998. What follows are selected works, publications, and outcomes of phase one of the project.

- A data bank of 30 videotaped elementary classroom performances of Dowling College/Project SCOPE II's student teachers. Videotaped performances are analyzed in action research studies and used to train observer/supervisors.
- A data bank of curriculum-lesson plans/units of instruction in elementary school subjects developed by Dowling College/ Project SCOPE II's student teachers. The lessons/units are analyzed and used to assist teacher candidates in preparing standards-based lessons.
- Four working partnership seminars attended by 60 administrators, teachers, professors and student teachers representing two partnering school districts, the purpose of which was to remove any existing barriers between the College and schools and create a collaborative atmosphere.
- Training of (35) graduate education students in action research.
- Two collaborative publications (Catelli & Carlino, 2001; Catelli, Padovano, & Costello, 2000).
- Two Project SCOPE II action research studies and presentations (Catelli & Dowling's First Action Researchers, 2001).
- Three paper and program presentations (Catelli & Costello, 2000; Catelli, Goldsmith, & Costello, 2001); and one poster presentation with a partnering teacher (Catelli & Carlino, 2000).

REFERENCES

Albert, L. (1991). Introduction and overview of the partnership movement: The partnership terrain. In F. Wilbur & L. Lambert (Eds.), *Linking America's schools and colleges* (pp. 1-4). Washington, DC: American Association for Higher Education.

American Association for Higher Education. (1990, June). *Faculty pioneers in school-college collaboration* [Special Ceremony and Brochure]. First National Conference on School-College Collaboration of the American Association for Higher Education, Chicago, IL.

Anderson, W.G. (1971). Descriptive-analytic research on teaching. *Quest, 15*, 1-8.

Anderson, W.G. (1974). *Teacher behavior in physical education. Part I: Development of a descriptive system*. Unpublished manuscript. New York: Teachers College, Columbia University.

Argyris, C., Putnam, R., & Smith, D.M. (1985). *Action science. Concepts, methods and skills for research and intervention*. San Francisco, CA: Jossey-Bass.

Bellah, R., Madsen, R., Sullivan, W., Swidler, A., & Tipton, S. (1990). *Habits of the heart*. New York: Harper & Row Publishers.

Beyrer, M., Montoye, H., & Placek, J. (1990, May). *Review of programs of the department of health and physical education: Report of the review committee*. Flushing, NY: Queens College/CUNY.

Byrd, D., & McIntyre, D. J. (Eds.). (1999). *Research on professional development schools: Teacher education yearbook VII*. Thousand Oaks, CA: Corwin Press.

California State University Presidents' Group. (1996, June 26). *Mission statement of the CSU presidents' group on teacher preparation and K-18 education*. California: Author.

Capra, F. (1997). *The web of life*. New York: Doubleday.

Catelli, L.A. (1985, Spring). On the move at the Louis Armstrong Middle School. *School/Community Connections: The Queens College Center For The Improvement of Education, 10*, 4.

Catelli, L. A. (1989). *School-college partnership: An insider's view*. Unpublished manuscript. Flushing, NY: Queens College/CUNY.

Catelli, L. A. (1990a). School-college partnership: Development of a working model for the Louis Armstrong middle school curriculum. *Middle School Journal, 21*(4), 36-39.

Catelli, L. A. (1990b). School-university partnerships: The transference of a model. In K. Vandergrift & S. Intner (Eds.), *Library education and leadership: Essays in honor of Jane Anne Hannigan* (pp. 127-140). Metuchen, NJ: Scarecrow Press.

Catelli, L. A. (1992). Against all odds: A holistic urban school/college partnership—Project SCOPE. *Action in Teacher Education, 14*(14), 42-51.

Catelli, L. A. (1993, January). *A new perspective for school-university partnerships in the 21st century*. Paper presented at the annual conference of the National Association for Physical Education in Higher Education, Fort Lauderdale, FL.

Catelli, L. A. (1995). Action research and collaborative inquiry in a school-university partnership. *Action in Teacher Education, 16*(4), 25-38.

Catelli, L. A. (1997). An holistic perspective on school-university partnerships in the twenty-first century—theory into practice. In D. Lambert & A. Hudson (Eds.), *Exploring futures in teacher education: Changing key for changing times* (pp. 228-246). London: Institute of Education, University of London.

Catelli, L. A. (2000). Action research to effect change for adolescent girls at an urban middle school: A matter of life and death. *Research in Middle Level Education-Annual, 23*(1), 133-148.

Catelli, L. A., & Carlino, J. (2000, June). *Collaborative action research to assess student learning and effect institutional change and improvement—Project SCOPE II*. Poster session presented at the annual assessment conference of the American Association for Higher Education, Charlotte, NC.

Catelli, L. A., & Carlino, J. (2001). Collaborative action research to assess student learning and effect change. *Academic Exchange Quarterly, 5*(1), 105-112.

Catelli, L. A., & Costello, J. (1998, April). *Collaborative action research as a powerful tool for improving curriculum and professional education in a school-university partnership program*. Paper presented at the annual meeting of the American Educational Research Association, San Diego, CA.

Catelli, L. A., & Costello, J. (2000, April). *An overall strategic model of school-college partnerships to effect change and improvement in teacher education and K-12 student learning*. Paper presented at the annual meeting of the American Educational Research Association, New Orleans, LA.

Catelli, L. A., & Dowling's First Action Researchers. (2001, February). *Action research in a K-18 school-college partnership project—Project SCOPE II*. Papers accepted at the annual meeting of the Association of Teacher Education, New Orleans, LA.

Catelli, L. A., & Franco, M. (1998). *Action research to effect change for urban youngsters in health and fitness: A school-college endeavor*. In the U.S. Department of Health and Human Services/ACYF with Columbia University's School of Public Health's Conference Proceedings of Head Start's Fourth National Research Conference on Children and Families in an Era of Rapid Change. Washington, DC: U.S. Department of Health and Human Services/ACYF, 584-585.

Catelli, L. A., & Johnston, D. (1994, March). *Descriptive analysis of conferencing behaviors of SCOPE student-teacher supervisors.* Paper presented at the annual meeting of the Eastern District Association of the American Alliance for Health, Physical Education, Recreation and Dance, Philadelphia, PA.

Catelli, L. A., & Mongiello, B. (1994, March). *A longitudinal study of individual and group change in health-related fitness performances of an urban middle school pupil population.* Paper presented at the annual conference of the Eastern District Association of the American Alliance for Health, Physical Education, Recreation and Dance, Philadelphia, PA.

Catelli, L. A., & Moskowitz, K. (1994, March). *A survey of preferred curriculum goals of parents, students, teachers, and administrators.* Paper presented at the annual conference of the Eastern District Association of the American Alliance for Health, Physical Education, Recreation and Dance, Philadelphia, PA.

Catelli, L. A., & Nix, W. (1992). Project SCOPE: An urban partnership venture—descriptions and predictions. In G. Graham & M. Jones (Eds.), *Collaboration between researchers and practitioners: An international dialogue—Proceedings from the 1991 AIESEP-NAPEHE World Congress* (pp. 105-110). Atlanta, GA: AIESEP/NAPEHE.

Catelli, L A., & Nix, W. (1994, March). *The use and effects of goal-setting procedures and videotaped analysis on the instructional performances of student teachers at SCOPE school settings.* Paper presented at the annual conference of the Eastern District Association of the American Alliance for Health, Physical Education, Recreation and Dance, Philadelphia, PA.

Catelli, L. A., Franco, M., & Mongiello, B. (1996). Linking assessment, instruction, and curriculum change: A collaborative school-college process model. In T. Fay (Ed.), *Developing Assessment—Monograph Series Vol. 2* (pp. 53-60). Latham, NY: New York State Alliance for Health, Physical Education, Recreation and Dance.

Catelli, L. A., Goldsmith, R., & Costello, J. (2001, February). *East meets west: Three school-college partnership projects for student achievement and improvement in teacher education.* Paper accepted for the annual meeting of the Association of Teacher Educators, New Orleans, LA.

Catelli, L. A., Johnston, D., & Franco, M. (1996, November). *What do teachers say in a student-teacher conference? A school-university action research study.* Paper presented at the annual conference of the New York State American Alliance for Health, Physical Education, Recreation and Dance. Long Island, NY.

Catelli, L. A., Nix, W., & Papapetrou, P. (1996, April). *Teachers as action researchers in a school-university partnership: What do they do and what is it for?* Paper presented at the annual meeting of the American Educational Research Association, New York.

Catelli, L. A., Padovano, K., & Costello, J. (2000). Action research in the context of a school-university partnership: Its value, problems, issues and benefits. *Educational Action Research, 8*(2), 225-242.

Catelli, L. A., Mongiello, B., Moskowitz, K., & Jordan, J. (1993). *Collaborative action research to effect change and improvement in urban middle-school physical education* (A Preliminary Report of Research Findings to the Administrators of The Louis Armstrong Middle School-Queen College Collaboration). Flushing, New York: The Queens College Center For The Improvement Of Education, Queens College/CUNY.

Catelli, L. A., Johnston, D., Nix, W., Stack-Lennon, M., Turner, W., & Escobar, S. (1994, March). *Changing the school practitioner's role in student teaching and teacher education: A school-college partnership endeavor.* Program presentation at the annual conference of the Eastern District Association of the American Alliance for Health, Physical Education, Recreation and Dance, Philadelphia, PA.

Catelli, L. A., Anslow-Chakrian, N., DeCurtis, P., Johnston, D., Jordan, J., McLaughlin, P., Mongiello, B., Moskowitz, K., Nix, W., Shurgin, S., & Stack-Lennon, M. (1987). *Competency-based teacher education: The pedagogical component.* Unpublished document. Flushing, NY: Queens College of the City University of New York.

Catelli, L. A., DeCurtis, P., Johnston, D., Nix, W., Mongiello, B., Moskowitz, K., & McLaughlin, P. (1993, March). *A holistic school-university partnership model for reforming education for the 21st century: New professional roles.* Program presentation at the national convention of the American Alliance for Health, Physical Education, Recreation and Dance, Washington, DC.

Catelli, L. A., DeCurtis, P., Nix, W., Johnston, D., McLaughlin, P., Mongiello, B., & Moskowitz, K. (1995, November/December). Collaborate: Become a new professional. *Strategies, 9*(3), 8-12.

Catelli, L. A., Foglia, G., Lettera, J., Loret, J., Lovins, H., Pardew, D., & Schwartz, S. (1980). *Competency based teacher education for the preparation of physical education teachers* (Document, Department of Health and Physical Education and New York State Education Department). Flushing, NY: Queens College/CUNY.

City University of New York (1991, December 10). *Access to excellence—The faculty of the City University of New York* [Program Booklet and Special Ceremony]. Distinguished faculty and faculty award recipients honored. New York: Author.

Clark, R. (1988). School-university relations: An interpretive review. In K. Sirotnik & J. Goodlad (Eds.), *School-university partnerships in action: Concepts, cases, and concerns* (pp. 32-65). New York: Teachers College Press.

Daniel, J. (1999, March). *How to sleep comfortably with an elephant: A view from the Open University*. Paper presented at the national conference of the American Association for Higher Education, Washington, DC.

Darling-Hammond, L. (Ed.). (1994). *Professional development schools*. New York: Teachers College Press.

De Geus, A. (1997). *The living company*. Boston: Harvard Business School Press.

Fullan, M., with Stiegelbauer, S. (1991). *The new meaning of educational change*. New York: Teachers College Press.

Gentile, A.M. (1972). A working model of skill acquisition with application to teaching. *Quest, 17*, 3-23.

Gips, C., & Stoel, C. (Eds.). (1999). *Making a place in the faculty rewards system for work with K-12: A project report of four universities*. Washington, DC: American Association for Higher Education.

Goodlad, J. (1988). School-university partnerships for educational renewal: Rationale and concepts. In K. Sirotnik & J. Goodlad (Eds.), *School-university partnerships in action: Concepts, cases, and concerns* (pp. 3-31). New York: Teachers College Press.

Goodlad, J. (1990). *Teachers for our nation's schools*. San Francisco, CA: Jossey-Bass.

Goodlad, J. (1994). *Educational renewal: Better teachers, better schools*. San Francisco, CA: Jossey-Bass.

Goodlad, J. (1999). Rediscovering teacher education: School renewal and educating educators. *Change, 31*(5), 28-33.

Goodlad, J., & Sirotnik, K. (1988). The future of school-university partnerships. In K. Sirotnik & J. Goodlad (Eds.), *School-university partnerships in action: Concepts, cases, and concerns* (pp. 205-225). New York: Teachers College Press.

Grundy, S. (1987). *Curriculum: Product or praxis*. London: Falmer Press.

Haberman, M. (1988). *Preparing teachers for urban schools*. Bloomington, IN: Phi Delta Kappa Educational Foundation.

Haycock, K., Hart, P., & Irvine, J. (1992). *Improving student achievement through partnerships*. Washington, DC: American Association for Higher Education.

Hollingsworth, S. (Ed.). (1997). *International action research: A casebook for educational reform*. London: Falmer Press.

Holly, P. (1991). Action research: The missing link in the creation of schools as centers of inquiry. In A. Lieberman & L. Miller (Eds.), *Staff development for education in the '90s* (pp. 133-157). New York: Teachers College Press.

Holmes Group. (1986). *Tomorrow's teachers: A report of the Holmes Group*. East Lansing, MI: Author.

Holmes Group. (1990). *Tomorrow's schools: A report of the Holmes Group*. East Lansing, MI: Author.

Holmes Group. (1995). *Tomorrow's schools of education: A report of the Holmes Group*. East Lansing, MI: Author.

Hyman, R. (1971). *Contemporary thought on teaching*. Englewood Cliffs, NJ: Prentice Hall, Inc.

Hyman, R. (1974). *Ways of teaching*. Englewood Cliffs, NJ: Prentice-Hall.

Jones, B., & Maloy, R. W. (1988). *Partnerships for improving schools*. Westport, CT: Greenwood Press.

Joyce, B. (1967). *The teacher and his staff: Man, media, and machines*. Washington, DC: National Education Association and the Center for the Study of Instruction.

Joyce, B. (1969). *Alternative models of elementary education*. Waltham, MA: Xerox College Publishing.

Joyce, B. (1972). The teacher innovator: A program for preparing educators. In B. Joyce (Ed.), *Perspectives for reform in teacher education* (pp. 1-22). Englewood Cliffs, NJ: Prentice-Hall.

Joyce, B., Calhoun, E., & Hopkins, D. (1999). *The new structure of school improvement: Inquiring schools and achieving students*. Buckingham, UK: Open University Press.

Joyce, B., & Weil, M. (1972a). *Models of teaching*. Englewood Cliffs, NJ: Prentice Hall.

Joyce, B., & Weil, M. (Eds.). (1972b). *Perspectives for reform in teacher education*. Englewood Cliffs, NJ: Prentice-Hall.

Kindsvatter, R., & Wilen, W. (1982). A systematic approach to improving conferencing skills. In E. Grimsley & R. Bruce (Eds.), *Readings in educational supervision* (pp. 105-109). Alexandria, VA: Association for Supervision and Curriculum Development.

Kochan, F. K. (1999). Professional development schools: A comprehensive view. In M. Byrd & D.J. McIntyre (Eds.), *Research on professional development schools: Teacher education yearbook VII* (pp. 173-190). Thousand Oaks, CA: Corwin Press.

Maeroff, G. (1983). *School and college: Partnerships in education*. Princeton, NJ: Carnegie Foundation for the Advancement of Teaching.

Molar, A. (1999). *Smaller classes and educational vouchers: A research update*. Harrisburg, PA: Keystone Research Center.

New York State Regents Task Force on Teaching. (1998, July). *Teaching to higher standards: New York's commitment*. Albany, NY: The University of the State of New York—The State Education Department.

Northwest Regional Educational Laboratory. (1998). *Catalog of school reform models: First edition*. Portland, OR: Northwest Regional Educational Laboratory.

Oja, S. N., & Smullyan, L. (1989). *Collaborative action research: A developmental approach*. London: Falmer Press.

Pignatelli, F., & Pflaum, S. (Eds.). (1993). *Celebrating diverse voices: Progressive education and equity*. Newbury Park, CA: Corwin Press.

Schaefer, R. (1967). *The school as a center of inquiry*. New York: Harper and Row.

Scheffler, I. (1960). *The language of education*. Springfield, IL: Charles C. Thomas.

Scheffler, I. (1965). *Conditions of knowledge*. Glenview, IL: Scott, Foresman Co.

Scheffler, I. (1966). Intellect and skill. In I. Scheffler (Ed.), *Philosophy and education*. Boston, MA: Allyn and Bacon.

Schlechty, P., & Whitford, B. (1988). Shared problems and shared vision: Organic collaboration. In K. Sirotnik & J. Goodlad (Eds.), *School-university partnership in action: Concepts, cases, and concerns* (pp. 191-204). New York: Teachers College Press.

Schmidt, B., Badillo, H., Brady, J., MacDonald, H., Ohrenstein, M., Roberts, R., & Schwartz, R. (1999). *The City University of New York: An institution adrift: A report of the mayor's task force on the City University of New York.*

Sirotnik, K. (1988). The meaning and conduct of inquiry in school-university partnerships. In K. Sirotnik & J. Goodlad (Eds.), *School university partnerships in action: Concepts, cases and concerns* (pp. 169-190). New York: Teachers College Press.

Slater, J. (1996). *Anatomy of a collaboration: Study of a college of education/public school partnership*. New York: Garland.

Smith, B.O. (1960). A concept of teaching. *Teachers College Record, 61*, 229-241.

Smith, B.O. (1962). Conceptual frameworks for analysis of classroom social interaction. *Journal of Experimental Education, 30*(4), 325-326.

Smith, B.O. (1963). A conceptual analysis of instructional behavior. *Journal of Teacher Education, 14*, 294-298.

Soltis, J. (1968). *An introduction to the analysis of educational concepts*. Reading, MA: Addison-Wesley.

Soltis, J. (1978). *An introduction to the analysis of educational concepts* (2nd ed.). Reading, MA: Addison-Wesley.

The California State University Institute for Education Reform. (1996, February). *Teachers who teach our teachers: Teacher preparation programs at the California State University* (popularly known as The Hart Report). California: Author.

Trubowitz, S., Duncan, J., Fibkins, W., & Longo, P. (1984). *When a college works with a public school*. Boston, MA: Institute for Responsive Education.

Trubowitz, S., & Longo, P. (1997). *How it works: Inside a school-college collaboration*. New York: Teachers College Press.

U.S. Department of Education. (1984). *Partnerships in education*. Washington, DC: U.S. Government Printing Office.

U.S. Department of Education. (1998, September). *Promising practices: New ways to improve teacher quality*. Washington, DC: Author.

U.S. Department of Education. (1999a). *Partnership grants for improving teacher quality*. Washington, DC: Author.

U.S. Department of Education. (1999b, June 4). *Preparing tomorrow's teachers to use technology: Capacity building implementation catalyst grants*. Washington, DC: Author.

Weiner, L. (1993). *Preparing teachers for urban schools: Lessons from thirty years of school reform*. New York: Teachers College Press.

Whiting, C., Whitty, G., Furlong, J., Miles, S., & Barton, L. (1996, July). *Partnership in initial teacher education: A topography* (Research Report from the Modes of Teacher Education Project—Institute of Education, University of London and Universities of Bristol and Sheffield). London: Health and Education Unit, Institute of Education, University of London.

Wilbur, P., & Lambert, L. (1995). *Linking America's schools and colleges*. Washington, DC: American Association for Higher Education.

Wilson, E. (1967). *A model for action: Rational planning in curriculum and instruction*. Washington, DC: National Education Association and the Center for the Study of Instruction.

Wilson, E. (1972). Can the school become a center of inquiry? A design for institution building. In B. Joyce & M. Weil (Eds.), *Perspectives for reform in teacher education* (pp. 23-47). Englewood Cliffs, NJ: Prentice-Hall.

PART II

The Present—A New Era

Five

How a Suburban College Educates Teachers for Diversity: A Working Model for Teacher Education

Kathryn Padovano
Roberta Senzer
Sarah Church

Classrooms in today's schools are very dynamic due in part to changes in population, family, socioeconomic conditions, and diversity of students. In order to function well, new teachers must acquire an understanding of the meaning of cultural and ethnic diversity. They need to develop the knowledge and strategies necessary to work effectively with students from diverse ethnic and cultural groups. It is imperative that new teachers reflect on and clarify their own cultural assumptions to be able to successfully meet the needs of diverse children in our schools.

Dowling College's School of Education examined its existing teacher education program and recognized that three significant issues should be addressed in the field experiences component of the program. First, a gap exists between the suburban college classroom and the elementary, middle school, and secondary classrooms of today. Second, suburban schools, as a result of changing demographics, serve children with increasingly diverse backgrounds. Third, field experiences in the inner city or multiethnic environments are an essential component for preparing new teachers. New teachers must be prepared for a student population that reflects multiracial, multicultural, and multiethnic backgrounds, like their urban counterparts. Thus, the School of Education sought collaborative partnerships with New York City community school districts and multiethnic Long Island school districts in order to provide its students with opportunities for enriched field experiences. Through the authors' participation on the New York State Regents visiting Committee on Low Performing Schools, relationships developed that led to establishing suburban/urban partnerships.

This chapter describes the New York City collaborative field-based model in which participants in the teacher education programs at Dowling College acquire essential teaching skills in urban school settings that foster development of academic and social skills in order to meet the education needs of children in the 21st century. The first section of the chapter is an overview of relevant national and state educational reform efforts and events. The second section explains the development of the School of Education's suburban-urban partnership model for teacher education. The authors' intent is to set forth a working model for the preparation of new teachers and their continued professional growth in teaching culturally and ethnically diverse student populations in the inner city.

NATIONAL AND STATE REFORM EFFORTS AND EVENTS

> After a decade of reform, we have finally learned in hindsight what should have been clear from the start: Most schools and teachers cannot produce the kind of learning demanded by the new reforms—not because they do not want to, but because they do not know how, and the systems in which they work do not support them in doing so. (National Commission on Teaching and America's Future [NCTAF], 1996, p. 5)

The National Commission's report, *What Matters Most: Teaching for America's Future*, was the result of a two-year study that emphasized the single most important strategy for achieving America's education goals: to recruit, prepare, and support excellent teachers for every school. "On the whole, the school reform movement has ignored the obvious: What teachers know and can do makes the crucial difference in what children learn. Standards for students and teachers are the key to reforming American education. Access to competent and caring teachers must become a new student right. Access to high-quality preparation, induction, and professional development must become a new teacher right" (NCTAF, 1996, p. 5). The Commission recommended that all children be taught by teachers who have the knowledge, skills, and commitment to teach children well, and that all teacher education programs meet professional standards of accreditation. A fundamental reorganization of teacher preparation programs was implicit in the Commission's conclusions.

The urgent need for restructuring teacher preparation programs has been proposed by scholars such as John Goodlad (1990a, 1990b), as well as the work of such groups as the Carnegie Task Force and the Holmes Group (1986, 1990). The initial call for restructuring the nation's schools began with the National Defense Act of 1958, a response to the perceived failure of American education prompted by the launch of Sputnik by the Russians in 1957. In 1983, *A Nation At Risk* was released by a presidential commission and indicated that the country's schools had deteriorated precipitously. The negative commentary on American education continued into the 1990s, wherein teachers and teacher education were seen as the problem.

Since the mid-1980s, the Holmes Group and the Carnegie Forum have been key players in promoting ideas for changes in the way teachers are prepared. In 1986, *A Nation Prepared* (Carnegie Forum) and *Tomorrow's Teachers* (Holmes Group) were released. These reports presented a vision for the teaching profession. At this time, the National Council for Accreditation of Teacher Education (NCATE) pursued a national agenda for raising standards for teacher education. NCATE has committed to strengthening the knowledge base as one of its top priorities. In a booklet titled *What Teachers Should Know and Be Able to Do* (1994), the National Board of Professional Teaching Standards (NBPTS) outlined rigorous professional standards. *Tomorrow's Schools of Education* (1995, pp. 2-3) challenged institutions to ". . . design a new curriculum . . . develop a new faculty . . . recruit a new student body . . . create new locations for much of their work . . . and build a new set of connections to those they serve. . . ."

Concurrent with these events, the New York State Education Department created a plan to put in place the processes that support and nurture the climate and conditions necessary for both teachers and organizational growth. This has resulted in new state initiatives. In 1994, New York developed *A New Compact for Learning* as the foundation for building a system in which every child masters what is needed to become an educated and competent adult. In 1996, the New York State Regents Task Force on Teaching began to look at teacher competency and certification issues and in 1998 concluded its work with a report, *Teaching to Higher Standards: New York's Commitment*.

In addition to improving the quality of teachers and raising standards, the Commission stressed the need and urgency to address the special problems of the urban school systems. Attracting and retaining talented teacher candidates are essential in order for the urban schools to succeed.

Each year, a large number of new teachers enter the profession with the potential to be effective teachers and leaders in their schools. In many cases, however, they receive little guidance to support their early teaching efforts. The New York State Board of Regents noted that the research indicated that a substantial percent of new teachers leave during the first five years of their teaching careers. Inner-city and urban classrooms experience a phenomenal level of teacher attrition: a 50% rate in the first three years of teaching (Summers, 1987). Huling-Austin (1990) contended that this alarmingly high attrition rate for new teachers was due to their feelings of isolation and frustration, need for support, and lack of practical classroom knowledge. There is evidence that those who do continue in the profession work diligently to overcome negative initial experiences, but ultimately may never reach their full potential as teachers (Huling-Austin, 1986).

American students today represent greater ethnic, cultural, and linguistic differences than at any other time in the past. In *We Can't Teach What We Don't Know* (Howard, 1999), the research indicates that American classrooms are experiencing the largest influx of immigrant students since the turn of the century. A survey conducted in the early 1990s revealed that in 50 of the nation's largest urban public school systems African Americans, Latinos, Asian Americans, and other students of color made up 76.5% of the student population (Council of the Great City Schools, 1994). Also, it has been estimated that by year 2020 students of color will make up approximately 46% of the nation's student population (Pallas, Natriello, & McDill, 1989). Thus, in tomorrow's classrooms teachers will more than likely instruct students from diverse ethnic, cultural, and linguistic groups. This is true for both inner-city and suburban teachers.

Noting that New York State's schools mirror this national trend, the New York State Board of Regents has made an attempt to address the growing disparity between cultural backgrounds of teachers and students by including provisions to ensure that teaching candidates develop an understanding of the nature of cultural diversity. A state-mandated requirement of field experience could support the need for these culturally diverse student populations.

In many cases, the cultural backgrounds of teachers—including their socioeconomic status—contrast markedly with those of their students. Whereas students of color presently comprise a significant number in 23 of the 25 largest school districts in the United States with a projected percent reaching as high as 40% of the total student population in the United States by 2000, the teaching profession has become increasingly European American and middle class. The represents a serious gap in equity.

Finally, the research indicates that there is a significant number of women and European Americans in the teacher force. Seventy-three percent of all public school teachers are women, and 87% of those teaching in public schools are "white" (U.S. Department of Education, November, 1995, p. 29). Profiles of teacher candidates and beginning teachers show similar gender and ethnic patterns. Most of these teachers, moreover, come from relatively stable family backgrounds. The majority of teachers and future teachers in our classrooms, then, come from very different backgrounds than many of the students they teach.

Teachers need training to become sensitized to the commonalties and differences among students, as well as to provide methods and techniques for addressing a context in which a multitude of cultures and learning styles must co-exist. The place to examine and practice effective teaching strategies is during the various field experiences designed for students in teacher education programs. Contact with students in actual diverse classroom situations serves a variety of purposes for the student teacher, including learning the teaching role, gaining an understanding of how learning actually takes place, and developing an understanding of the nature of school environments themselves.

The importance of teacher preparation to address cultural diversity needs is obvious. This has been examined over recent years through the creation and implementation of partnerships between universities and public schools. Professional Development Schools have taken on increased importance as a model for bringing together school district and higher education personnel. Such models are based upon a collaborative partnership that stimulates and supports coaching teacher candidates and strengthens teaching and learning for both school and college faculty. The literature strongly recommends a continued effort to commit to these kinds of partnerships.

THE DEVELOPMENT OF COLLABORATIVES AND A WORKING SUBURBAN-URBAN PARTNERSHIP MODEL

In an effort to fill this need, a collaborative pilot project was undertaken between Dowling College's School of Education and a New York City Intermediate School (IS 218). Under the direction of the then-dean Kathryn Padovano, a number of collaboratives with New York City schools were started during the late 1990s. The dean, having been involved in the desegregation of the Los Angeles schools in the 1970s, and more recently in the 1990s with members of the New York State Board of Regents on matters of equity gaps in the New York City school system, was personally and professionally committed to seeing that Dowling's teacher candidates become adequately prepared to meet the challenges associated with diversity. Concurrent with developing collaboratives with New York City schools, the dean also forged new partnerships with administrations at numerous school districts on Long Island, including those districts with large minority populations. The primary focus of these partnership programs was to provide professional and program development to working administrators and teachers.

The many conferences and meetings with state and New York City officials, and the numerous conversations with Long Island administrators and teachers as well as conversations with Dowling's students pointed more and more to the fact that many, if not all, of our students had no first-hand knowledge of any dimension of working in inner-city schools, nor did they have knowledge of working with student populations that were widely different in culture and ethnic diversity. Thus, there was an obvious need for Dowling College, a suburban college, to begin addressing this void in its teacher education programs.

In addressing these needs, it was determined that the purpose of the working school-college partnerships is threefold:

1. to facilitate a partnership with a district that focuses on the education and development of urban youth,
2. to offer future teachers who are primarily European American the opportunity to begin studying the problems of culturally diverse students, and
3. to mentor teacher candidates to develop culturally responsive and pedagogically sound instructional practices for the children in urban schools and communities.

The dean and her associates involved the Dowling College faculty through a faculty committee in conversations to determine what Dowling students needed to know in order to face the challenges of the 21st century. The question asked was how we could engage our predominantly European American, culturally mainstream corps of teacher candidates in a type of experience that would not only help them to understand cultural differences but also prepare them to effectively negotiate the complexities of urban communities. Recognizing that changes in current field experiences were necessary in order to prepare teachers for urban settings, the pilot partnership projects required that practicing teachers in urban elementary and intermediate schools work closely with teachers candidates to enable them to learn what it means to be committed to education and its impact in a diverse environment. The outcomes of such a collaboration include:

- an expected willingness or desire to teach in an urban setting;
- an understanding of culturally diverse pupil populations; and
- a foundation in community-building approaches, service-learning approaches, and other approaches that target the real goals of community constituencies to improve the development and achievement of its children.

To that end we developed urban partnerships with (1) schools that were identified as low performing with a highly underserved population and (2) urban schools with many resources and a reputation that attracted middle-class families. Presently, we are working with schools in Community School Districts 2 (Lower Westside/Manhattan), 6 (Inwood/Manhattan), 24 (Corona/Queens), and 28 (Rego Park, Jamaica/Queens).

The special skills that are targeted for the teacher candidates to develop in these settings are those that are described by Haberman (1995) in his analysis of teachers of children of poverty. He found that teachers are successful when they shift the focus of learning from extrinsic rewards, that is, a job in the unforeseeable future, to learning for the purpose of learning itself. This requires strategies that include the following characteristics: consistently seeking new activities for the children, using numerous and different types of materials to engage the children's interest, elaborating on topics and problems that the children experience in their day-to-day lives, identifying the special talents of some children in order to interest other children in these activities, modeling learning behavior by bringing to the classroom the teacher's own interests, capitalizing on leadership within student groups, and asking questions of interest to the children to raise their curiosity. To facilitate the acquisition of these skills, Dowling faculty members have recently begun to develop curriculum content and materials for the site-based seminar that accompanies the field experience.

For the most part, teachers have traditionally conceived their role as working primarily with students in the classroom and helping them learn academic material. In our complex society, teachers need to utilize all resources available, including parents and other professionals. There is a growing emphasis on collegiality; teachers are beginning to take charge of their occupation and move toward greater professionalism. *The Condition of Teaching: A State-by-State Analysis*, a teacher survey conducted by the Carnegie Foundation for the Advancement of Teaching, confirms that in the early 1990s, teachers in Connecticut, Iowa, Minnesota, Mississippi, New Jersey, and Wisconsin seemed most positive about the success of reform in their respective states. Local teacher organizations, inspired by the success of the American Federation of Teacher (AFT) locals in Rochester, Miami-Dade County, Toledo, Cincinnati, and other urban schools districts involved in site-based management, empower teachers and provide them a greater stake in making the school better. Empowerment (Maeroff, 1993) "signifies a transformation through which more teachers become confident and knowledgeable practitioners—very possibly as members of teams—who are able to play a part in changing their own teaching and in changing their schools" (p. 10).

In Bellah's (1985) work on individualism and commitment in American life, he points to the serious conflict that American society still faces today in construing meaning, the conflict between the individual's need for commitment and community and the belief that ultimately the individual is alone and answerable only to oneself.

Therefore, working in partnership with the administrative staff and faculty of urban schools to equip our teacher candidates for their responsibility to teach all children gives meaning and coherence to the field experience. We know that teachers who work together with shared goals are a positive, powerful force in effectively teaching children, and we know that teachers who labor alone rarely understand that their colleagues share many of the same problems inside and outside the classroom. Thus, we have taken an inclusive and comprehensive approach to the partnerships, soliciting the participation from all members of the school community.

In addition, we know that teacher candidates need to be active participants in their own learning and in the creation of a new belief system that has community as the core of its value system. This site-based partnership model is an ideal mechanism to enable teacher candidates to learn how to work successfully with children in constantly changing times. Total immersion in meaningful and relevant field experiences is an important means of assisting the learners to cope with the social changes in the schools.

As mentioned previously, the urban school the authors chose for the pilot project is Intermediate School 218, also known as the Salome Urena Middle School. The school evolved into a partnership with the Children's Aid Society, one of the oldest social welfare agencies in the United States. The Salome Urena Middle School was selected because it had (1) an enthusiastic teaching staff and principal, (2) a diverse student body, and (3) a strong interest from the parents and community. Of particular interest to the authors was the fact that the State Board of Regents had designated IS 218 as a School Under Regents Review (SURR School) because of consistently low performance on standardized tests. The school was able to ameliorate this problem, and today IS 218 holds an average attendance of 92%, the highest in the district. The school averages 2.2 suspensions per 100 students, versus 6.8 for all New York City intermediate schools. Math and reading scores have continued to rise steadily, with math scores rising nearly 40% over a two-year period.

The strength and power of community alliances have had a positive effect on student learning, often with unprecedented results. An underlying theme in the creation of the Dowling College New York City partnerships was to tie theory directly to practice. The college was inspired to work with IS 218 because it is an exemplary school that has successfully made this connection. In order to facilitate a strong link between theory and practice, the principal, who served as the seminar leader for the teacher candidates, provided discussions on educational philosophy and teaching strategies. The school-site provided a real-life laboratory in which the principal had the ability to demonstrate relevant experiences. One of the goals of this field experience was to expose students to committed urban teachers, to help develop commitment and a sense of efficacy among the teacher candidates. In such a setting, our teacher candidates learned that they can make a significant difference. Direct communication with the school community enabled the Dowling teacher candidates to seek out and build the relationships that support collaborative and cooperative interactions among community members which in turn afforded them the opportunity to make wise decisions that positively affected their teaching.

Dowling College in collaboration with New York City schools developed a model for field-based teacher training that benefited all parties involved in the field experience process. The model's foundation is based on information obtained through the collective experiences of professionals working with new teachers in inner-city settings. It provided an opportunity for students who had virtually no inner-city experience with experiences that will aid them in achieving success in their first year of teaching.

The process for developing the model included input and evaluation from teacher candidates, cooperating teachers, and district administrators as well as information obtained from visits to other inner-city schools throughout New York State. Every two years, the School of Education surveys all of its teacher candidates, cooperating teachers, field supervisors, seminar leaders, principals, and administrators in order to receive feedback on its field experience programs. The survey analysis has provided direction for these partnership programs.

Integrated into the theoretical framework of our teacher education program is a belief that when future teachers are immersed into a culture different from their own, it is likely that they will develop a personal theory that accepts students as individuals. Experiences teaching in communities with diverse populations should contribute to developing an understanding of the importance of diversity to a quality learning environment. In the urban-suburban partnerships we have developed, our students are offered enriched opportunities.

Our recent pilot partnership with IS 218 is only a beginning. Perhaps there is more good news on this front than we realize. If the mix of the student population in the School of Education is any indication, it appears that more and more ethnic minorities are entering the education field on Long Island.

The European American population of education students at Dowling has decreased from 90% in 1993 to 78% at the undergraduate level and from 87% to 82% at the graduate level. The current education student population is 515 undergraduates and 1,554 graduate students.

It is too early to make a case for a specific cause and effect relationship between increases in our ethnic minority population and our many community partnerships; however, the general belief of the people involved in the partnerships is that there has been positive influence in this regard.

During the last decade, the School of Education has moved toward increased community involvement through the numerous partnerships it has developed. This is indeed a critical dimension of the College's mission and its evolving suburban-urban partnership model in teacher education. It is only through the continued pursuit of an understanding of the changing needs of the community regarding diversity and other critical issues that the School of Education will meet the comprehensive needs of its students. Our mission of the personal college serves the needs of the students only if it reaches out to the world community at large. Seen in Figure 5.1 are the major components of our working model for the suburban-urban partnerships we have developed in teacher education.

Clarity of Purpose for the Partnership

Selection of School Sites and Personnel	College's Teacher Education Program
• Schools that are designated as exemplary in the inner city • Schools that work effectively with social services agencies and community business leaders • Schools that have an active and successful parent group • Experienced teachers who are professionally committed to teaching inner-city students, pedagogically adept, and willing to collaborate and mentor teacher candidates • Principals who are willing to participate in or teach a seminar that accompanies the teacher candidate's field experience	• Involvement of key committees, faculty, and administrators • Development by school and college personnel of a special seminar to accompany field experiences in the inner-city school site • Inclusion of topics and issues focusing on diversity in course syllabi • Development of mechanisms for ongoing input and evaluation • Grant-writing activity to support partnership projects

Theoretical Framework and Themes

- Total immersion in a culture of diversity for the teacher candidate
- Empowerment and sense of community for all participating members
- Collective professional experiences as the foundation for the model

Figure 5.1. Suburban-Urban Partnership Model in Teacher Education

As we reflect on our ultimate goal of continually creating better ways to educate, one dimension of the challenge is crystal clear. An elitist approach to higher education is unacceptable and leads to isolationism. Isolation from a world that is changing at the speed of light will doom us to failure. Evolution to more and more diversity is now the norm. We cannot ignore this reality. Higher education needs to prepare its students for this evolving cultural phenomenon. In order, to do this we must better understand students, parents, administrators, communities, and ourselves. We must be prepared to work closely with representatives from all of these constituencies, including social service and business organizations. Only in this fashion will we ensure a journey with a destination, a journey that continues to take us to more profound levels of learning, understanding, and accomplishment. The challenge for us will be to continue to change and grow as we blend distinct institutions to enhance the learning of children and youth and the preparation and professional development of the educators who work in them.

The chapters following this one exemplify the ongoing curriculum work of our colleagues in the School of Education. Their chapters are representative of their efforts to transform the elementary teacher education program to an effective program for preparing teachers who will teach in urban and suburban settings in the next century.

REFERENCES

Bellah, R.N., Madsen, R., Sullivan, W.M., Swidler, A., & Tipton, S.M. (1985). *Habits of the heart*. Berkeley: University of California Press.

Carnegie Forum on Education and the Economy. (1986). *A nation prepared: Teachers for the 21st century*. Report of the Carnegie Task Force on Teaching as a Profession. Washington, DC: Author.

Carnegie Foundation for the Advancement of Teaching. (1990). *The condition of teaching: A state-by-state analysis*. Princeton, NJ: Princeton University Press.

Council of Great City Schools. (1994). *National urban education goals: 1992-1993 Indicators report*. Washington, DC: Author.

Goodlad, J.I. (1990a). Better teachers for our nation's schools. *Phi Delta Kappan, 3*, 184-194.

Goodlad, J.I. (1990b). *Teachers for our nation's schools*. San Francisco: Jossey-Bass.

Haberman, M. (1995). *Star teachers of children in poverty*. West Lafayette, IN: Kappa Delta Pi.

Holmes Group. (1986). *Tomorrow's teachers: A report of the Holmes Group*. East Lansing, MI: Author.

Holmes Group. (1990). *Tomorrow's schools: Principles for the design of professional development schools*. East Lansing, MI: Author.

Howard, G.R. (1999). *We can't teach what we don't know: White teachers, multiracial schools*. New York: Teachers College Press.

Huling-Austin, L. (1986). What can and cannot be reasonably expected from teacher induction programs. *Journal of Teacher Education, 1*, 2-5.

Huling-Austin, L. (1990). Teacher induction programs and internships. In W.R. Hustin (Ed.), *Handbook of research in teacher education* (pp. 535-548). New York: Macmillan.

Maeroff, G.I. (1993). *Team building for school change: Equipping teachers for new roles*. New York: Teachers College Press.

National Board of Professional Teaching Standards. (1994). *What teachers should know and be able to do*. Detroit: Author.

National Commission on Excellence in Education. (1983). *A nation at risk: The imperatives of educational reform*. Washington, DC: Author.

National Commission on Teaching and America's Future. (1996). *What matters most: Teaching for America's future*. Teachers College, Columbia University. New York: Author.

Pallas, A.M., Natriello, G., & McDill, E.L. (1989). The changing nature of the disadvantaged population: Current dimensions and future trends. *Educational Researcher, 18*(5), 16-22.

Summers, J.A. (1987). *Summative evaluation report: Project CREDIT*. Terre Haute: Indiana State University, School of Education.

U.S. Department of Education. (1995). *National Center for Educational Statistics: Digest of Educational Statistics*. Washington, DC: Author.

Six

Asian American and Latino Literature and Culture: An Instructional Module for Preservice Teacher Education

Bernadyn Kim Suh

Children of Asian and Latino ethnic minority groups have special needs and interests. Their needs are not being met by the current school curricula, which primarily focus on the European American majority. The Asian and Latino populations are growing at a rapid rate. According to the U.S. Census Bureau, approximately 31 million Spanish speaking people live in the United States (Larmer, 1999, pp. 48-51). In the 1980s, the United States absorbed more than 8.6 million immigrants, mostly from Asia, Latin America, and the Caribbean (Loeb, Friedman, & Lord, 1993). This was the largest influx since the last great wave of immigration in the 1920s. It was been projected that the current population of 31 million Latinos will reach 96 million by the year 2050, an increase of more than 200% (Larmer, 1999). This population must be educated in school systems with teachers who can effectively deliver a new type of education to a diverse population of students. The 21st century presents many challenges to the United States, and the status of the United States in the world arena depends on the contributions of all of its citizens. Therefore, it is important to prepare quality teachers who will not only examine their own beliefs, biases, and prejudices, but also develop appropriate attitudes, knowledge, and skills to facilitate the successful achievement of a culturally and ethnically diverse population of learners.

At Dowling College, a small private college on Long Island 50 miles from New York City, over 90% of the preservice and inservice teachers are European American. They have lived in suburbia most of their lives and have had little contact with ethnic minorities. In teacher education courses at Dowling College, we are working to assist our students in becoming knowledgeable about the needs of ethnic minority children. Many of our students will secure teaching positions in schools on Long Island, a region of New York State that is fast becoming culturally and ethnically diverse, and others will obtain teaching positions in schools in New York City.

As a professor of education who has taught in Harlem, and as an Asian American who has grown up in this society, I am in a unique position to guide teacher candidates in understanding and teaching minority children. Having left Hawaii in 1962 with a bachelor's degree from the University of Hawaii, I then went on to enroll in a master's degree and doctoral program at Teachers College, Columbia University. Upon graduating from the program, I secured a teaching position in Harlem in two New York City public schools, P.S. 113M and P.S. 125M. It was immediately evident to me that my teacher preparation courses did not adequately prepare me for teaching in the inner city. I was not aware of the chasm that existed culturally between the students, who were mainly African American and Puerto Rican, and me. I was the only Asian American in the school, and they found me an oddity. I had innumerable adjustments to make as I tried to teach the children and learn about their culture, about which I knew very little. I learned Spanish words and become familiar with the foods my students' mothers so generously provided me. I eagerly searched through books and magazines to find pictures of ethnic minorities to integrate into lessons in order to foster a sense of ethnic pride in my students. This was in the 1960s, and we have come a long way since then. As a result of my experiences in Harlem, which left lasting impressions, I stress the importance of intercultural competence to the teacher candidates at Dowling College, and I encourage them to be sensitive and caring about the needs of all groups. I believe that teacher candidates have to learn in the same manner we ask them to teach their students: to actively involve them in the learning process, have them become totally immersed in the different cultures they are studying, and encourage them to respect one another's differences.

One of the tools that I utilize in this endeavor to assist my students in achieving intercultural competence is an instructional course/field module that I have developed for use in preservice teacher education. In this new era of teacher education, professional course work that is linked to field experiences is essential for blending theory with practice. My intent in this chapter is to present excerpts from some of the major components of this course that can be replicated and utilized in other preservice teacher education programs. The overall purpose of the module is to prepare teacher candidates in elementary education to design quality learning experiences for ethnic minority children so that they ultimately become effective teachers of a diverse population of students. More specifically, the purposes of the instructional module are to (1) sensitize teacher candidates to the cultural realities and needs of Asian American and Latinos in the United States; (2) have teacher candidates examine and acquire a working knowledge of Asian and Latino literature; and (3) prepare teacher candidates to design relevant instructional lessons directed at national and state learning standards for pupils in the areas of social studies, language arts, and cultural understandings.

The chapter includes excerpts from the module that consists of objectives, learning activities, and assignments, as well as available resources in Asian American and Latino literature and culture. The learning experiences and assignments that have been created for the module are based on information drawn from research and other writings that range in topics from multiculturalism to teacher beliefs (e.g., Cabello & Burstein, 1995; Pajares, 1993; Pignatelli & Pflaum, 1993), as well as my 30 years of experience. In implementing the module, instructional technology is used to assist teacher candidates in completing various learning activities and exercises. It is suggested that the module be used as part of a teacher candidate's course work and accompanying field experience. In presenting the module, it is my intent to have teacher educators, teacher candidates, and researchers join us at Dowling in a type of collaborative, participatory action research effort to further develop and refine the instructional module.

The chapter is arranged in two sections. The first section provides contextual information in the form of an overview of the teacher education program at Dowling College and a brief description of the new courses and related field experience. The second section presents excerpts from the module and its component parts. At the end of the section, I identify a series of general research questions to supply readers with a framework for assessing the effects and impacts of the module on teacher candidates' learning. The information obtained from the assessment will contribute to future use and collaborative development and dissemination of a researched-based teacher education module. Future research on the effects of the module-experience on teacher candidates is particularly important for us at Dowling College, as well as at other colleges and universities that are preparing preservice teachers to teach diverse populations of children. In Appendix A, I identify a short list of additional resources for the module. I hope that this introductory module on increasing preservice teachers' intercultural competence will serve as a springboard for dialogue among teacher educators, researchers, and preservice education students as well as a catalyst for interinstitutional research.

OVERVIEW OF THE PROGRAM, COURSES, AND FIELD EXPERIENCE

At Dowling College, as well as at colleges and universities across the country, preservice teacher education programs emphasize the education of ethnic minority children. Teacher candidates take introductory courses and a series of content-related teaching methods courses that include strategies for teaching diverse populations of children. The introductory courses expose teacher candidates to contemporary pedagogical theories, relevant learning theories, standards of learning and teaching, and an array of critical issues confronting education and society today. At Dowling College, teacher candidates then enroll in a series of methods courses, the first of which focuses on social studies, language arts, and literacy acquisition. These courses afford teacher candidates opportunities to focus on the needs of ethnic minority children. Teacher candidates learn how to develop lesson plans and units of instruction that focus on national and New York State curriculum standards in the subject areas cited above. The curriculum standards in social studies, in particular, include the study of the major social, political, economic, cultural, and religious developments in New York State and in our nation's history. The standards are integrated with those of language arts and literacy acquisition. Teacher candidates develop lessons to actively engage pupils in achieving the learning standards. They then implement lessons in a teaching or microteaching situation. They consider and plan for multisensory learning strategies and differing learning styles of their students. A focus on multiculturalism, racism, literacy acquisition, and an integration of relevant fiction and nonfiction literature (language arts standards) are an integral part of the courses.

The courses that make up the first set of teaching methods courses are intended to be taken in conjunction with a field experience. In the field experience, the teacher candidates participate in module instruction; guided observation of children, teachers, and schools; and tutoring of and practice teaching with diverse populations of students. The field experience can take place in a variety of settings, for example, schools, museums, social agencies, and so forth. All courses including the field experience are linked so that teacher candidates are oriented to the school community; life in the classroom; diverse student populations;

multicultural issues; pedagogy in social studies, literacy, and language arts; and the teaching profession. For a specified number of hours, teacher candidates participate in varied experiences in field settings including ones in high-need schools, with parent/caregivers, and with socioeconomically disadvantaged students. They are afforded opportunities to apply what they are learning in the college classroom to real-life settings along with opportunities to discuss, analyze, and reflect upon their experiences.

This instructional module is part of the program's first set of methods courses. It consists of a number of exercises and assignments that are carried out during teacher candidates' work in the field, coordinated with the social studies and language arts courses. The principle idea, as supported by research, is to coordinate the teacher candidates' field experience with what they are learning in the teacher education classroom (see Bondy, Schmitz, & Johnson, 1993; and Grant & Secada, 1990) and to sequence the learning activities in such a way so as to ensure development of necessary competencies. What follows in the next section of the chapter are excerpts from some of the major components of an introductory instructional module on Asian American and Latino literature and culture designed for preservice teacher education students in elementary education. I have added comments in a subsection entitled Instructor's Note, for purposes of either (1) clarifying learning activities for readers, (2) identifying areas of research, or (3) providing readers with additional information that may enhance their understanding of a topic under discussion. The module is intended to be used by other teacher educators in courses with teacher candidates in clinical settings, professional development schools, school/college or university partnership programs, or other partnerships, for example, social service agencies. It should also be mentioned that the excerpts are written as instructional sets for teacher candidates and can be directly used by teacher candidates as they explore issues attendant to their own intercultural competence.

EXCERPTS FROM AN INSTRUCTIONAL MODULE

Introduction and Instructional Set for Teacher Candidates

This module, entitled Asian American and Hispanic Literature and Culture, is designed primarily for preservice students who have entered the initial phases of a program in elementary teacher education. It is an introductory module that begins to prepare you, the teacher candidate, with the skills, knowledge, and attitudes needed to become an effective teacher of diverse student populations. The objectives of the learning activities, experiences, exercises, and assignments included in this module are to:

1. help you become sensitive to the cultural realities and needs of the Asian American and Latino populations in the United States;
2. assist you in examining your beliefs, biases, prejudices, and myths held about the Asian and Latino cultures;
3. provide you with the opportunity to develop attitudes, knowledge, and skills that will assist you in facilitating learning and academic achievement of culturally and ethnically diverse learners;
4. assist you in acquiring a working knowledge of Asian American and Latino literature;
5. foster the development of an initial concept of teaching a diverse student population; and
6. prepare you to design relevant instructional lessons directed at national and state learning standards for students in the areas of Language Arts, Social Studies, and Cultural Understandings.

The learning activities, experiences, assignments, and exercises you will engage in will take place in your field settings, in class, at home, and in other designated educational sites, e.g., museums, libraries, regional corporations, and businesses. This module will integrate the areas of social studies, language arts, multicultural education, and instructional technology.

You will be required to (1) keep a journal of your experiences and a portfolio of completed assignments, writings, essays, sample lessons, etc.; (2) participate in group discussions and individual conferences; and (3) engage in role playing, tutoring, and team teaching.

Finally, through structured study, reading, observation, and participation in this module you will be expected to achieve competence in the following areas:

1. demonstrate cultural sensitivity to teaching Asian American and Latino student populations, and
2. demonstrate an initial pedagogical and intercultural competence for becoming an effective teacher of diverse student populations in the areas of social studies and language arts.

In the next major component of the module, the learning activities are clustered around an area of competence they support and the objective(s) to which they contribute. The learning activities, exercises, and assignments that are presented here are exemplars of activities that enable teacher candidates to develop the desired competence or achieve the identified objective(s). They were selected not only to illustrate how the instructional module assists teacher candidates in developing intercultural competence but also to identify for other teacher educators the areas in which research can or needs to take place and suggest methods by which to conduct investigations on the effects and impacts of this module. They also provide evidence of student learning that can be utilized with teacher education accrediting agencies such as the National Council for the Accreditation of Teacher Education. Finally, the learning activities are categorized according to where they take place, for example, in the teacher education classroom, on site at a partnering school, at the college or university, in the elementary classrooms to which the teacher candidate is assigned, at home, or by computer. I also suggest the phase of the semester the teacher candidate should engage in the learning activity. It should be noted that this is a developmental process for the teacher candidate. Thus, the sequence of learning activities in this module is an important feature and relevant factor to research. Additional or optional learning activities are offered either to extend the teacher candidates' thinking or to embellish their learning experience.

I. Developing and demonstrating a cultural sensitivity to teaching Asian-American and Latino students.

The following learning activities, exercises, and assignments are intended to facilitate the acquisition of objectives 1 through 3.

Learning Activities, Exercises, and Assignments

- Exploring educational histories and examining attitudes, myths, and beliefs (activities suggested for the first five weeks of a semester).

In Class

A. Think of your most memorable educational incident or experience and the ways in which your ethnicity, class, culture, and gender have shaped your schooling and academic achievement, success or failure. (Open discussion is led by the instructor.)

Instructor's Note: See Francis-Okongwu & Pflaum, 1993, pp. 125-128 for a further explanation of this exercise and related research.

B. Identify someone in this class that has come from a different cultural background than yours and interview that person. Formulate at least 5 questions to ask that person. Identify any differences or similarities with regard to how the individual perceives the world, past experiences and future challenges, perception of opportunities for a successful future, including perceived opportunities for academic success and a successful career.

Instructor's Note: Students are requested to keep a list of the educational practices or factors that contribute to or detract from their academic success.

Assignment at Home

A. On a one-page sheet, indicate in outline form your responses to the following questions:
   1. What are your past experiences of working with Asian American students, e.g., Chinese, Japanese, Korean, Vietnamese, and Latino students, e.g., Cuban, Mexican, Puerto Rican, El Salvadoran?
   2. What are your present beliefs and ideas about Asian Americans and Latinos living in the United States today who have come from various parts of the world such as China, Korea, Japan, Mexico, Central America, South America, Cuba, and Puerto Rico?
   3. What do you think it would be like to teach Asian American and Latino children?

B. Write a three-page paper on your concept of teaching a diverse student population.

Instructor's Note: The responses to the questions and the "teaching concept" paper are sources of data for research studies to establish baseline information for each teacher candidate and groups of candidates in the program. Toward the end of the module, teacher candidates are asked to repeat the assignment along with answering a questionnaire to identify any change in their attitudes, beliefs, and/or previously held notions about Asian American and Latino children and teaching diverse populations of student in general.

C. Read the two-page article entitled "To The Second and Third Generations of Koreans," by Bernadyn Kim Suh (1976). Write a paragraph or two describing your own family background.

In the Field

A. Observe and diagram the physical setting of the class and the seating arrangement of students in class.

B. Chart the interactive behaviors of an Asian American or Latino child during one class period (sociogram techniques will be explained by your course instructor). Shadow the child for a morning or afternoon. Write a brief summary of relevant events and your impressions of the experience.

C. Interview the teacher regarding his or her impressions, beliefs, and perceptions of teaching Asian American and Latino children.

D. Have the teacher of the class to which you are assigned select an Asian American or Latino student for you to tutor. Introduce yourself to the child and get to know one another. Have the child talk about subjects that are of personal interest, for example, what the child enjoys, dislikes, or finds difficult in school; what challenges the child faces in and outside of school, etc. The instructor of the course and your peers will assist you in formulating additional questions.

Assignment At Home (Assigned the first week of class and due at the end of the first month of the course experience.)

Select two of the following books (one from the Asian American Experience listing and one from the Latino Experience). The books depict contemporary experiences of either Asian Americans or Latinos (fiction and nonfiction).

A. Identify any myths or erroneous beliefs you might have had about Asian or Latino people and their cultures. Cite a few examples mentioned in the book.
B. In a paragraph, portray the main character's challenges and struggles. Summarize the main storyline in two to three paragraphs. What does it mean for the protagonist to fit in to the society?

The Asian American Experience

Typical American (Jen, G., 1991, Boston: Houghton Mifflin).
Mona in the Promised Land (Jen, G., 1996, New York: Alfred A. Knopf).
Eating Chinese Food Naked (Mei Ng, 1998, New York: Scribner).
Native Speaker (Lee, C., 1996, New York: Riverhead Books).
The Fruit'n Food (Chang, L., 1996, Seattle, Washington: Black Heron Press).
Asian: The Accidental Notes of a Native Speaker (Liu, E., 1998, New York: Random House).
Why She Left Us (Rizzuto, R., 1999, New York: Harper Collins).
A Gesture Life (Lee, C., 1999, New York: Riverhead Books).
The Joy Luck Club (Tan, A., 1994, Paperback, Mass Market, Ivy Books).

The Latino Experience

Dreaming in Cuban (Garcia, C., 1992, New York: Knopf)
How the Garcia Girls Lost Their Accents (Alvarez, J., 1991, Chapel Hill, NC: Algonquin Books).
Bronx Primitive: Portraits In A Childhood (Simon, K., 1982, New York: Viking Press)

Additional Works

New Strangers in Paradise (Muller, G., 1999, Lexington: University Press of Kentucky)—analyses of the new immigrant writers who tell of an immigrant's experience in contemporary America.
The NuyorAsian Anthology—Asian American authors writing about life in New York City (Edited by Realuyo, Henry, & Rizzuto,1999).

Social Studies and History

Optional Assignment: Compare and contrast what life was like for an Asian or Latino immigrant living in the United States during the 1920s with an Asian or Latino immigrant living in the United States today. Explain the differences and similarities. What prejudices and discriminatory acts did the individual confront? Portray American society during each period and explain how Asian Americans and Latinos view their lives in America today. (Your course instructor will direct you to specific resources to complete this assignment.)

Outside of Class

A. Interview a successful Asian American or Latino entrepreneur, business person, chief executive officer, president of a college, educator in a school or college, or museum director or educator in your region. Formulate a series of questions regarding this person's perceptions of past experiences in school and in college; life challenges and struggles; and the events, experiences, or persons that contributed significantly to his or her success in life. Ask the individual to identify the prejudices she or he may have personally encountered from others, in or outside of the school setting. Have the person identify one way a teacher or school system might prevent problems faced by Asian American and Latino children.

B. Visit a school (elementary, middle, or high school) that has a high percentage of Asian American and/or Latino student populations. (For example, in New York City in Chinatown, the Cascades High School for Teaching and Learning has 192 students half of whom are Asian [Chinese, Korean, or Burmese]; 25% are Latino; 20% are African American; and 5% are European American or American Indian.) Formulate questions with your classmates and the instructor of your social studies course to ask (1) students, (2) teachers, (3) administrators, and (4) parents of the school. Schedule a visit and record the responses from your interview and your reactions to the experiences. (The assignment is to be completed by the end of the first 4 weeks of class.)

In Class (The second or third week of class)

A. View the video Shadow of Hate (Guggenheim, 1995) and respond to the following two questions during a class discussion led by the instructor.
   1. What is your general reaction to the events seen in this video? How do you feel about what you saw, and what do you think?
   2. Based on the events seen in this video, how has prejudice affected the United States, and what can you do as a citizen to eliminate prejudice?

Instructor's Note: In the video Shadow of Hate (Guggenheim, 1995), all groups who came to America, starting from the early colonial period to the present, are shown coping with racism and discrimination. Specially, the video portrays how groups of Chinese people, who had built railroads through the Sierra Mountains, were then herded into ghettos and killed. The video also shows scenes of Japanese Americans who were placed in concentration camps during World War II, lost their homes and property, and, in many cases, were separated from family members. Teacher candidates usually have an intense reaction to the video and are interested in knowing more. I refer them to Yoshiko Uchida's books: Journey to Topaz, Journey Home, and The Invisible Thread and request that they read at least one. The Invisible Thread describes Uchida's childhood as a Nisei (second generation). The books describe the tragic herding of innocent Japanese people into desert concentration camps. They are excellent choices to accompany the video seen in class.

II. Developing and demonstrating initial pedagogical and intercultural competencies that are needed to become an effective teacher of a diverse student population in the areas of Social Studies And Language Arts

Learning Activities, Exercises, and Assignments

Assignment at Home

A. Identify and summarize a recent newspaper/magazine article dealing with racial problems in an urban or suburban setting.
B. Describe three ways you might alleviate racist and discriminatory acts against Asian American and Latino children in the classroom.
C. Develop a short 20-30 minute lesson plan promoting multiculturalism for a group of children in the classroom to which you are assigned in your field setting. Formulate in the lesson three ways in which racism and discrimination can be eliminated and explain how you would explore this with students.

1. Read in the journal Educational Leadership (Association for Supervision and Curriculum Development, April, 1999) 3 of the 6 articles identified below—one of the three must be "Bridging Cultures with Classroom Strategies":
   - "A Different Mirror: A Conversation with Ronald Takaki" by Joan Montgomery Halford.
   - "Reducing The Effect of Racism in Schools" by Sandra Parks.
   - "Deepening the Meaning of Heritage Months" by Deborah J. Menkart.
   - "The Changing Face of Bilingual Education" by Russell Gersten.
   - "Bridging Cultures with Classroom Strategies" by Carrie Rothstein-Fisch, Patricia M. Greenfield, and Elise Trumbull.
   - "Respect in the Classroom: Reflections of a Mexican-American Educator" by Eva Midobuche.

For each of the three articles you have selected to read, write three ideas, facts, concepts, etc. you have learned either about the ethnic group(s) identified in the article, the topic highlighted, or the instructional strategies suggested by the authors. In addition, explain in a paragraph or two, the use of the Collectivism vs. Individualism framework as a tool for understanding cultural differences (see Rothstein-Fisch, Greenfield, & Trumbull, 1999).

Instructional Technology

A. Go to the following web sites and explore the information and links at the site and/or respond in writing to the question(s) asked.
   - Asian American Culture—articles and links on Asian American film, music, and literature and issues such as politics and racial discrimination. [http://asianamculture.about.com]
   - The Lifestyles & Cultures of Asians Today—Asian-Life is an ezine devoted to promote the lifestyles and cultures of Asians today. [http://www.asian-life.com]
   - Latinos (Encyclopedia. com)—Links, sites and books. [http://www.encyclopedia.com/ articles/05926.html] At this site (1) answer the question: What are the 3 largest Spanish-speaking groups in America today, and where do they live? (2) Go to related books at this site and identify one children's book, e.g., Meet Josephina (1997) by Valarie Tripp and Susan McAliley (Pleasant Co. Publishers), and record what the book is about from the description given. Identify and describe one software package for youngsters. (Keep a running list of children's books and software focused on Asian-American and Latino literature).

Literacy Acquisition and Language Art

A. Aspectos Culturales—Children's books, songs, games, Latino culture, and language.
   [http://www.aspectosculturales.com] (1) Click on Overview and read the information; then click on Teacher Resources and select two resources you would use in your classroom (Books and Videos) and with the child you tutor. (2) Click on Examples and view samples of 4 reading levels from Amigos (monthly periodical in English and Spanish); select the reading level that would be appropriate for the child you are tutoring or the class you are teaching. Assess the child's/children's level of skill, and design an appropriate developmental lesson incorporating the material found at the website.

Children's Asian-American and Hispanic Literature

Instructor's Note: In Literature and the Child (1998), the authors clearly identify the importance of children's literature in the development of the child. They outline the social nature of learning, the need for interaction, and the ways in which literature can play an important role in development. Literature can help children understand life. Children's literature is arranged in ten categories or genres: (1) picture and early books, (2) poetry, (3) folklore, (4) fantasy, (5) science fiction, (6) realistic fiction, (7) historical fiction, (8) biography, (9) non-fiction, and (10) culturally diverse literature.

Starting in the primary grades, children can learn about the contributions of all the different groups that make up the population of the United States and thereby may learn intercultural competence and appreciation. Reading about the lives of people who have made contributions from their respective ethnic backgrounds is essential. Readers shape their view of the world and of themselves partly through the books they read. If children never see themselves in books, then this absence subtly tells them that they are not important enough to appear in books. In addition, stereotyped images of an ethnic group are harmful not only to the children of that group but to others who may get a distorted view. European American children are often given a distorted image of U.S. society. They are not prepared to value the United States' multi-ethnic and cultural character because they are surrounded by literature and other instructional materials that either present groups stereotypically or make ethnic minorities invisible by omitting them entirely.

"Bookalogues: Multicultural Literature" included in the 1993 issue of the Language Arts Journal (Harris, Yokota, Johnson, & de Cortez, 1993), cites specific guidelines in selecting Hispanic literature for children.

- Choose works that best provide readers with an in-depth view of a culture, one that goes beyond the superficiality of the tourist mindset.
- Select books that include Latino children as protagonists. Other children need to see children from cultures other than their own as protagonist.
- Select a variety of books in order to offer readers a view of Latino cultures in all of their diversity.
- Select books in which children learn about the major changes in our society's transformation from a rural to industrial to a post industrial society and the impact of those change on Latinos (pp. 221-222).

It should be mentioned that although Latinos (Puerto Rican, Cuban, Mexican, etc.) share a common language, they are not all culturally the same. They are all very different and have their own cultural practices. This module has identified Latinos as Spanish-speaking individuals. I suggest that the facilitator-instructor of the module select one specific ethnic group on which to focus.

In Class

The instructor will give a focused presentation on child development and children's literature, integrating the areas of English Language Arts and Social Studies.

<u>Assignment At Home and In the Field</u>

A. Go to Kay Vandergrift's web site on Children's Literature. [http://www.scils.rutgers.edu/special/kay/childlit.html] (1) Read the introduction and explore the site; for example, click on "care about children and their literature." (2) Go back to the first page and read the section "Illustrated Materials for Young Children." In the section entitled "How do we evaluate illustrations as a means of portraying positive multicultural images of childhood," click on Asian American and Hispanic American children's literature and read the information. (3) Compile your own list of books from those identified by Dr. Vandergrift, and select one you will use with the child you tutor and/or with the class you teach. Prepare a written lesson plan. Make sure you design an appropriate objective for the child's level of ability and developmental stage and a method by which you can assess the achievement of the objective. Identify the national or state standard the lesson supports or to which it contributes.

B. Implement the lesson with the child you tutor and/or the class you teach. After the lesson record your reflections and analyses in your journal.

ASSESSING THE MODULE EXPERIENCE THROUGH RESEARCH

Researching and assessing the impact and effects of the module experience on teacher candidates are important aspects of the module's development and usefulness. As mentioned previously, it is important to know if we have been successful in achieving the objectives of the module. The information that we obtain through research studies will not only be used to change and improve the experiences included in the module but also contribute to the body of knowledge focused on teacher education. It is recognized quite clearly by the education community that becoming an effective teacher of a culturally and ethnically diverse population of students is an ongoing, collaborative process, and that it must be continued throughout one's professional education. As a faculty at Dowling College, we recognize that assessment of the module must be built in to its original design. The written materials produced by the teacher candidates, for example, the "teaching concept paper," as well as questionnaires that target specific competencies of the module, are the sources of data for action research studies. The questions below are general and are offered as a means of beginning the research process:

1. How has the module experience impacted or affected the teacher candidates' attitudes toward and beliefs about Asian Americans and Latinos and their cultures, and their perceptions regarding teaching Asian-American and Latino children as well as diverse population of students?
2. In what ways have teacher candidates altered or changed a preconceived notion, attitude, or belief they had prior to the module in regard to Asian American or Latino people?
3. In what ways do the learning activities and exercises included in the module enable teacher candidates to develop and demonstrate the desired competencies?
4. Which learning activities are rated by teacher candidates as being more meaningful in helping them develop the competencies? Which do they feel are less meaningful or helpful?
5. Which learning activities are most helpful and meaningful to teacher candidates who have lived most of their lives in communities lacking in diversity?
6. Are there learning activities or exercises that are more meaningful to male teacher candidates than to female teacher candidates, those who self-identify as European American, and those candidates who self-identify as an ethnic minority?

Although this is not an exhaustive list of possible questions, it can serve as a springboard toward deeper levels of assessment of the module experience.

All children deserve effective and equitable instruction in U.S. public schools. As the United States becomes increasingly more diverse, teachers must be able to see children through the children's own cultural lenses; create instruction that is inclusive, meaning-laden, and multicultural; teach in an inclusive fashion; and affirm the value and worth of all children who enter their classroom doors. In order for this level of intercultural competence to be achieved, teacher candidates must be afforded the opportunity to examine their own beliefs, biases, and stereotypes in a safe environment where they are provided with ample time for reflection. They also need to examine U.S. society and the ways in which the societal structure in this country creates opportunity for some at the expense of others. Finally, they need to enter their classrooms armed with knowledge of themselves and of the inequities inherent in the society, the diverse cultures of their students, the ways in which culture can impinge upon learning, and the ways to maximize the academic success of every student. It is only through this kind of knowledge and awareness—personal, societal, and pedagogical—that teaching and learning in public school classrooms will truly be transformed.

APPENDIX A
ADDITIONAL RESOURCES

The following are offered as additional resources for the course/field module.

Children's Literature:

Latino Children's Literature

Favorites of mine are books written by Gary Soto: *Baseball in April and Other Stories* (2000, Harcourt Brace); *Jesse* (1994, Harcourt Brace); *Taking Sides* (1992, Harcourt Brace); and *Pacific Crossing* (1992, Harcourt Brace). Two of his poetry works I recommend are *Neighborhood Odes* (1994, Mass Market Paperback) and *A Fire In My Hands* (1999, EconoClad Books).

Two books written and illustrated by Tomie de Paola—*The Lady of Guadalupe* and *The Legend of the Poinsettia*—reflect Latino culture, as does one by Arthur Durros entitled *The Abuela* (1997, New York: Penguin).

Asian-American Children's Literature

The book *Momotaro* (Illustrator, Suyeoka, G., 1972, Australia: Island Heritage Limited) was created for the children of Hawaii. Two others that I would recommend are *The Korean Cinderella* by Shirley Climo and illustrated by Ruth Heller (1993, Mexico: Harper Collins Publishers) and *The Big Wave* by Pearl S. Buck, a true classic (1947, New York: The John Day Co.).

Multiculturalism

From the Video Workshop, I recommend a 20-minute video entitled *Diversity in the Elementary Classroom: Implications For Teaching* (1995). The Video Workshop is published by the National Association of Elementary School Principals. The video contain excellent practical suggestions for teachers.

A favorite children's book of mine that I suggest to teacher candidates is *Old Turtle*, which won the Abby Book of the Year Award for its wonderful story of humankind learning to live together in harmony. Other children's books dealing with multiculturalism are Sheila Hamanaka's *All the Colors on the Earth* and *On the Wings of Peace*, and one by Veronica Lawlor entitled *I Was Dreaming to Come to America: Memories from the Ellis Island Oral History Project* (1995).

REFERENCES

Alvarez, J. (1991). *How the Garcia girls lost their accents.* Chapel Hill, NC: Algonquin Books of Chapel Hill.

Association for Supervision and Curriculum Development. (1999, April). Understanding race, class, and culture. *Educational Leadership, 56*(7).

Bondy, E., Schmitz, S., & Johnson, M. (1993). The impact of course work and fieldwork on student teachers' reported beliefs about teaching poor and minority students. *Action in Teacher Education, 15*(2), 37-52.

Cabello, B., & Burstein, N.D. (1995). Examining teachers' beliefs about teaching in culturally different classrooms. *Journal of Teacher Education, 46*(4), 285-294.

Chang, L.W. (1996). *The fruit'n food.* Seattle, WA: Black Heron Press.

Francis-Okongwu, A., & Pflaum, S. (1993). Diversity in education: Implications for teacher preparation. In F. Pignatelli & S. Pflaum (Eds.), *Celebrating diverse voices* (pp. 112-132). Newbury Park, CA: Corwin Press.

Galda, L., & Cullinan, B. (1998). *Cullinan and Galda's literature and the child* (4th ed.). Philadelphia: Temple University.

Garcia, C. (1992). *Dreaming in Cuban.* New York: Knopf.

Grant, C., & Secada, W. G. (1990). Preparing teachers for diversity. In W. R. Houston, M. Haberman, & J. Sikula (Eds.), *Handbook of research on teacher education* (pp. 403-422). New York: Macmillan.

Guggenheim, C. (1995). *The shadow of hate: A history of intolerance in America* [Video, VHS 40 minutes]. Montgomery, AL: Teaching Tolerance.

Harris, V., Yokota, J., Johnson, G., & de Cortez, O.G. (1993). Bookalogues: Multicultural literature. *Language Arts, 70*(3), 215.

Jen, G. (1991). *Typical American.* Boston: Houghton Mifflin.

Jen, G. (1996). *Mona in the promised land.* New York: Knopf.

Larmer, B. (1999, July 12). Latino America. *Newsweek*, pp. 48-51.

Lee, C. (1999). *A gesture life.* New York: Riverhead Books.

Lee, C. (1996). *Native speaker.* New York: Riverhead Books.

Loeb, P., Friedman, D., & Lord, M.C. (1993, October 4). To make a nation: How immigrants are changing America for better or worse. *U.S. News and World Report,* pp. 47-54.

Liu, E. (1998). *Asian: The accidental notes of a native speaker.* New York: Random House.

Mei, N. (1998). *Eating Chinese food naked.* New York: Scribner.

Muller, G. (1999). *New strangers in paradise: The immigrant experience and contemporary American fiction.* Lexington: University Press of Kentucky.

Pajares, F. (1993). Preservice teachers' beliefs: A focus for teacher education. *Action in Teacher Education, 15*(2), 45-54.

Pignatelli, F., & Pflaum, S. (1993). *Celebrating diverse voices: Progressive education and equity*. Newbury Park, CA: Corwin Press.

Realuyo, B.A., Henry, K., & Rizzuto, R. (Eds.). (1999). *The Nuyorasian anthology: Asian American writing on New York City*. New York: Asian American Writers Workshop.

Rizzuto, R.R. (1999). *Why she left us*. New York: Harper Collins.

Rothstein-Fisch, Greenfield, P., & Trumbull, E. (1999, April). Bridging cultures with classroom strategies. *Educational Leadership, 56*(7), 64-67.

Simon, K. (1982). *Bronx primitive: Portraits in a childhood*. New York: Viking Press.

Suh Kim, B. (1976). To the second and third generations of Koreans. *Korean News*, pp. 30-31.

Tan, A. (1994). *The joy luck club*. New York: Ivy Books.

Tripp, V., & McAliley, S. (1997). *Meet Josephina*. Middleton, WI: Pleasant Co.

Seven

Teaching Youngsters Science in a Culturally Diverse Urban Classroom

Stephen Farenga
Beverly Joyce

Since 1954, the American classroom has become increasingly diversified due to desegregation actions, immigration patterns, and higher birth rates of some ethnic groups. National statistics indicate that, as we enter the 21st century, African Americans, Asian Americans, Hispanics, and Native Americans will compose 33% of the K-12 enrollment (National Center for Education Statistics [NCES], 1997; Rittenhouse, 1998). Currently, in some of the larger school districts, these culturally diverse groups are a minority majority. This ethnic diversity is accompanied by language diversity and disproportionate levels of poverty. The profile of the urban classroom is markedly different from that of some affluent suburbs. In contrast, today's preservice teachers are predominantly European American and female—not unlike their predecessors—and most expect to teach in a European American, middle-class school. However, this is not the reality of the 21st century classroom. Without appropriate education and experience, these teachers may undergo culture shock upon entering an urban classroom and become part of the two-thirds of new teachers who leave the classroom after four years (Huling-Austin, 1986).

At suburban colleges, such as Dowling College, teacher education for the urban classroom presents challenges and opportunities to both the faculty and preservice teachers. To be successful in the culturally diverse urban classroom, teachers must be given the opportunity to develop a strong pedagogical content knowledge base and foster heightened sensitivity to pupils' prior knowledge and skills. The process of developing new teaching skills and knowledge bases, and the pleasure of experiencing new cultures, languages, and customs in the appropriate field settings provide unique opportunities to new teachers. Thus, changes in teacher education based on the National Standards and reform movement in science are necessary to prepare the suburban teacher to meet the challenges and embrace the opportunities to teach elementary science in urban classrooms.

The chapter focuses on the changes in (1) curriculum, (2) delivery of instruction, and (3) pupil outcomes and assessment as they relate to the study and teaching of elementary science in an urban model. The chapter is organized around the above themes. The first section is devoted to the specific changes in curriculum that have come about as a result of the new national and state learning standards in science education. Included in the section are subsections entitled *standards in action*, which portray a standards-based or student-centered classroom. Here we are attempting to provide preservice teachers with an illustration of how the new standards might operate in an elementary science classroom. Also included in the first section are profiles of the preservice teachers we teach as well as a profile of the pupils they will teach in urban settings.

The second section focuses on the instructional strategies that are relevant to teaching the learning standards in science education. A newer instructional strategy entitled *adaptive inquiry*, which integrates elements from direct instruction and open-ended inquiry, is presented. As a teaching model, *adaptive inquiry* is a student-oriented instructional system that is based on an authentic assessment of the youngster's needs. In this section, we also offer applications of the concepts and ideas we have identified as well as promote to the reader a conservative constructivist approach to teaching science.

In the third section on assessment, we explain an approach to assessing pupil outcomes in the context of a constructivist learning environment. Simply put, the purpose of assessment is to accurately evaluate the pupil's ability to do science. Performance assessment tools are identified and briefly explained.

Finally, we make general recommendations to preservice students that address their desire to be effective teachers of elementary science in urban school settings, and we offer specific exercises for teachers to enhance their development as teachers of science. Additional resources, web-site addresses, and on-line teacher links are listed at the end of the chapter.

CHANGES IN SCHOOL CURRICULUM AND PUPIL LEARNING OUTCOMES

Principles underlying the National and State Science Education Standards address the need to raise the level of science learning and instruction. The thrust of the Standards is to foster critical thinking and promote scientific literacy. (The National Science Standards are available at http://www.nap.edu/readingroom/books/intronses. The New York Learning Standards are available at *http://www.cnyric.org/cnyric/standards/standards.html.*) The integration of three distinct subject domains—science, mathematics, and technology—is strongly advocated by educators, scientists, and various community members. According to the National Research Council (1996), a pupil who is a critical thinker and is science literate is able to ask for clarification, make decisions based on empirical evidence, and determine answers to questions stimulated by curiosity.

> *Standards in action.* In Mrs. Norbert's fifth grade classroom, pupils were asked to determine which brand of paper towel was most absorbent. In collaborative groups, they posed a science research question, "Which of three brands of paper towel absorbs the greatest amount of water?" Then, with their classmates, they identified the manipulated variable (i.e., brand of paper towel) and the outcome variable (i.e., amount of water absorbed). Through this process, the groups were able to identify assumptions and influences surrounding the problems. Based on these variables they were able to design a controlled experiment to test their hypothesis. The pupils realized that experimental controls are like rules in a game, keeping conditions fair. Upon completion of their experiment, the collaborative group members compared, analyzed, and discussed their solutions. As critical problem solvers, pupils recommended necessary adaptations to produce a more absorbent paper towel with respect to unit cost. This allowed them to reflect on both topic and process.

The new emphasis in science education is to bring systemic reform to grades K-12. This effort is widespread, occurring at national, state, and community levels. The goal is to heighten scientific literacy while increasing science achievement. The reform movement in science identifies standards for science curriculum, delivery of instruction, professional development, and methods of assessment. It has been suggested that the science curriculum should cover fewer topics in depth to achieve greater understanding of the subject. Pedagogy should stress constructivist teaching strategies that promote inquiry and recognize that inquiry is the energetic force to advance scientific knowledge. Compulsory participation in staff development activities that are continuous, constructivist in nature, collaborative, and supported by research will become the norm in the next decade. Finally, effective assessment techniques need to be aligned with the goals of the science program.

Standards in action. Ms. Thomas has planned several days of activities to provide her pupils experience with concepts of constructing simple circuits. She first questioned her pupils to determine what they already knew about circuits. After the discussion, they were given materials (i.e., wire, bulbs, and dry cell). Working in collaborative pairs, the pupils were challenged to design a solution to the problem of lighting the bulbs using only the supplied materials. Ms. Thomas observed the pupils working toward a solution and asked them about how they were constructing the circuits. She was aware that, at this stage, the ability to work together and communicate their ideas was critical. Through observation and facilitation, Ms. Thomas realized that many of her students were at the concrete stage, requiring the testing of each solution to determine if they were successful. At this point, she used a developmental checklist to determine whether her pupils were using process skills (e.g., predicting, testing, communicating) to arrive at a solution.

During a follow-up lesson, Ms. Thomas had her students diagram how the bulb would light. They needed to develop symbols to communicate their results and convert the symbols into words to develop a set of written instructions. As the pupils began to write instructions, the need for precise terminology became evident. They realized the importance of appropriate terminology to communicate effectively (e.g., contact points, collar of the bulb). Throughout these activities, assessment of pupils' understanding matched the progression of the lesson.

The National Standards require multiple means of formative assessment rather than a single summative evaluation. The youngsters in Ms. Thomas's class were actively engaged in continuous assessment of their work and that of their peers at each stage of the activity. Ms. Thomas focused on the youngsters' process skills (e.g., prediction, inquiry, communication) and the structure of their content knowledge (e.g., developing a simple circuit). Based on her knowledge of the National Standards, Ms. Thomas put less emphasis on assessing lower level skills and content knowledge that is easily measured.

Science performance and content standards have been proposed to assist teachers in determining levels of student competence. The combination of these proposed changes are intended to affect systemic reform in grades K-12 (see Table 7.1). Changes in today's science classroom and student learning are driven by the National and State Science Education Standards, as well as the reform movement in science, and require new approaches in teaching science in the classroom. New emphases require teachers to understand and respond to individual student interests, strengths, experiences, and needs.

PUPIL PROFILE

Preparing our preservice teachers for their inner-city classrooms includes discussing the diversity of the student population. The

Table 7.1. National Science Education Standards

National Science Education Standards Encompass the Following Emphases:

Less Emphasis On	More Emphasis On
• Treating all students alike and responding to the group as a whole • Rigidly following curriculum • Focusing on student acquisition of information • Presenting scientific knowledge through lecture, text, and demonstration • Asking for recitation of acquired knowledge • Testing students for factual information at the end of the unit or chapter • Maintaining responsibility and authority • Supporting competition	• Understanding and responding to individual student's interests, strengths, experiences, and needs • Focusing on student understanding and use of scientific knowledge, ideas, and inquiry processes • Guiding students in active and extended scientific inquiry • Providing opportunities for scientific discussion and debate among students • Continuously assessing student understanding • Sharing responsibility for learning with students • Supporting a classroom • Community with cooperation • Shared responsibility and respect • Working with other teachers to enhance the science program

youngsters in an urban classroom reflect their neighborhood population in terms of ethnicity, family structure, home environment, language, extracurricular experiences, and academic achievement. This diverse composition creates new challenges and opportunities for classroom teachers.

We remind our preservice teachers that ethnic background, family characteristics, and home environment are often predictors of later academic participation, progress, and achievement. As inner-city public school teachers, they will find that approximately 32% of their pupils are African American and nearly 25% are Latino (NCES, 1997). African American and Latino children are more likely than European American children to live in poverty, live in single-parent families, and live in urban areas. In addition, Latino youngsters who speak Spanish at home and outside of school may have difficulties in speaking and reading English. These characteristics have been identified as risk factors for future academic difficulties (Sable, 1998; Sable & Stennett, 1998).

In our classes, we discuss the factors, such as preprimary education, that are significant predictors of later academic success. Early childhood educational experiences of ethnic minority children differ significantly from those of European American children (Sable, 1998; Sable & Stennett, 1998). Whereas African American and European American children participate in preprimary education at similar rates, African Americans lag behind European Americans in mastering early literacy skills, such as identifying primary colors, reading stories, and writing their own names. Latino children are less likely than European Americans to be enrolled in preprimary education, and their literacy skills are lacking. Heightening our preservice teachers' awareness of these differences in early educational experiences assists them in responding to the needs of their pupils.

Opportunities for preprimary educational experiences should be fostered in the home where family members are active participants in their children's education. Once again, European American children have the advantage over African Americans and Latinos (Sable, 1998; Sable & Stennett, 1998). At ages 3 to 5, European American children (89%) are more likely to have been read to three or more times in the past week than their African American (76%) or Latino (65%) peers. European American pupils (43%) are also more likely than their African American (34%) or Latino (26%) classmates to have visited a library in the past month. Without a strong combination of these primary literacy experiences, African American and Latino youngsters run the risk of developing inquiry skills deficits. Youngsters with strong primary literacy experiences are taught to recognize similarities and differences, form patterns, and identify regularities. These inquiry-related behaviors play an important role in building literacy skills. For example, a youngster with strong primary literacy experiences can look at two word lists (e.g., HOP, RAT, BIT, CAP and HOPE, RATE, BITE, CAPE), recognize the pattern of regularity, and conclude that the "E" makes the vowel long. This represents an important connection between the skills in science (i.e., pattern recognition) and emerging literacy through inductive reasoning.

As we have seen in our research, educational opportunities for youngsters are often found in a variety of activities after school and during school vacations. Ethnicity and socioeconomic background play key roles in student participation in extracurricular activities. Pupils from lower socioeconomic backgrounds seem to reap the greatest benefits from participation in after-school and summer activities (Frailer & Morris, 1998; NCES, 1996; Siege, 1989). However, because inner-city schools offer far fewer opportunities, their pupils have limited access. Thus, the after-school hours of lower income, ethnic minority youngsters are often unstructured (Rittenhouse, 1998). During summer vacation, European American pupils (45%) and pupils from high-income families (57%) are far more likely to participate in organized summer activities than are their African American (25%) and Latino (19%) peers or classmates from lower-income families (12%). Research indicates that extracurricular activities must be in line with classroom curriculum to effectively support the academic goals of the school (Majoribanks, 1991; Midwinter, 1995).

As science educators, our preservice teachers know that science proficiency is an important outcome of schooling in the 21st century. They subscribe to the belief that critical thinkers are pupils who can apply scientific information, interpret data, and make inferences. However, they must be prepared to work with youngsters with varying levels of science proficiency. As reflected in national fourth grade science achievement scores, the science proficiency gap significantly favors European American pupils (average score = 239) over their African American (202) and Latino (207) classmates (Sable, 1998; Sable & Stennett, 1998). As society increasingly demands a technologically advanced work force, those pupils who are science literate will enjoy a distinct advantage. Therefore, our preservice teachers must be prepared to meet the challenges of the inner-city classroom and take advantage of the opportunities presented by a diverse student body. Youngsters' science literacy can be fostered by encouraging them to identify science problems in their own environment (e.g., building model bridges, using subway schedules to determine train speed, identifying and classifying vegetation native to city parks), develop their own plan of study, recognize the integration of subject matter (e.g., mathematics/science, communication skills/science), and interpret the outcome.

PRESERVICE TEACHER PROFILE

The majority of Dowling College preservice teachers reflect the national profile of public school teachers—predominantly European American (91%) and female (74%) (NCES, 1997). Their family backgrounds and life experiences are likely to be quite different from that of their inner-city pupils. In our classroom conversations, the teachers admitted that they had limited knowledge about the history and culture of inner-city pupils. To ameliorate this deficit, we developed a science education research program that provided preservice teachers opportunities to read, research, and reflect on these topics to better prepare them for their inner-city classrooms. Furthermore, they expressed concern that their lack of familiarity with these youngsters' backgrounds would inhibit their ability to be successful in the urban classroom. We know that few teachers are aware of the many scientific contributions made by African American, Latino, and other ethnic minorities, and this information is not readily available in most teacher training programs (Atwater, 1994).

As preservice teachers develop techniques to involve, interest, and include their inner-city pupils in science, they are encouraged to consider the following approaches:

1. The teaching of science should be infused with youngsters' culture and language. Preservice teachers are encouraged to examine how different cultures approach and solve problems that all people encounter.
2. The community should be encouraged to work collaboratively with the school and science classroom. Schools should establish partnerships with community resources such as museums, zoological parks, and industries, thus fostering reality-based learning.
3. The scientific pedagogy should be oriented toward reciprocal interaction. In reciprocal teaching, the teacher initially takes on the role of coach enabling pupils to develop questions. Feedback from the teacher is given through summaries of pupils' questions, comments, and work product.
4. The goal of science assessment should be one of advocacy, not legitimacy of failure. Working from a model of strength rather than a deficit model, teachers can identify what youngsters can do. Based on results of formative assessment, instruction can be modified to fit the needs of the pupils (Cummins, 1986).

Through these approaches, it becomes apparent that the teachers' role is not to empower their pupils. Rather, they are creating an environment in which pupils are able to empower themselves.

DELIVERY OF INSTRUCTION

Hands-on science means just that: pupils require concrete objects to manipulate as they develop concepts and understandings through direct observation. Scientists formulate hypotheses and then place these ideas under rigorous experimentation, demonstration, observation, and possible revision. Youngsters, like scientists, need to experience science. Abstract concepts need to be made concrete through the use of manipulatives. The pupils need to practice inquiry-based science strategies. The development of these strategies may appear difficult at first due to a lack of prior knowledge making pure inquiry-based teaching ineffective. The teacher's pedagogical repertoire requires a blended fluency of direct instruction and inquiry learning strategies.

Science instruction can be thought of as a continuum ranging from teacher-centered direct instruction to pupil-centered open-ended inquiry (see Figure 7.1). Direct instruction entails delivery of content in small amounts (knowledge level instruction) and testing. It is designed to build a knowledge base and is reported to be highly effective. Open-ended inquiry encourages pupils to use their prior knowledge to structure future investigations.

Direct instruction and inquiry-based teaching are two classroom practices supported by empirical data. The essence of direct instruction is to help the student acquire the basic cognitive and communication process-skills. Principles culled from direct instruction methods are useful in satisfying the youngsters' knowledge gaps that may hinder inquiry-based science instruction. In this situation, the locus of control is external and rests with the teacher. The teacher's function is to monitor

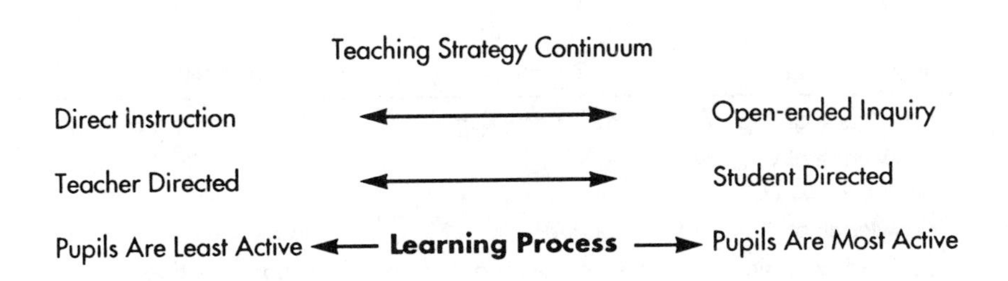

Figure 7.1. Adaptive Inquiry

and direct youngsters' classroom concentration and persistence, rather than to encourage independence. It has been demonstrated that on-task classroom behavior and positive reinforcement are essential to modifying and improving pupil behavior (Becker & Gersten, 1982; Meyer, Gersten, & Gutkin, 1984). Direct instruction necessitates that the curriculum be carefully sequenced and rigidly controlled throughout the instructional process.

The format of the inquiry process is less structured, requiring increased locus of control to be situated with the pupil. The process of inquiry requires pupils to start with a question, design an investigation, develop a hypothesis, collect data, use data to answer the original question, determine whether the original question requires modification, and communicate results. The true inquiry process is open-ended, generally leading to additional questions. The process seems linear; however, the skills necessary to proceed through the investigation have varying levels of difficulty. Based on years of science teaching, it is evident that all pupils are not at the same starting point in terms of prior knowledge, abilities, and interests. To maximize the benefit of inquiry, the teacher tailors the activity to accommodate the pupils' experiential profiles. This tailoring process produces a new strain of inquiry that integrates techniques from direct instruction and open-ended inquiry that is called *adaptive inquiry* (see Figure 7.2).

Direct instruction and open-ended inquiry are purported to be effective strategies for teaching science. However, when used exclusively, each strategy leaves gaps in the delivery of instruction. Teachers need to assess prior knowledge and the design of the delivery of instruction to match the cognitive level of the pupil. As instruction is delivered, the teacher must assess pupil responses and move the pupil from concrete understandings to more abstract conceptual development. Parallel processing of information is obtained from the delivery of instruction, pupils' outcomes, and prior knowledge. This continuous feedback and interpretation of information is the basis of adaptive inquiry. Adaptive

Suburban Teacher	Urban Pupil	Pupil Outcomes
Knowledge of Pupils/ Knowledge of Content and Pedagogy	Prior Knowledge	Driven by Standards
Knowledge of Standards	Language	Performance Assessment
Self Understanding	Ethnic Background /Culture	Traditional Testing

Figure 7.2. Integrated Components of Adaptive Inquiry

inquiry requires the teacher to conceptualize and respond to pupil outcomes, background, and the teacher's own input factors.

Adaptive inquiry is the product of the synergistic relationship between what a youngster brings to the classroom and the teacher's ability to shape a lesson in response to the needs of the youngster. This synergistic energy is not only evident between teacher and pupils, but also among classmates. It is the process of designing lessons that have divergent outcomes. The divergent nature of the lesson is primarily influenced by pupils' prior knowledge and what they want to know. Flexibility in the design, assessment, and communication of results is paramount to foster the concept of science as inquiry at work. By implementing a focus and review strategy in a lesson, the teacher is able to assess pupils' prior knowledge and understanding of the topic.

Questioning and discussion at this juncture are rudimentary means of assessment which allow the teacher to clear vocabulary and establish understanding.

Standards in action. Ms. Stevens wanted her sixth grade class to understand the relationship between heat absorption and color. She divided the class into teams of four. Each team received four cans: black, yellow, white, and silver-colored. Ms. Stevens had the pupils fill the cans with soil. Each team received four thermometers which they inserted in the soil at a depth of 5 cm. The cans were then placed under a 150 watt lamp, equidistant from the heat source. The pupils were directed to read the thermometers every three minutes and record their readings on a chart. Ms. Stevens assesses the pupils' understanding of the activity by posing the following questions and activities. Pupil responses demonstrate their levels of understanding indicating when they are ready to move from direct instruction to inquiry.

Knowledge	"What are the variables in the experiment?"
Comprehension	"What was the purpose of the experiment?"
Application	"Why might the color of the containers be significant?"
Analysis	"Diagram the dependent and independent variables and the controls necessary to complete the experiment."
Synthesis	"Based on your own experiences, what could you predict about color and heat absorption?"
Evaluation	"What criteria would you use to evaluate the results of the experiment?"

EARLY EXPERIENCE

Research suggests that early experiences in science help children of all socioeconomic levels improve readiness, language, logic, and mathematical skills (Koballa & Bethel, 1991). All children have the capacity to question. As children's experiences broaden, their ability to question matures. Young children tend to explore their environment through trial-and-error tests, gathering empirical data through their five senses to build experiential knowledge. Older children explore questions through experiments using variables and setting controls. Therefore, teachers need to be prepared to provide developmentally appropriate inquiry experiences.

Inquiry-based teaching strategies that are dependent on the pupils' prior knowledge require teachers to recognize and evaluate the differences in prior learning relative to cultural difference. In our classes, preservice teachers are exposed to constructivist teaching strategies that focus on building knowledge bases from experiential foundations, thus maximizing the learning potential of the individual pupil. Teachers are trained to use assessment techniques that measure the informal learning experience of their pupils. Once recognized, differences between the expected and observed experiential backgrounds of culturally diverse urban youngsters can be used to offer them a greater advantage in an inquiry-based science classroom (Duit & Treagust, 1995; Lemke, 1990; Lowery, 1996).

In the field, teachers must be prepared to put aside preconceived beliefs about their pupils' prior knowledge and sociocultural backgrounds. It appears that urban students' informal science-related experiences may not parallel those of suburban students (Joyce & Farenga, 1999). Without awareness of these differences, teachers may inaccurately presume that youngsters have had many visits to a zoo or museum, thus missing an opportunity to provide those experiences. Our teachers recognize the need to supplement their lessons to maximize their students' experiential backgrounds by connecting new information with preexisting mental constructs. Research theory implies that learning is constructed by a synergistic interaction of prior knowledge and new learning experiences. Therefore, children construct their own knowledge by comparing new sensory experiences with previous concepts and use this information to develop new levels of understanding. Studies have demonstrated that pupils who come from homes with background experience that parallels the school's curriculum function productively in classroom activities (Majoribanks, 1991; Midwinter, 1975).

One advantage of an inquiry-based science classroom is that it advances affective, cognitive, and psychomotor objectives. It is a mentally and physically active classroom designed to foster a variety of hands-on lessons that encourage doing and thinking as opposed to simply listening. Active participation in science that is child-centered, driven by the youngsters' natural interest in the world around them, meets the needs of the urban classroom.

In addition, the teacher needs to clarify for the pupils what it means to talk science and to help them understand the nuances of the language used in science. Language, therefore, is critical, for it is the vehicle that forwards the development of meaning. (See Lemke, 1990, for an extensive discussion of language, culture, science, and knowledge.)

> *Standards in action.* In a discussion with a fifth grade class regarding the properties of a fluid, it became obvious that certain pupils could not distinguish between the terms clear and colorless. Probing further, we found that many pupils believed that if a liquid had color of any amount it could not be clear. The pupils' ideas were entrenched complete with rationales that made sense to them even though they were incorrect. These ideas were strongly held and only after numerous examples, observations, and discussion were the pupils able to distinguish between the two concepts of clear and colorless. To have continued with the lesson without clarifying the terms would have advanced misconceptions. Left unchecked, the anticipatory set would have created confusion in future lessons. Further discourse was encouraged among pupils as they worked in collaborative groups to develop initial questions that may be suitable for later inquiry.

Facilitated discussions need to address defining problems, identifying variables, collecting data, graphing results, recognizing cause and effect relationships, and building and modifying models. Collaborative learning is a teaching strategy at which we encourage our teachers to be adept in their classrooms. This approach assists pupils who are underrepresented in science to benefit from working collaboratively and collectively. Well-structured collaborative activities encourage pupils through discourse and hands-on problem solving to internalize the use of inquiry.

Our philosophy of science teaching is to the right of Piaget. Our conservative constructivist approach provides the pupil enough structure to effectively recognize the relationships between facts to build concepts and to recognize the relationships among concepts to form generalizations. The pupils are required to build their own scientific knowledge and understanding. The key to this process is pupil progression from a dependent learner to an independent investigator. At each step in the science learning process, the teacher assesses understanding and readiness for the independence necessary for inquiry. Behaviors that we have identified as necessary for baseline level of inquiry are: ability to make choices, locate answers, use resources, organize time, set goals, persevere to complete project, and discuss results. Building upon these behaviors, a collaborative teacher/pupil relationship develops, where the teacher assesses abilities and prepares pupils to progress to a level of greater independence. At this level, the pupil is ready for increased responsibility and freedom in owning the inquiry process.

The parallel teaching process includes: (a) pupils pose questions to investigate, and the teacher helps to refine them; (b) pupils plan, execute, and evaluate their investigation and the teacher is available for facilitation; and (c) the teacher helps pupils document outcomes. The monitoring and assessing process furnishes the greatest opportunity to determine conceptual change.

The key to the model is awareness of pupil outcomes guided by standards, urban pupil background and prior knowledge, and teachers' awareness of self. The teacher needs a clear understanding of what the standards are and who the pupils are, as well as a clear understanding of themselves.

ASSESSMENT

Science education is moving away from a behaviorist paradigm of stimulus-response learning toward a constructivist model of inquiry-based learning dependent on prior knowledge and conceptual development. Educators, informed by research, are aware that learning is context dependent and is fostered by the social interactions among teachers and pupils.

In a constructivist learning environment, the purpose of assessment is to accurately evaluate pupils' ability to do science. This requires a comprehensive approach to assessment that includes alternative tools in addition to traditional tests. The challenge of developing assessment instruments that are congruent with a constructivist classroom was raised by former secretary of education, William Bennett, who stated:

> The problem of assessment also constrains the spread of "hands-on" science. It is relatively easy to test children's knowledge when they have been asked to memorize lists of data for a test. It is much harder to design tests that measure learning derived from experience. (Bennett, 1986, p. 3)

This approach to assessment involves the student, the teacher, and the curriculum. Of course, teachers need to evaluate their pupils' academic progress. However, as part of the assessment process, they also need to evaluate their own teaching and curriculum. In order for teachers to measure their professional growth and the progress of their pupils, they must collect data regarding pupils' prior knowledge, teachers' goals and objectives, and pupils' achievement. This comprehensive approach to assessment requires an array of tools, such as performance assessment, prior knowledge scales, and traditional standardized tests.

PERFORMANCE ASSESSMENT

A fundamental rule in developing a valid achievement test is matching what went on in the classroom (i.e., delivery and content) with the means of assessment. In a constructivist classroom, pupils acquire scientific knowledge through discussion and participation in hands-on, minds-on activities that support abstract concepts. They construct their own scientific knowledge. For a valid assessment of their achievement, pupils must be evaluated based on a hands-on, minds-on test; that is, if they are not passive learners, then they should not be evaluated in a passive manner.

Performance assessment tools provide an opportunity for pupils to demonstrate their ability to successfully complete an activity using concrete manipulatives to demonstrate abstract concepts. This assessment technique integrates cognitive and psychomotor abilities. Through the use of a performance assessment, a youngster's problem-solving skills are observable and his level of cognitive ability can be benchmarked to the National Science Education Standards. At Dowling College, our preservice teachers are trained to administer and interpret New York State's Elementary Science Program Evaluation Test (ESPET), a performance assessment that is administered to all fourth graders. The ESPET and an eighth grade version of the skills-based test establish New York State as a pioneer in the area of performance assessment.

Performance assessment is especially appropriate for culturally diverse pupils, particularly those who may have difficulties in speaking and reading English, because it is not language-anchored. Pupil performance may even be enhanced because they can receive context cues from the manipulative materials. These context cues will allow the pupils to convert their abstract thinking into a concrete product.

Prior Knowledge Scales

Young children bring a variety of experiences to the classroom. A constructivist approach requires teachers to engage pupils in learning experiences that build upon prior knowledge. To connect new data with preexisting mental constructs, teachers need to be aware of pupils' prior experiences. Because conventional assessment techniques are often limited to standard readiness screenings in reading and arithmetic, broad areas of experience are neglected.

The importance of environmental influences outside of school has been the focus of numerous studies (Kahle, Parker, Rennie, & Riley, 1993; Majoribanks, 1991; Mason & Kahle, 1989; Walberg, 1991). Midwinter (1975) states that the home is such a powerful influence that no change is possible without its informed support. Studies indicate that pupils who come from homes primed with experiences that parallel the school's curriculum function productively in school activities (Majoribanks, 1991; Midwinter, 1975).

Experiential differences affect future learning outcomes in science (Harlen, 1985; Kahle, 1990). If experiential differences are not ameliorated, the continuance of educational inequalities occurs by capitalizing on experiences present in certain segments of the population (Walberg, 1991).

Awareness of pupils' prior experiences provides a referent to incorporate curricula that encourage all youngsters to actively participate. Therefore, teachers need access to effective means of assessing their pupils' informal science experience to understand how these experiences and to translate into science knowledge. In an effort to form the foundation of an experiential science checklist for the identification of specific strengths and deficits, we developed the Science Technology Scale (STS) (Farenga & Joyce, 1997c), an instrument designed to measure pupils' out-of-school science- and technology-related experiences (see Mason & Kahle, 1989).

STS items defined the factors that underlie extracurricular experiences in science and focused on four types of out-of-school science-related activities experienced by youngsters: physical science-related (e.g., "taken something apart to see how it works"), life science-related (e.g., "visited a zoo or aquarium"), technology-related (e.g., "used a computer to study, do homework, or write a report"), and science-related inquiry skills (e.g., "used a ruler, thermometer, measuring cup, or measuring scale"). Each item was evaluated using a four-point scale (ranging from "never" to "about once a week") indicating the frequency with which a student participates in a particular activity.

Our research suggests that differences exist in the number and kind of science-related experiences reported by young pupils. For example, gender analysis revealed that boys were likely to engage more frequently in science-related activities, especially those in physical science. Girls participated in more observational and life science activities (Farenga & Joyce, 1997a, 1997b, 1999). Diverse socioeconomic groups also show different science-related backgrounds. Youngsters from higher socioeconomic areas reported more frequent and a broader base of informal science-related activities. Teachers must recognize student diversity not only in terms of background, culture, and language, but also opportunities and experiences.

In the science classroom, pupils' prior knowledge, language abilities, and real-world experience can be assessed through content pretesting, concept mapping, and experience inventories, such as the STS. We alerted our preservice teachers to the risk of assuming that inner-city youngsters shared the same experiences as those of suburban or rural children. The teachers may have to broaden the youngsters' backgrounds to include exposure to environmental and life sciences, such as beach ecology, stargazing, or pond studies before they can build upon this knowledge. Often parents are the child's first and most influential teachers. Therefore, we encouraged our preservice teachers to partner with parents. Participating in simple science-related activities with friends, siblings, and parents provides youngsters with opportunities to enhance scientific thinking.

Traditional Testing

A comprehensive approach to assessment includes traditional standardized tests, such as the California Achievement Test (CAT), Stanford Achievement Test (SAT), and the Iowa Test of Basic Skills (ITBS). The results of these tests are used to compare pupils to others at the same age and grade levels. The inner-city teacher must be cognizant of some basic assumptions about testing and assessment often held by traditional test makers (Samuda, 1986). These assumptions do not recognize the diversity in background, culture, language, opportunities, and experiences of inner-city pupils. The belief that there is a communality of experience, opportunities, languages, and backgrounds may result in a systematic misrepresentation of the achievement levels of culturally diverse, inner-city youngsters.

Therefore, preservice teachers learn that it is important to evaluate the validity of a test in terms of the nature of the content and pupils to be tested. While the debate regarding test bias continues, inner-city teachers can best serve their class of culturally diverse pupils by using a variety of assessment techniques to evaluate their levels of understanding science.

RECOMMENDATIONS

Our experience suggests that preservice teachers need to recognize, assess, and build upon the experiences that youngsters bring to the classroom. Ignoring the differences that culturally diverse pupils bring to the classroom will only exacerbate further inequalities. Due to differential socialization patterns, youngsters come to school with vastly different science-related experiences.

Educators need to focus on breaking the mold in teaching to allow for individual differences. Science programs must integrate what we know about youngsters' experiential backgrounds to develop a more productive and inclusive science pedagogy. A major goal of science education should be to identify techniques that encourage active participation of all pupils in science.

Good teaching for urban youngsters has been described as good teaching for all youngsters (Haberman, 1996). Good teaching in the science classroom can be recognized when pupil behavior includes solving problems that are of interest and importance to them, seeing major concepts and ideas, conducting experiments, reflecting on their life experiences, working collaboratively with classmates, and critically evaluating their own work. This should be the goal of all science classrooms, including urban classrooms, as our youngsters prepare for their contributions to society in the 21st century.

EXERCISES FOR PROFESSIONAL DEVELOPMENT

1. Teaching science in a diverse inner-city classroom, you will encounter youngsters' science misconceptions. Describe how pupils' previous informal science-related experiences may foster their common science misconceptions. Develop strategies for correcting them.
2. As an inner-city elementary school teacher, you will discuss student assessment profiles with parents. What assessment tools would be included in the profile? How would you explain pupil progress to parents in a meaningful way? Develop a letter to the parents discussing their child's profile without using technical jargon.
3. You need to develop an inquiry checklist to measure your pupils' process skills. Identify the process skills that you want to measure. List specific items that would be included on the checklist. How would you use the information to develop science activities?
4. Based on what you have read in this chapter, how might inquiry-based science teaching be adapted for youngsters with limited process skills, content knowledge, and psychomotor abilities? Develop a list of specific adaptive techniques.

RESOURCES

National Oceanic and Atmospheric Administration (NOAA)
NOAA Homepage http://www.noaa.gov
NOAA's Internet Sites for Teachers
The National Oceanic and Atmospheric Administration (NOAA) is the Federal agency dedicated to predicting and protecting our environment. NOAA has more than 300 homepages. Those listed below are especially useful for teachers.
Answers From NOAA For students and teachers
gopher://esdiml.esdim.noaa.gov/11/NOAAA_systems/education/
NOAA Teacher at Sea Program
http://www.tas.noaa.gov
Sea Grant Schools Teacher Resources
http://www.mdsg.umd.edu/NSGO/WhatisSeaGrant.html#EDUCATION
El Nino Page
http://www.pmel.noaa.gov/toga-tao/el-nino/
Estuarine Research Non-point source pollution
http://www.nos.noaa.gov/ocrm/nmsp/education.html

SCIENCE CENTERS AND MUSEUMS

The Association of Science-Technology Centers Incorporated (ASTC) has more than 400 museum members located in the United States and around the world. Here are a few of the museum web sites. For all web site addresses, visit the ASTC home page.
ASTC Homepage http://www.astc.org
Exploratorium, San Francisco, CA
http://www.exploratorium.com
American Museum of Natural History, New York, NY
http://www.amnh.org/
The Franklin Institute Science Museum, Philadelphia, PA
http://www.fi.edu
The Computer Museum, Boston, MA
www.tcm.org
The Bronx Zoo, New York, NY
http://www.bronxzoo.com

TEACHER LINKS

Here are some of our favorite educational web sites. We use them in our classes and recommend them to our preservice teachers.

Online with ERIC
http://205.174.118.254/resource/erichtm
National Science Teachers Association (NSTA)
www.nsta.org
Stennis Space Center Weather Page: Education Edition
http://education.ssc.nasa.gov/htmls/weather.htm
National Earthquake Information Center: Earthquake Bulletin
http://gldss7.cr.usgs.gov/neis/bulletin
ERIC Clearinghouse
http://eric.net
National Science Standards Matrix
http://www.ucmp.berkeley.edu/fosrec/Matrix.html
The National Science Standards
http://www.nap.edu/readingroom/books/intronses
The New York: Learning Standards
http://www.cnyric.org/cnyric/standards/standards.html

REFERENCES

Atwater, M. M. (1994). Research on cultural diversity in the classroom. In D. L. Gabel (Ed.), *Handbook of research on science teaching and learning* (pp. 558-576). New York: Macmillan.

Becker, W. C., & Gersten, R. (1982). A follow-up of follow through. *American Educational Research Journal, 19*, 75-92.

Bennett, W. J. (1986). *First lessons: A report on elementary education in America*. Washington, DC: U.S. Government Printing Office.

Cummins, J. (1986). Empowering minority students: A framework for intervention. *Harvard Educational Review, 56*, 18-36.

Duit, R., & Treagust, D. F. (1995). Students' conceptions and constructivist teaching approaches. In B. J. Fraser & H. J. Walberg (Eds.), *Improving science education* (pp. 46-69). Chicago: National Society for the Study of Education.

Farenga, S. J., & Joyce, B. A. (1997a). Beyond the classroom: Gender differences in science experiences. *Education, 117*(4), 563-568.

Farenga, S. J., & Joyce, B. A. (1997b). What children bring to the classroom: Learning science from experience. *School Science and Mathematics, 97*, 248-252.

Farenga, S. J., & Joyce, B. A. (1997c, November). *Uncovering children's science and technology experiential backgrounds: Development of the Science Technology Scale (STS)*. Paper presented at the Annual Meeting of the American Evaluation Association, San Diego, CA.

Farenga, S. J., & Joyce, B. A. (1999). Intentions of young students to enroll in science courses in the future: An examination of gender differences, *Science Education, 83*, 55-75.

Frailer, J. A., & Morris, F. J. (1998). The influence of extended-year schooling on growth of achievement and perceived competence in early elementary school. *Child Development, 69*(2), 495-517.

Haberman, M. (1996). The pedagogy of poverty versus good teaching. In W. Ayers & P. Ford (Eds.), *City kids, city teachers* (pp. 118-129). New York: The New Press.

Harlen, W. (Ed.). (1985). *The teaching of science*. London: David Fulton.

Huling-Austin, L. (1986). Factors to consider in alternative certification programs: What can be learned from teacher induction research? *Action in Teacher Education, 8*(2), 51-58.

Joyce, B. A., & Farenga, S. J. (1999). *Informal science experience profiles of urban students*. Manuscript in preparation.

Kahle, J. B. (1990). Why girls don't know. In M. Budd Rowe (Ed.), *What research says to the science teacher: The process of knowing* (Vol. 6, pp. 55-67). Washington, DC: National Science Teachers Association.

Kahle, J. B., Parker, L. H., Rennie, L. J., & Riley, D. (1993). Gender differences in science education: Building a model. *Educational Psychologist, 28*(4), 374-404.

Koballa, T. R., & Bethel, L. J. (1991). Is there a relationship between science and other subjects taught in schools? In D. Holdzkom & P. B. Lutz (Eds.), *Research within reach: Science education* (pp. 79-107). Washington, DC: National Science Teachers Association.

Lemke, J. L. (1990). *Talking science: Language, learning and values*. Norwood, NJ: Ablex.

Lowery, L. F. (Ed.). (1996). *Pathways to the science standards*. Washington, DC: National Science Teachers Association.

Majoribanks, K. (1991). Educational productivity and talent development. In B. J. Fraser & H. J. Walberg (Eds.), *Families, schools, and students' educational outcomes* (pp. 75-99). New York: Pergamon.

Mason, C. L., & Kahle, J. B. (1989). Students' attitudes toward science and science related careers: A program designed to promote a stimulating gender-free learning environment. *Journal of Research in Science Teaching, 26*(1), 25-39.

Meyer, L., Gersten, R., & Gutkin, J. (1984). Direct instruction: A Project Follow Through success story. *Elementary School Journal, 2*, 241-252.

Midwinter, E. (1975). Toward a solution of the EPA problem: The community school. In J. Rushton & J. D. Turner (Eds.), *Education and deprivation* (pp. 159-183). Manchester: Manchester University.

National Center for Education Statistics. (1997). *Digest of education statistics*. Washington, DC: U.S. Government Printing Office.

National Center for Education Statistics. (1996). *Urban schools: The challenge of location and poverty*. Washington, DC: U.S. Government Printing Office.

National Research Council. (1996). *National science education standards*. Washington, DC: National Academy Press.

Rittenhouse, G. (Ed.). (1998). *The condition of education*. Washington, DC: U.S. Government Printing Office.

Sable, J. (1998). The educational progress of black students. In G. Rittenhouse (Ed.), *The condition of education* (pp. 2-10). Washington, DC: U.S. Government Printing Office.

Sable, J., & Stennett, J. (1998). The educational progress of Hispanic students. In G. Rittenhouse (Ed.), *The condition of education* (pp. 11-19). Washington, DC: U.S. Government Printing Office.

Samuda, R. J. (1986). The role of psychometry in multicultural education: Implications and consequences. In R. J. Samuda & S. L. Kong (Eds.), *Multicultural education: Programmes and methods* (pp. 47-98). Toronto: Intercultural Social Science Publication.

Siege, D. F. (1989, March). *The acquisition of reading skills across development: A process model for achievement*. Paper presented at the annual meeting of the American Educational Research Association, San Francisco, CA.

Walberg, H. J. (1991). Improving school science. *Review of Educational Research, 61*(1), 25-69.

Eight

Helping Teachers Recognize and Connect the Culturally Bound Nature of Young Children's Mathematical Intuitions to In-School Mathematics Concepts

Daniel Ness

The literature on mathematical thinking clearly shows that young children do mathematics well before they enter formal schooling (Brush, 1978; Ginsburg, Pappas, & Seo, 2001; Ness, 2001). To be sure, evidence of youngsters' knowledge of mathematical ideas has been documented and published as far back as the early nineteenth century. Balfanz (1999) refers to a number of pioneers in early childhood education and early writers on young children's often sophisticated mathematical thinking. In 1818, Samuel Goodrich proposed that young children were capable of discovering basic arithmetic concepts on their own. Warren Colburn (1833), who has been considered by some as the first constructivist, extended on Goodrich's ideas by proposing that children can learn arithmetic inductively and through objects used in their everyday lives.

Two main points are important to keep in mind. First, mathematical ideas in particular and knowledge in general do not arbitrarily begin from the time the child enters formal schooling.

Instead, these ideas are constructed by the individual and are based on experience from the time of birth. Indeed, children, whether in or out of school, young or older, have a propensity to learn and search for efficient ways of tackling mathematical (and other) problems. The second point to consider is that young children's mathematics differs in many ways from the mathematics presented in school. This is not to say that their mathematics is any less accurate or efficient than school mathematics. Rather, it is essential for teachers to identify the strengths of youngsters' mathematical ideas and facilitate ways in which connections, patterns, and relationships can be made once children enter school.

A major goal of this chapter is to show that young children are engaged in very interesting and often sophisticated mathematical activity in the everyday context, and much of this form of mathematics plays a critical role in the way they begin to work with mathematical ideas presented in school. The term mathematical activity is defined here as action that occurs specifically when children are engaged in tasks that demonstrate their conceptual knowledge of mathematical ideas (e.g., number and geometric concepts). A parallel goal is to show that the notion of culture, specifically as it relates to the mathematical ideas of children of low-, middle-, and upper-income households, goes far beyond the idea of ethnicity. The "ethno" in "ethnomathematics" does not solely refer to one's ethnic background; rather, it describes culture in its broadest context. That is, the concept of culture can refer to members of certain age groups, gender, social class, and even a group's moral or ideological mindset.

When D'Ambrosio (1985) defines the term ethnomathematics, he includes the mathematics of all cultural groups, including the culture of young children and that of socioeconomic class. D'Ambrosio's framework demonstrates the culturally bound nature of young children's mathematical activities. In particular, young children, as opposed to older children and teens, comprise a culture that does mathematics in oftentimes creative and effective ways. Moreover, nearly all children, regardless of socioeconomic class, have been shown to engage in quite complex mathematical activity in the everyday context (Ginsburg et al., 2001; Ness, 2001). In fact, Ginsburg and his colleagues, whose data were collected in inner-city preschools and daycare centers in New York City, found no significant differences among low-, middle-, and upper-income preschool children in terms of the time they spend engaged in mathematical activity during free play. Their data support the concept that young children, in both urban and suburban settings, naturally exhibit a high degree of mathematical ability. This concept is integrated in my Mathematics Methods classes at Dowling College in which preservice teachers learn to recognize this natural ability and connect it with the potentially powerful formal mathematics curriculum.

Although few, if any, differences in mathematical thinking exist in terms of socioeconomic class, why does the mathematical performance of inner-city school children still lag behind that of suburban and even rural children? Some of the reasons that may account for this might be: (1) the tracking of children into programs that limit their access to full mathematics curricula, (2) the limited mathematical knowledge and preparedness of many—but certainly not all—teachers in inner-city schools, (3) the hasty administrative decisions having to do with labeling oftentimes mathematically competent children as learning disabled, and (4) the severe shortages of funding and resources allocated to inner-city school districts (Anyon, 1997; Oakes, 1990; Payne & Biddle, 1999). Given the greater diversity of learners in the inner city, standardized testing measures alone would serve only to impede the progress of these students and not necessarily help them. Alternative approaches to standardized testing procedures, such as those discussed below, are desperately needed.

In addition to the issue of inequity between inner-city children and those attending schools in suburban and rural districts, the inner-city environment affords certain types of activity fostering mathematical activity that are lacking in suburban or rural environments, and vice versa. For example, a child residing in Harlem, an area of Manhattan in New York City, may have little difficulty in determining the distance between home and school, given that 20 street blocks is equal to one mile, 10 blocks equal to one-half mile, and so forth, whereas the very task of determining mileage for children residing in suburban or rural regions may be more difficult. Similarly, suburban and rural children may experience certain aspects of mathematics and measurement (e.g. acreage, the example of the golden mean ratio in nature) that may be lacking in the city environment. The main idea here is that the experiences of inner-city and urban children differ from those of suburban and rural children, and because children construct their own knowledge based on prior experiences, it is important for teachers to recognize these differences and tailor mathematics curricula to the needs of all youngsters. To this end, alternative methods of mathematical assessment are necessary when evaluating students' knowledge.

My experience and research with young children demonstrate that alternative methods of mathematical assessment are more sensitive to the unique strategies of individuals from all ages and ethnic backgrounds (Ginsburg, 1997; National Council of Teachers of Mathematics, 2000). Before discussing three alternative methods of mathematics assessment, I define the notion of samples of behavior. Then, three scenarios stemming from my work with young children in and out of school are presented. The first scenario is based on a method I refer to as contextual observation. The second involves the use of tacit dialogues, and the third demonstrates a class engaged in learning multiplication through the teaching method of structured analysis. I then summarize how the alternative methods of assessment presented in this chapter allow for versatility in teaching children of diverse backgrounds.

MATHEMATICS ASSESSMENT IN ACTION

Before discussing the three methods of alternative assessment in mathematical thinking and understanding presented in this chapter, it is necessary to define the manner in which teachers may implement such assessment procedures in their mathematics lessons. Given that alternative methods of assessment can be laborious processes for teachers and may not adequately cover the gamut of mathematical knowledge that each student is expected to learn, is it possible to extract specific elements of existing techniques that benefit and enhance teachers' and pupils' expectations? In an attempt to maximize the mathematical potential of students and minimize the excess labors of teachers, it would be to both the students' and teachers' advantage to focus on small bits of information that demonstrate conceptual understanding rather than several aspects of a given mathematical topic or concept. Most alternative methods seem to hone in on the latter, yet teachers may not have the time, experience, or resources to do so. Therefore, it would be worthwhile to underscore the sample of behavior that is defined here as the elicited response of each mathematical question posed by the teacher.

A word of caution, however, is necessary. Samples of behavior are not simply student responses (mathematical questions in this case) that involve rote and mechanical production or procedural knowledge alone. Asking the child, for instance, to fill in the blanks to several single-digit number facts without any connection to patterns and relationships would fall into this category. Rather, well-developed samples of behavior should be based on tasks that allow the teacher to evaluate responses from the child that are indicative of conceptual knowledge or understanding of a particular mathematical topic. One such example of this would be when a teacher poses a question involving the connection between squares and rectangles, and the student may or may not identify this relationship. Three alternative methods and their accompanying scenarios are now presented.

Contextual Observation

Only recently have there been studies focusing on young children's mathematical thinking and abilities in the everyday context (Ginsburg et al., 2001; Ness, 2001). Ginsburg and his colleagues identified six mathematical categories in which four- and five-year-old children are engaged: classification (grouping, sorting, or classifying); magnitude/comparison (ordering, measuring, comparing length, size, or weight); enumeration (numerical judgments, counting, subitizing); dynamics (exploration of change or transformation involving arithmetic or geometric operations); patterns and shapes (identification of relationships or awareness of shape concepts); and spatial relations (awareness of direction, location, or placement of objects). My earlier work has drawn on naturalistic observation methodology and focuses on young children's engagement in spatial, geometric, and architectural activities in the everyday context. Despite the advantages of naturalistic observation methodology, one major obstacle concerns educators. The concern revolves around the question: how can teachers use alternative assessment methods as a means of optimizing their time so as to serve the needs of all students?

Naturalistic observation methodology, then, can be an extremely useful tool for researchers and practitioners in the development and learning of mathematics. However, although this method is effective in understanding young children's mathematical potential, naturalistic observation methodology alone may not always benefit teachers. One reason is because this potentially powerful alternative assessment tool is a time-consuming undertaking and may limit the amount of time that each teacher allocates for all classroom activities.

Therefore, it is essential to extract certain components of naturalistic observation that focus on specific samples of behavior of each child. Earlier, I have discussed samples of behavior, a term that refers to responses from individual questions or problems with which the student is confronted. Samples of behavior serve as hotbeds for alternative methods of assessment because they provide the teacher great autonomy in terms of time management. Using observational techniques when focusing on samples of behavior of each student is what undergirds the concept of contextual observation. The following scenario is an example of how teachers can use contextual observation as a means of maximizing their knowledge about youngsters' abilities in mathematical understanding.

SCENARIO I: STAN AND LORRAINE'S "BIG SQUARE"

It seems to be commonplace in so-called popular culture to believe that young children cannot do mathematics and that the subject is initially encountered upon entering formal schooling. Quite to the contrary, empirical evidence suggests that mathematical thinking begins shortly after birth (Bryant, 1995; Simon, Hespos, & Rochat, 1995, Wynn, 1992, 1995). Wynn's experiment, which shows that young infants can count, involved the use of a display of a small number of objects. The sequence of events in Wynn's experiment is the following:

1. An object is placed in the infant's view by hand in a large open box; a screen rotates up so that the object is hidden from view.
2. The hand leaves the scene empty.
3. A second object is then added and the addition of a second object is also in the infant's view. So, behind the screen, one of two possibilities may arise: two objects are present, or one object is present, and the second object "added" is placed out of sight behind the screen.
4. The hand leaves the scene empty.

Two situations may occur: (1) The screen drops, and two objects are revealed; or (2) the screen drops, and only one object is revealed. Wynn's results show that infants were surprised when the number of objects remaining (one object in the above case) did not match the number of items in the change that had occurred, namely, the addition of another object; that is, the infant expected two items, not one.

Indeed, mathematical thinking continues well beyond infancy. Gelman and Gallistel (1978) argue that children develop a sense of identifying sets and one-to-one correspondence by three years of age. Ginsburg, Pappas, and Seo (2001) argue that although the amount of time spent on mathematical activity actually increases with age, preschoolers in general are engaged in mathematical activity nearly 50% of the time during free play. As a teacher of young children, I have observed children's samples of behavior involving mathematical activity in the everyday context. Stan and Lorraine's "Big Square" is a case in point.

Stan and Lorraine, both approximately 3 years 6 months, are two of 16 children between 3 and 4 years of age who attend a preschool in New York City. This preschool also caters to 10 two-year-olds and 21 four-year-olds. The children at this preschool are from both low- and middle-income families residing within New York City limits. Upon finishing their snack, Stan and Lorraine decide to walk over to the block area. Both children insist upon building a "big square" that they will use as a hurdle once it is complete, and perhaps most important, Stan and Lorraine demonstrate some really interesting mathematics as they are constructing their "big square" using different sizes of blocks.

What, if any, mathematical ideas stem from this account of Stan and Lorraine's episode? First, although their rendition of the "big square" appears more like a rectangle than a square (given that the opposite sides of their figure are equal in length and any two adjacent sides are not), they do know that the term *square* is also associated with a four-sided figure with four right angles, seemingly a major achievement for a three-year-old. A second striking aspect of their construction is their desire to be meticulous and precise in making certain that the "big square" is enclosed and resembles a four-sided figure with four right angles. In working together to construct the "big square," both children used four types of blocks for their structure: the half-unit, unit, double-unit, and the quadruple-unit block. Stan initially places one quadruple-unit block parallel to the wall at a distance equal to approximately five unit blocks. Interestingly, the children do not begin to build the perpendicular sides. Instead, they place another quadruple-unit block next to and parallel with the wall and also parallel with the initial quadruple-unit block.

The children then construct the left perpendicular side, using a double unit block and two unit blocks. Next, knowing that they need to close the gap, they use two half-unit blocks to do so. The right perpendicular side was the last to be constructed. At this point, they were running out of double-unit and single-unit blocks. In order to complete the "square," Stan and Lorraine knew that they needed four half-unit blocks to finish the shape (see Figure 8.1). The main idea is

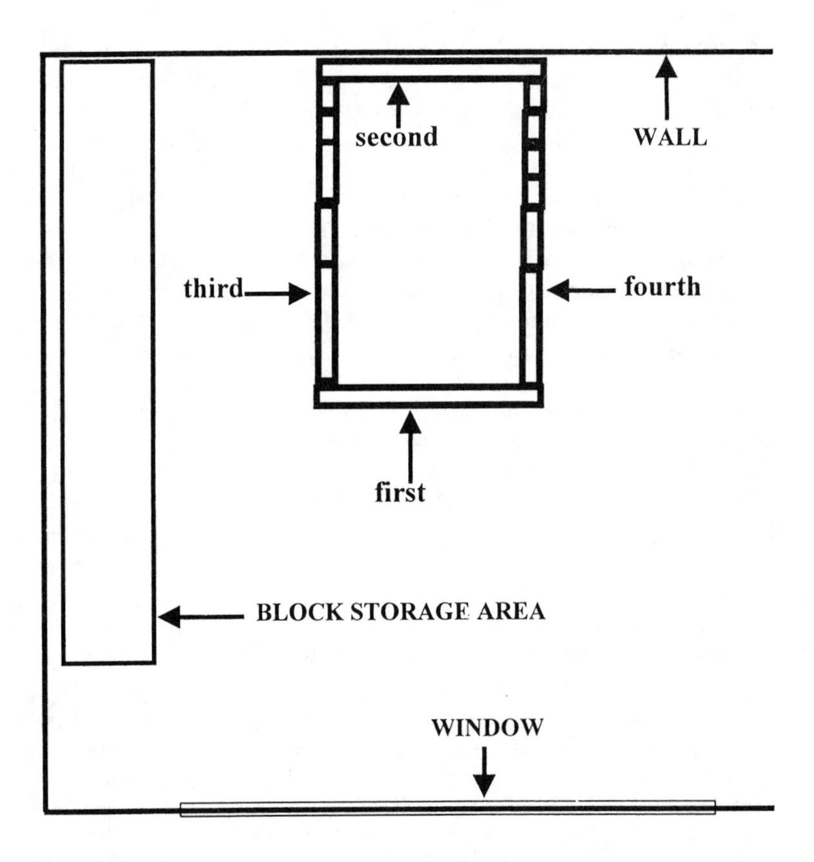

Figure 8.1. Stan and Lorraine's "Big Square"

this: both children possess clever ways of producing a legitimate geometric shape, and this idea further demonstrates their considerable potential for doing mathematics in school. Further, Stan and Lorraine's thinking goes beyond identification of shape alone. They are able to recognize shape properties as well. Again, that these three-year-olds referred to a rectangular object as a square is not what is important here; this does not mean that they are bereft of geometric ideas. They are not. It would be a worthwhile task for the Kindergarten or first-grade teacher to make note of such interesting creations and facilitate situations in which the children can perhaps eventually identify the differences between shapes having sides with differing lengths and those whose sides have equal length.

CONTEXTUAL OBSERVATION AND STANDARDS FOR SCHOOL MATHEMATICS

How can the role of contextual observation enhance the quality of teaching and learning in the early grades? For one thing, the contextual observation technique surely requires an authentic activity-based situation. In the context of nearly all preschools and classrooms in the early elementary grades, the use of objects (such as Legos and blocks) for play and intellectual creativity is the norm, so one of the contextual factors that affect early mathematical outcomes are those involving specific objects that are used in the course of free play. (Other contextual influences are social interaction and particular play activities.) In fact, it has been shown that children's play with Lego and block objects is highly correlated with the amount of time that these children are engaged in mathematical activity (Lin & Ness, 2000).[1]

The *Principles and Standards for School Mathematics* (NCTM, 2000) also advocate *supportive learning environments* as a means for teachers to detect strengths that may serve to students' advantage in later grades. As stated in the Geometry Standard for grades pre-K to 2 (NCTM, 2000, p. 97), "Teachers must provide materials and structure the environment appropriately to encourage students to explore shapes and their attributes." Moreover, as stated in the "Learning Principle" of the National Mathematics Standards, "Students must learn mathematics with understanding activity building new knowledge from experience and prior knowledge" (NCTM, 2000, p. 20). In this sense, then, one of the most effective ways to allow youngsters to construct their knowledge is through alternative methods of standardized testing. As seen from the scenario above, contextual observation provides such an

---

[1]One important caveat is that one should not automatically assume that mathematical activity will always occur given access to Lego and block materials.

outlet. Moreover, a highly conducive environment for contextual observation is a classroom in which play assumes an important role. A major problem, however, is that in many contexts, adults often misinterpret play as being "just play" or a type of random or unorganized recreational activity, devoid of intellectual interaction (Clements & Sarama, 2000). However, research in play shows otherwise (Ginsburg, Pappas, & Seo, 2001; Van Hiele, 1999). In fact, play fosters intellectual growth among children, and contextual observation is one way in which teachers can tap into children's cognitive strengths. This method is not the only one, however. It is also important for teachers to expand their repertoire when considering ways in which to enrich the diverse students in their classes. Another important method for doing this is through the tacit dialogue technique.

TACIT DIALOGUES

Piaget (1926) developed the clinical method to assess children's thinking. This method evolved into what is currently referred to as the clinical interview. In Piagetian terms, when performing a clinical interview, interviewers do not teach or instruct children; instead they examine how children think and whether they understand the underlying concepts of a particular topic being discussed (Ginsburg, 1997). Based on the results of these interviews, they can review the areas in which problems arise for individual students.

However, in the context of the elementary mathematics classroom, the clinical interview has some shortcomings. Does the Piagetian clinical interview method serve as a practical device for assessing individual students' knowledge, and is it possible for all students of any given class size to be assessed through the clinical interview technique, given that teachers must accommodate all students simultaneously? Keep in mind that the clinical interview attempts to provide a generalizable account of an individual student's mathematical abilities. To perform a clinical interview will require a large segment of time, perhaps 45 minutes for each student. Can an inner-city teacher of 40 students or more afford to do so?

This is precisely where the tacit dialogue comes into play. Tacit dialogues are defined here as moments of verbal exchange between teacher and student whereby the former is able to extract information or understanding of the latter through samples of behavior. Instead of performing the clinical interview to focus on particular students' mathematical knowledge at the expense of neglecting others, tacit dialogues allow teachers to hone in on each of their students' understanding of mathematical concepts in a variety of classroom settings. As the students are engaged in authentic mathematics activities, the teacher extracts pertinent mathematics concepts that evidence students' understanding. Janelle's case of addition and subtraction provides insight in this technique.

SCENARIO II: JANELLE'S ADDITION AND SUBTRACTION STRATEGIES

In this scenario involving tacit dialogues, a teacher attempts to tap in to what a six-year-old child is thinking and how the child thinks about a particular mathematics problem. As you see in the excerpt below, the teacher-interviewer presents Janelle with two similar scenarios, and Janelle is asked to solve the mathematical problems presented in each. Each scenario is only a few minutes, and can certainly be performed in the context of a first- or second-grade classroom of 25 or more students. The first scenario is the following:

Interviewer: OK, Janelle. Here we go. Jimmy has 3 marbles and Amanda has 5 marbles. So Jimmy has how many marbles?
Janelle: 3.
Interviewer: And Amanda has how many?
Janelle: 5.
Interviewer: OK. How many marbles are there altogether?
Janelle: (Approximately 10 seconds elapse.) 7.
Interviewer: Seven. How did you figure that out?
Janelle: Hmm. I was thinking a 5 and a 3. Well, there was 5. Then I moved one of the marbles from Jimmy to the 5, and it was 6. Then I moved another marble over to the 6 and it was 7.

In general, Janelle was moving mental images of the marbles as she was thinking about how many marbles there are in all. Also, keep in mind that the goal of the teacher-interviewer is not to teach the child during the course of the dialogue in the form of telling or instructing but to identify how the child thinks and then to lead the child in the right direction to solve the problem. The second scenario is the following:

Interviewer: Let's try another one. Jimmy has 8 marbles, and he gives 2 of them to Amanda. How many marbles does Jimmy have now?
Janelle: 5?
Interviewer: OK. How did you do that?
Janelle: Well, I know that 5 and 2 is 8. And if Jimmy has 8 marbles, and he wants to give 2 of them to Amanda, then he must have 5 left.

Interviewer: And that's because 5 and 2 is 8?
Janelle: Mm hmm.

What can we learn from the tacit dialogue between Janelle and her teacher? On the surface, one may notice in the above excerpt that Janelle gave incorrect answers to the two problems. Are we to conclude, then, that Janelle is less mathematically able than other students her age? Is she possibly learning disabled? Should we conclude that she simply lacks intelligence? Through alternative methods of assessment, like tacit dialogues, we can identify some really interesting and logical thinking processes of children who may be considered less able than their peers. Unfortunately, most students, whether in first grade or twelfth grade, are all too often evaluated solely on the accuracy of their answers through standardized tests and not on the process in which they arrived at them. In Janelle's case, many educators and administrators seeing her mathematics score might falsely conclude that she is mathematically learning disabled or might label her as such merely from the number of correct answers she produces.

A closer examination of the above excerpt, however, tells a completely different story, and, in fact, a much more accurate picture of Janelle's mathematical abilities. To begin with, the results from the tacit dialogues between student and teacher demonstrate that Janelle is a bright six-year-old whose thought processes were mathematically logical and even precise. In the second scenario, when the teacher asked Janelle how she knew that Jimmy had 5 marbles left, she responded in a way that clearly revealed her understanding of subtraction as being the reverse process of addition. Logically, her explanation was precise, but there is more.

In the first scenario, Janelle used the strategy of *counting on* to arrive at her answer. Counting on is a procedure that young children develop outside of the school context which serves as an invaluable tool for adding two or more sets. This procedure is an extension of *counting all* in which a child counts all the objects or images in two or more sets starting from the number one. Janelle demonstrated her understanding of an additional mathematical concept as well. In attempting to find the answer to 3+5, Janelle argued that the answer would be the same as the one for 5+3, hence, revealing her understanding of commutativity in the process of addition; that is, Janelle recognizes the fact that no matter how you add the two numbers, namely 5 and 3, you get the same result. Clearly, then, tacit dialogues can help teachers better understand the thinking processes of students, what they really know about mathematics, and the concepts that underlie important areas.

TACIT DIALOGUES AND STANDARDS FOR SCHOOL MATHEMATICS

School children, particularly those in inner-city school districts with inadequate facilities and resources, are frequently mislabeled as learning disabled (Anderson, 1997). This is often due to erroneous responses. However, similar to Janelle's excerpt described above, children's errors in mathematical problems often have sensible origins. Tacit dialogues provide an outlet for preventing such misappropriation and inept diagnoses of one's abilities because they allow for much greater latitude of an individual student's knowledge when grappling with various aspects of a particular mathematical topic. At the same time, teachers will find the tacit dialogue approach feasible and within easy reach, that is, not as protracted and unachievable for large and diverse classes as the Piagetian clinical interview.

As stated in "The Assessment Principle" of the NCTM *Principles and Standards* (2000), "Assessment should support the learning of important mathematics and furnish useful information to both teachers and students" (p. 22). Performing tacit dialogues summons useful information by detecting youngsters' thought processes when dealing with mathematical concepts. In Janelle's case, the useful information had to do with her understanding of advanced mathematical definitions for a first-grader, namely, her ability to appreciate the reversibility of addition and subtraction, as well as her understanding of commutativity.

The "Assessment Principle" further claims that assessment should be "a valuable tool for making instructional decisions" (p. 23). As stated above, school children are commonly misdiagnosed as learning disabled. These conclusions are frequently based on the lack of time teachers devote to individual student differences in conceptual understanding. Moreover, this is most widespread in urban schools, where diversity is abundant, yet where funding and resources are limited or perhaps lacking altogether. To correct this problem, teachers can employ tacit dialogues as a means of extracting pertinent information about each student's mathematical problem area. It may very well not be so problematic, especially if the teacher has identified that a student's errors have sensible origins.

Structured Analysis

Another way to consider children's unique strategies in solving mathematical problems and in essence to respect the child's preschool or out-of-school mathematical experiences is to allow children to share their own strategies before teaching the standard algorithms to those problems. To do this, it is crucial that teachers involve all of their students in the process of explaining their processes in arriving at an answer. One effective way of carrying this out would be to have students present their unique ways of doing a problem at the chalkboard. Samples of behavior that are used to elicit this method of assessment are known as Structured Analysis.

SCENARIO III: MS. DUARTE'S LESSON ON MULTIPLICATION

One illustrative example of this way of teaching is based on one of my experiences observing an inner-city second-grade class. The teacher, Ms. Duarte, had begun the class by presenting the students with a multiplication problem: 4 x 13. Most of the children seemed to understand the meaning of the numerals and the multiplication sign; however, they were not taught the so-called standard column-format algorithm for multiplication, nor was the problem used for drill or review. The students spent the next ten minutes or so attempting to solve this problem using their own, unique strategies. At the end of ten minutes, the teacher asked four students to present their own ways of solving the multiplication problem 4 x13 on the chalkboard at the front of the classroom. Perhaps the most fascinating result is that not one of the four students went about solving this problem in the same way. Further, not one of the students used or was taught the standard algorithm to solve the problem. (Incidentally, as a means of making connections, the teacher did in fact discuss the standard algorithm after the children presented their unique invented strategies.) In analyzing each student's process, you will see that their procedures in going about the problem clearly revealed that they were aware of the important concepts that form the underpinnings of multiplication. For the first student, Gabrielle, the problem was simply one of repeated addition, namely:

$$\begin{array}{r} 13 \\ +\underline{13} \\ 26 \end{array} \qquad \begin{array}{r} 13 \\ +\underline{13} \\ 26 \end{array} \qquad \begin{array}{r} 26 \\ +\underline{26} \\ 52 \end{array}$$

However, repeated addition is not the only multiplication concept exhibited by these students. A second student, Mary, demonstrated her understanding of place value and its role in the process of multiplication:

$$\begin{array}{rrr} 10 & 3 & \\ 10 & 3 & 40 \\ 10 & 3 & \underline{12} \\ \underline{10} & \underline{3} & 52 \\ 40 & 12 & \end{array}$$

Clearly, Mary knows that when you attempt to solve 4 x 13, you multiply the number of tens that are present (one ten) by four, and the number of units (three) by four. She is also aware of the fact that the sum of four 10s is 40, and the sum of four 3s is 12, also a form of repeated addition, and, of course, the sum of 40 and 12 will yield the answer. However, that does not seem to be all that Mary knows; even though she did not explicitly write it on the board, Mary also seems to have a good understanding of the distributive property: 4x13=4(10+3) which can be written as 4(10)+4(3).

A third student, Jim, seemed to make use of his number facts and his understanding of base 10. First, Jim wrote down 3x4=12. He then wrote 1x4=4 followed by 10x4=40. He then added the sum of 40 and 12 to arrive at the answer of 52. Jim seems to know his number fact 1x4=4. What is most interesting is his extension of this idea, namely, that if you multiply the first number, 1, by 10 and multiply that product by 4, the resulting product will be 4x10 or 40. A fourth student, Wayne, used yet another strategy. His solution to 4 x13 was the following:

4x15=60
4x2=8
60-8=52

This is a fascinating example because it demonstrates how the ability to estimate can be extremely useful in solving problems. In this case, Wayne seemed to be familiar with the idea or number fact that 4x15=60. He also knows that 4x13 is 4x2 less than 4x15, or 52 is 8 less than 60.

Again, as is common in most mathematics lessons in the elementary school, the teacher of this second-grade class could have simply started the period teaching the standard algorithm to multiplication without paying any attention to children's unique strategies. As shown above the children's strategies elicited conceptual understanding. Teaching only with the standard algorithm, however, may not necessarily demonstrate the important inherent multiplication concepts, like repeated addition or place value. The most important idea here is that children need to know that different methods at arriving at solutions to mathematical problems are useful, and that some methods may be more or less efficient than others.

Structured Analysis and Standards for School Mathematics

As stated in the "Number and Operations" Standard for Grades Pre-K to 2 in the *Principles and Standards for School Mathematics*, "Flexibility in thinking about numbers . . . is a hallmark of number sense" (NCTM, 2000, p. 80). As elicited in the above scenario, Ms. Duarte provided a conducive environment for her students by fostering a structured lesson, yet at the same time allowing her students to arrive at their own solutions to a mathematical problem. Allowing them to solve the problems using their own method was not the only important factor, however. After the students at the chalkboard provided their own unique solutions, Ms. Duarte expected the students sitting at desks to analyze and question their peers' process of solving the problem. Further, the NCTM *Standards* contend that "students . . . develop understanding of place value through the strategies they invent to compute" (p. 82). We have clearly seen this occur in Ms. Duarte's classroom. If you recall, a number of her students developed a sensible method for finding the answer to 4x13 by referring to the "13" as one "10" and three "1s". Also, research shows that students often rely on their own computational strategies before they connect them with standard algorithms (Cobb et al., 1991; Gravemeijer, 1994; Steffe, 1994). The structured analysis approach, then, allows for versatility in connecting various mathematical ideas and concepts and in demonstrating the many different approaches in students' processes in arriving at solutions.

A REVIEW OF ALTERNATIVE METHODS OF MATHEMATICS ASSESSMENT

We have seen how mathematical thinking is clearly an intrinsic part of a young child's life in the everyday context. Moreover, research has shown that children are able to construct their unique, often abstract, and complex methods of arriving at a solution to a multiplication problem, let alone their understanding of the concepts involved in multiplication itself (Ginsburg & Seo, 1999). How then can educators alter their methods of mathematical assessment so as to be more sensitive to and respectful toward a student's unique mathematical knowledge? How can ethnomathematics assessment play a role in the classroom and still consider the everyday mathematics of young children?

Teaching and Learning Mathematics Through Contextual Observation. One type of ethnomathematical assessment deals with observing young children in their everyday context. In one sense, the elementary teacher of mathematics can observe the mathematics occurring during children's free play. This will help in providing the teacher with ideas in how to connect everyday mathematical experiences with the mathematics presented in the school context. As Greenes (1999) would argue, for this to happen, teachers will need to know the mathematics content very well, in addition to knowing what their young students know about the subject. In another sense, observation can involve the teacher in terms of identifying and respecting the uniqueness of each student's strategies in solving particular problems before the so-called standard algorithm is presented. Allow students to present their own methods at arriving at solutions and foster an environment that allows students to become acquainted with the solutions of others.

Teaching and Learning Mathematics Through Tacit Dialogues

The tacit dialogue technique is a form of assessment that is sensitive to an individual's way of knowing. From an ethnomathematics perspective, tacit dialogues may serve as an invaluable tool as well. My observations of teachers and educators of mathematics have shown that the curriculum should begin from the point where the educator discovers what a particular child knows mathematically, in other words, the child's ethnomathematics. It is only at that point when educators can become more creative in assisting children in codifying their own knowledge and thinking. Educators need to begin by listening to students and finding authentic ways to incorporate students' own perspectives into educational research and practice. Educators must find alternative ways to identify what students understand. At the same time, with respect to what I refer to as tacit dialogues, Ginsburg (1997) argues in favor of the clinical interview method, for it enables the teacher-interviewer to gain "insight into the child's mind" and "requires that we treat [children]" with fairness and "in a special, non-standard way" (p. 68). Clearly, a rationale for using the tacit dialogue technique is compatible with the argument that researchers and educators must identify what children understand and listen to what they are saying. As Farenga and Joyce have argued in the previous chapter, children's experiential knowledge that they gain both in school and out of school may have strong affects on student outcomes.

However, this is not to say that producing correct answers is not important; rather, the tacit dialogue technique will allow teachers to identify how their individual students think about various mathematical problems. Once this is determined, facilitating an environment where each student can identify errors in the thinking process as a means of obtaining the correct answer would be the next step.

Teaching and Learning Mathematics Through Structured Analysis

Structured Analysis provides the opportunity to promote ethnomathematics by encouraging an environment that is conducive to learning mathematical ideas, one that promotes dialogue and allows students to explain their solutions and question or even challenge the solutions of others. Asking students to merely parrot or mimic their answers does not reveal their knowledge of the mathematical topic being presented. For Greenes (1999), preschools should also have meaningful learning environments that involve genuine and intellectually enjoyable mathematical thinking. This type of mathematical teaching and learning, involving discourse between student and teacher, is quite common in Japan and other East Asian societies (Hatano & Inagaki, 1999) and can also serve as a form of assessment if teachers encourage their students to explain their solutions both in the form of written work and as oral presentations.

CONCLUSION

As we have seen, these three forms of alternative assessment—contextual observation, tacit dialogues, and structured analysis—have been shown to be much more precise gauges for determining what individual students know and how they go about doing particular mathematical problems. At the same time, adopting an ethnomathematics program as a means of representing the diversity of students also asks that one deemphasize the role of standardized testing in mathematics. As we have seen earlier, such results may lead to unwarranted and even outright false conclusions about a particular student's mathematical ability. Administrative steps taken that classify individuals as learning disabled or low in intelligence solely on the basis of a poor performance on such tests are inequitable in that the accuracy of the answers in no way demonstrates that person's complete knowledge or understanding of mathematics. However, the deemphasis of standardized testing does not mean that we eliminate factual knowledge in our teaching. One major misrepresentation of constructivist methodology is that factual or procedural understanding does not allow for one's construction of mathematical knowledge. Children often use this form of knowledge to establish connections between numerous mathematical concepts and operations.

Finally, educators would be better served to recognize the similarities between the intuitive nature of both children's mathematical thinking and that of the mathematician or other professional who uses mathematics. That is to say, the mathematics of the mathematician is not solely what is published in the mathematics journal or textbook. Instead, mathematics also involves the thinking process and working out of proofs of theorems. As described throughout this chapter, children too think through their mathematical ideas in the everyday context.

RESOURCES

Goudreau Museum of Mathematics in Art and Science
http://www.mathmuseum.org
International Study Group on Ethnomathematics
http://www.rpi.edu/~eglash/isgem.htm
The International Study Group on the History and Pedagogy of Mathematics
http://earnie.bgsu.edu/~vrickey/hpm/index-hpm.html
Mathematics Association of America
http://maa.org
Please Touch Museum—an extension of The Children's Museum of Philadelphia
http://www.pleasetouchmuseum.org

Teacher Links
I highly recommend the following web sites for pre- and inservice elementary-school teachers who are interested in mathematics education resources. These web sites have been utilized in my own classes. I have listed mathematics teachers' organizations from two states (California and New York). However, other state mathematics teacher organizations are available, and many are linked to the National Council of Teachers of Mathematics (NCTM) web site (see below).

California Mathematics Council
http://www.cmc-math.org
National Council of Teachers of Mathematics
http://www.nctm.org
Association of Mathematics Teachers of New York State
http://www.amtnys.org

You can also log on to the Teachers College Record web site for information on the mathematics (and language arts) curriculum standards for each of the 50 states. The Teachers College Record URL is: *http://www.tcrecord.org*

REFERENCES

Anderson, S. (1997). Worldmath. In A. B. Powell & M. Frankenstein (Eds.), *Ethnomathematics: Challenging Eurocentrism in mathematics education* (pp. 291-306). Albany: State University of New York Press.
Anyon, J. (1997). *Ghetto schooling*. New York: Teachers College Press.

Balfanz, R. (1999). Why do we teach young children so little mathematics? Some historical considerations. In J. V. Copley (Ed.), *Mathematics in the early years* (pp. 3-10). Reston, VA: National Council of Teachers of Mathematics.

Brush, L. R. (1978). Preschool children's knowledge of addition and subtraction. *Journal for Research in Mathematics Education, 9*, 44-54.

Bryant, P. (1995). Children and arithmetic. *Journal of Child Psychology and Psychiatry, 36*, 3-32.

Clements, D. H., & Sarama, J. (2000). Early childhood corner: Standards for preschoolers. *Teaching Children Mathematics, 7*(1), 38-41.

Cobb, P., Wood, T., Yackel, E., Nicholls, J., Wheatley, G., Trigatti, B., & Perlwitz, M. (1991). Assessment of a problem-centered second-grade mathematics project. *Journal of Research in Mathematics Education, 22*, 3-29.

Colburn, W. (1833). *Arithmetic: Upon the inductive method of instruction.* Boston: Hilliard, Gray & Co.

D'Ambrosio, U. (1985). Ethnomathematics and its place in the history and pedagogy of mathematics. *For the Learning of Mathematics, 5*(1), 41-48.

Gelman, R., & Gallistel, C. R. (1978). *Children's understanding of number*. Cambridge, MA: Harvard University Press.

Ginsburg, H. P. (1997). *Entering the child's mind: The clinical interview in psychological research and practice.* New York: Cambridge University Press.

Ginsburg, H. P., & Seo, K. H. (1999). The mathematics in children's thinking. *Mathematical Thinking and Learning, 2*, 113-129.

Ginsburg, H. P., Pappas, S., & Seo, K. H. (2001). Everyday mathematical knowledge: Asking young children what is developmentally appropriate. In S. Golbeck (Ed.), *Psychological perspectives on early childhood education.* Mahwah, NJ: Erlbaum.

Gravemeijer, K. (1994). *Developing realistic mathematics instruction.* Utrecht, Netherlands: Freudenthal Institute.

Greenes, C. (1999). Ready to learn: Developing young children's mathematical powers. In J. V. Copley (Ed.), *Mathematics in the early years* (pp. 39-46). Reston, VA: National Council of Teachers of Mathematics.

Hatano, G., & Inagaki, K. (1999). Early childhood mathematics in Japan. In J. V. Copley (Ed.), *Mathematics in the early years* (pp. 219-226). Reston, VA: National Council of Teachers of Mathematics.

Lin, C. L., & Ness, D. (2000, April). *The everyday mathematics of Taiwanese and American four- and five-year-old children.* Paper presented at the Conference of the American Educational Research Association, New Orleans, Louisiana. (ERIC Document Reproduction Service No. ED 440 757)

National Council of Teachers of Mathematics. (2000). *Principles and standards for school mathematics*. Washington, DC: National Council of Teachers of Mathematics.

Ness, D. (2001). *The development of emergent spatial thinking, geometric concepts and architectural principles in the everyday context*. Ph.D. dissertation, Teachers College, Columbia University, New York.

Oakes, J. (1990). *Multiplying inequalities: The effects of race, social class, and tracking opportunities to learn mathematics and science*. Santa Monica, CA: Rand Corp.

Payne, K. J., & Biddle, B. J. (1999). Poor school funding, child poverty, and mathematics achievement. *Educational Researcher, 28*(6), 4-13.

Piaget, J. (1926). *The child's conception of the world*. Totowa, NJ: Littlefield & Adams.

Simon, T. J., Hespos, S. J., & Rochat, P. (1995). Do infants understand simple arithmetic? A replication of Wynn (1992). *Cognitive Development, 10*, 253-269.

Steffe, L. P. (1994). Children's multiplying schemes. In G. Harel & J. Confrey (Eds.), *The development of multiplicative reasoning in the learning of mathematics* (pp. 3-39). Albany: State University of New York Press.

Van Hiele, P. M. (1999). Developing geometric thinking through activities that begin with play. *Teaching Children Mathematics, 5*(6), 310-316.

Wynn, K. (1992). Addition and subtraction by human infants. *Nature, 358*, 749-750.

Wynn, K. (1995). Infants possess a system of numerical knowledge. *Current Directions in Psychological Science, 4*(6), 172-177.

Nine

Literacy Experiences of Young Children 3 to 8 Years of Age

M. Victoria Rodríguez

At the beginning of the new millennium, we face a technological revolution and important demographic changes, both of which will have unpredictable consequences. Through computers and the Internet, we have easy, inexpensive access to an enormous amount of information available in almost any part of the world. To be able to access this new world and its enormous opportunities, advanced literacy skills are indispensable. However, the goal of attaining advanced literacy for everyone as required by a high-tech economy has not been achieved. This is especially true for African Americans, Latinos, Native Americans, and poor children. Furthermore, there is an increasing number of students whose native language is not English, who have different traditions than the mainstream society, or who do not have literacy skills in their native language, for whom acquiring advanced literacy skills is particularly challenging (Burns, Griffin, & Snow, 1999; Dickinson, 1994; Snow, Burns, & Griffin, 1998).

This has been confirmed by the more recent *Reading Report Card for the Nation and the States* (Donahue, Voelkl, Campbell, & Mazzeo, 1999). In the national reading assessment of 4th-, 8th-, and 12th-grade students conducted in 1998 by the National Assessment of Educational Progress, 62% of students in fourth grade performed at or above the basic level; 31% performed at or above the proficiency level, but only 7% performed at the advanced level of achievement. The average reading score for European American students was higher than for African American, Latino, and American Indian students. The gap between European American and African American students was 33 points and 31 points between European American and Latino students. Students who were eligible for the free/reduced-price lunch program had lower average reading scores than students who were not eligible for the program.[1]

Factors that contribute to the students' difficulties in learning to read and write include lack of home exposure to the language and literacy traditions of the mainstream society that are either mostly or exclusively used in school, low socioeconomic background, which often translates into lack of exposure to a variety of interesting literacy materials at home and in school, nonstandard dialects of English or limited proficiency in English, biological factors, inappropriate instruction, and teachers who are not well prepared to teach beginning readers in low-income areas (Snow, Burns, & Griffin, 1998). Unfortunately, the same children who do not have intensive and extensive literacy experiences at home tend to attend schools that do not provide them with the kind of enriched literacy environments that they need.

In this chapter, I will first present the definition of emergent literacy based upon the research of the home literacy experiences of young children while focusing on a longitudinal study that I conducted in the homes of three young Dominican children from low-income backgrounds in an inner-city community in New York City (Rodríguez, 1995, 1999). Then I will discuss how both the research on teaching literacy to young children and the research on children's experiences with literacy at home and in their community should inform a developmentally appropriate practice.

---

[1]The National Assessment of Educational Progress 1998 *Reading Report Card for the Nation and the States* is available on the World Wide Web: http://nces.ed.gov/naep. The report provides detailed information about the methodology used to obtain the reading scores at the 4th, 8th, and 12th grades for three different achievement levels. It compares the reading scores attained in 1992, 1994, and 1998 for four regions of the country, as well as for student subgroups (gender, race/ethnicity, free/reduced-price lunch program, and parents' level of education). The results are also related to some school and home characteristics that affect literacy development.

EMERGENT LITERACY

During the last 20 years, research on early literacy development has undergone important changes. Young children are now considered "linguistically and cognitively competent," with the ability to engage in learning and understanding the world around them through their own actions with external objects (Ferreiro & Teberosky, 1982, p. 12), and through social interactions that involve language and other communication tools available in a specific society (Berk & Winsler, 1995; Vygotsky, 1978). The term "emergent literacy" has been used in the last 20 years to describe the development in reading and writing that children experience before being able to read and write conventionally by exploring print widely available to them in literate societies.

As a result of the shift in perception of the child's ways of approaching the world, researchers have studied early literacy development from the child's perspective. Research from an emerging literacy perspective has shown that reading and writing in young children are intertwined and grow out of oral language competency (Teale, 1986a), and that young children are extremely interested in making sense of the world around them. Literacy is part of that world and part of that sense-making process. Thus, children start inquiring into print well before they receive formal instruction in reading and writing in school (Anderson & Stokes, 1984; Cochran-Smith, 1984; Ferreiro, 1986; Goelman, Oberg, & Smith, 1984; Teale & Sulzby, 1989). Actually, some children learn to read and write before going to school (Durkin, 1966). Children's exploration of print does not happen in a vacuum but rather depends on the functions and uses assigned to literacy in a specific society at a certain time and in the children's home (Cook-Gumperz, 1986; Heath, 1983; Leichter, 1984; Schieffelin & Gilmore, 1986); the children's interaction with more mature literates (John-Steiner, Panofsky, & Smith, 1994; Moll, 1990; Vygotsky, 1978); and finally the way young children are involved in the literacy activities going on at home and in the larger society (Anderson & Stokes, 1984; Szwed, 1981; Teale, 1986b).

Home Literacy Experiences

The importance of the family's role in the development of literacy has been pointed out by the extensive research on the characteristics of homes in relation to literacy promotion. Homes have been studied as the first place in which literacy begins. In addition, Burns, Griffin, and Snow (1999) point out that "the more children know about language and literacy before they arrive at school, the better equipped they are to succeed in reading" (p. 8).

Most research involved in studying home literacy experiences of young children (3 to 8 years of age) aimed to uncover the functions and uses of literacy, print, and writing materials available in these homes, the ways in which children explore print on their own, and the ways adults or mature literates socialize children into literacy. The studies used ethnographic methodology including participant observation that involves the researcher being in the home over a period of time, audiotaped interviews of family members and children when appropriate, videotaping or audiotaping both children's literacy activities and significant interactions between children and more mature literates, and collection of parents' and children's writing samples.

Functions and Uses of Literacy and Literacy Materials Available at Home

With regard to the functions and uses of literacy, the research indicates that literacy was part of the everyday lives of most families regardless of their economic level. The purposes of literacy and the types of literacy used depended on the practical problems that the families had to solve. Both middle-class families and families living below the poverty level used literacy to maintain relationships with relatives and friends; to gain information about local, state, and national events; to provide entertainment; to confirm facts or beliefs; to educate; to replace oral communication in situations where it was not feasible; or to establish and maintain social relationships. Low-income families also used literacy to deal with different public agencies such as welfare, school, and the court system and to improve their financial situation through the use of coupons, food stamps, advertisements for apartments, and funds for educational purposes (Heath, 1983; Rodríguez, 1995; Taylor, 1983; Taylor & Dorsey-Gaines, 1988).

There is much variability in the literacy artifacts available to young children and adults. Cochran-Smith (1984) found that the families of 15 children ranging in age from 3 to 5 years owned from 40 to more than 100 children's books. In addition, children's magazines and comic sections from newspapers were also available in these households. Some children had books that had belonged to older siblings or to their parents when they were children. They also received books as gifts, had their own bookshelves in their rooms, and often selected their own books. They played games based on storybook characters, watched TV or movie productions based on children's stories, and read the original stories both before and after watching these shows. In addition, parents regularly took their children to public libraries and encouraged them to select and borrow books that they would later read to them. A few children also attended public library story hours and film programs. Heath (1983) studied three communities in the Piedmont Carolines, namely, Roadville,

Trackton, and the townspeople. She reported that compared with the townspeople, there were few magazines in Trackton and Roadville (African American and European American working-class communities respectively) and only books related to the school or church. In the study I conducted in 1995 in New York City, I found that in the household in which the mother had higher formal education and more economic means, there were more books for adults and more books for children. However, in all three households studied, most books were related to school (textbooks, dictionaries, encyclopedias), and very few were children's books (Rodríguez, 1995). In addition, some of the literacy artifacts in these households were in Spanish, as was the case for several Mexican families in Teale's study (Teale, 1986b).

Although writing materials were available in virtually all families studied, in some of these families children had difficulties finding paper and pencil when they wanted to write, and in fact did not own these literacy materials until they started school (Rodríguez, 1999; Teale, 1986b).

Purcell-Gates (1995) studied the home literacy experiences of Donny, a child whose parents were illiterate. She reported that although there were books available in Donny's home, his parents did not read or write in front of their children, and on the rare occasions in which they tried to read to their children, they did it by interpreting the story based on the pictures.

Children's Exploration of Print

All studies reviewed in this chapter highlight the fact that children were very interested in learning about print. Thus, they initiated and organized their literacy activities when print was used in front of them and asked for help from more mature literates when needed. However, Purcell-Gates (1995) observed that the lack of exposure to print and its functions at home made 7-year-old Donny reluctant to use literacy materials such as pencils, papers, and crayons for any other purposes than making or doing things such as crafts. Donny enjoyed being read to and would dictate stories, but he did not try to read or write himself. Even when he was with other children who were engaged in literacy activities at the university's Literacy Center, he was reluctant to initiate reading or writing on his own.

In the longitudinal study conducted in New York City in the homes of three low-income young Dominican children (Rodríguez, 1995, 1999), it was found that because literacy is also a tool easily available nowadays in highly technological societies and permeates most human endeavors, children explored print while engaging in their daily activities, which included watching TV, listening to music, singing, and playing. The three participant children in the study, Virginia Suarez, Roberto

Martínez, and Jesús Vázquez were observed watching commercial television for extended periods of time. Although they all were nonreaders, this did not discourage them from being attentive to the screen when it was filled with print. A lot of print is usually involved in commercials, in general, and especially in commercials about cereals, toys, and music, which are very attractive to children. Questioning the children about what the print on television meant to them indicated that Virginia and Jesus called anything written on screen "numbers" and tried to make sense of the function or meaning of the marks on the screen based on their knowledge of the TV program and the image. This is similar to what the young nonreaders did in the study by Ferreiro and Teberosky (1982); they looked at the picture to make sense of the text presented to them.

It seems that the movies on TV, the commercials, and the songs may have helped the three young participants in my study to understand that print is meaningful, that print can be turned into sound, and that written language is different from oral language, concepts that other children learned through being read to (Clay, 1979; Smith, 1976, 1978; cited in Teale, 1981). Furthermore, watching TV may have helped them develop a sense of story by trying to understand who the characters were, what objects were involved, where and when the action took place, what the main events consisted of, why the event occurred, and what the consequences of the event were (Snow, Nathan, & Perlmann, 1985).

Music was highly valued in these families and listening to music was part of the entertainment in all the households, especially during weekends and holidays. The participant children enjoyed listening to and dancing *merengue*, traditional Dominican music, and were often observed singing the songs at the beginning and the end of soap operas and some commercials.

These children's oral language was indeed enriched by listening to music and singing, activities that were highly valued in their homes. Perhaps singing and listening to songs plays an important role in the development of vocabulary and the development of a schema of story, given the fact that songs sometimes have the format of a story. As Snow & Tabors (1993) point out, "oral forms of language are in some sense prior to literacy language" and "oral language skills are the basis for the development of written language skills for children" (p. 6).

Play may be defined as behavior that is pleasurable, has no extrinsic goals, is spontaneous and voluntary, and involves some active engagement on the part of the player (Garvey, 1990). Literacy was explored by the children in a playful manner in the observed homes. Most of the literacy events observed were initiated when someone or many persons in the room were using literacy artifacts to fulfill one of the many social needs, such as completing homework, paying bills, or reading mail. However, if play is defined as above, then most of the literacy activities in which Virginia, Jesús, and Roberto engaged were play.

Some literacy events were initiated when a pencil, a pen, crayons, a piece of paper, or a book were in the child's way. This was especially the case for Virginia, whose interaction with a literacy artifact seemed an exploration of a new toy, as when she found crayons on the floor and took them out, one by one, while scribbling on the piece of paper at hand. This was also the case when Virginia "read" the book *Clifford's Family*. Virginia appeared to explore "reading" as another game.

Most of the episodes in which Virginia, Jesús, and Roberto engaged in a literacy event with their mothers, siblings, or neighbors were spontaneous and voluntary because they were initiated by the targeted children. In addition, the literacy event actively engaged the children and had an element of enjoyment that was not present at other moments, such as when older children were doing their homework, and their work was not as good as their mothers would have liked.

Virginia, Jesús, and Roberto seemed to explore writing, reading, and numeracy through play more than using writing and reading in play activities. However, using print during play was observed when Roberto played the game of school with his friend Tomás and his sister's friend, Valeria, and on other occasions when he played school with his sister. Virginia and Jesús also played school, but they focused more on school behavior and would say things such as "you have to behave" and "you have to do what the teacher tells you to do"; consequently, literacy activities were very seldom involved (Rodríguez, 1995, 1999).

WAYS IN WHICH CHILDREN ARE SOCIALIZED INTO LITERACY

There were significant differences regarding the ways children were socialized into literacy. In general, mothers, siblings, neighbors, and friends interacted with young children through being role models, reading stories aloud to their children, and informally teaching them about literacy. Except for the family studied by Purcell-Gates (1995) in which both parents were illiterate, virtually all studies reported that children had the opportunity to see adults at home reading and writing to some extent. Reading and writing were used every day and for many different purposes (e.g., paying bills, reading mail, purchasing different goods, entertainment, and relationships with different social institutions), and the children observed their parents in their daily practices of literacy (Anderson & Stokes, 1984). However, only certain families involved their young children in those practices by answering children's questions about print, initiating activities around print, or mediating parents-children and children-children relationships through reading and writing, as was the case in the families studied by Cochran-Smith (1984), Heath (1982), and Taylor (1983).

A practice widely used in print-oriented families is reading aloud to children.[2] Cochran-Smith (1984), Heath (1983), and Taylor (1983) found that all children they studied were read to on a regular basis, in some cases as early as when they were 3 to 6 months old. As the children were growing up, both they and their parents initiated storyreading. Parents read stories to their children at different times of the day, with bedtime reading being the most consistent and frequent. Storyreading also took place at other moments during the day, especially when the child and one parent were alone together and after periods of active play. Parents provided books or tape recordings of texts for children to read or look at on their own during long auto trips. Parents reported that children looked at books by themselves as they chose to play with specific toys during the day. Storyreading was both a solitary activity done in their rooms and an activity shared with siblings and or parents.

This practice was not used in all households. Heath (1983), Miller, Nemoianu, and Dejong (1986), Purcell-Gates (1996), Rodríguez (1999), and Taylor and Dorsey-Gaines (1988) reported that although some families read aloud to their children until they were 5 years of age, most families did not read aloud to children, or this was not done consistently. Rodríguez (1995) found that only one family of the three studied engaged in literacy activities before going to sleep. However, the activity did not always involve reading but singing and praying as well. In addition, it seems that there are important differences in the ways in which others read to children. Mothers read to their children in basically the same way: mother and child sat next to each other or in some cases the child sat on the mother's lap. Mother reads, asks questions, and interacts with the child while reading. The patterns of interaction change over time and are different depending on the type of book read, social group, and socioeconomic status (Sulzby & Teale, 1991). Middle-class mothers often linked the information in the book to other experiences in the child's life, used more explicit positive feedback, and did not use the "Say X" kind of prompts widely used in working-class families (Heath, 1983; Miller, Nemoianu, & Dejong, 1986).

Families intervene in their children's literacy development by teaching them. Most families reported that the firstborn got more attention, whereas the following children were more influenced by their siblings. Literacy-oriented families do not teach reading and writing formally, especially when children are young. Parents believe that exposure to books and reading activities in the context of the children's everyday lives and routines and for a variety of purposes helped them to learn to read when they went to school. Thus, any formal teaching is incidental and usually only happens when requested by the child. Heath (1982) pointed out that these families informally teach at home a way of

---

[2]For a detailed review of research in book reading, see Klesius and Griffith (1996) and Teale (1987).

talking and taking from print that will be used later in school and in their jobs. In contrast, many families for whom print is not a way of life may start teaching reading and writing formally but not necessarily in the way it is done in schools. However, low-income families often focus on teaching the mechanics of literacy (letters, sounds) but not the uses of literacy.

Developmentally Appropriate Practice

Developmentally appropriate practice alludes to the design of safe learning environments for young children that promote child development and learning in all domains (physical, language, cognition, social, and emotional) based on our knowledge of how children develop and learn, the individual needs and characteristics of the child, and the social and cultural contexts in which the development takes place, while taking into consideration the needs and preferences of the families (Bredekamp & Copple, 1996, pp. 8-9).

The review of literature presented in this chapter indicates that although most children come to school with some kind of exposure to print, the type, intensity, and quality of experiences of each specific child varies widely. Adams (1990) pointed out that most children from print-oriented families come to school at age 6 with at least 3,500 hours of experience with print such as storybook reading, watching *Sesame Street*, and participating in language and reading/writing activities at home. Children from families in which "reading and writing are peripheral and peripherally valued activities" (p. 87) had only about 25 hours of storybook experience and 200 hours of other literacy events (p. 89). These data may explain why certain children find reading and writing a difficult endeavor. However, teachers still need to make sure that all their students learn to read and write, and a developmentally appropriate practice recommends that children be treated differently based on their needs and previous experiences.

Research on home literacy experiences, developmentally appropriate practice, and emergent literacy indicate that in order to be successful with students who may encounter difficulty learning to read and write, teachers have to work on several fronts at the same time. High-quality literacy programs have to include not only effective literacy instruction in the classroom but parental and community involvement as well.

EFFECTIVE LITERACY INSTRUCTION

High-quality instruction is essential especially when teaching children who did not have home exposure to the language and literacy used in school or who have any of the characteristics that make reading and writing a difficult task. The International Reading Association and The National Association for the Education of Young Children (NAEYC, 1998) in a position statement about early reading pointed out that "no one teaching method or approach is likely to be the most effective for all children. Rather, good teachers bring into play a variety of teaching strategies that can encompass the great diversity of children in schools" (p. 38). Therefore, it seems that in order to be able to use the strategies adequate to the needs of the children in the classroom, it is of paramount importance to know what learning experiences each child brings to school.

The studies reviewed here provide useful information for the classroom teacher interested in learning about young children's early literacy experiences. However, because each child's experience is different, teachers have to arrive in the classroom with an inquiring attitude that allows them to ask questions and find answers. Thus, the first task should be to learn about how literacy is defined and used at home and in which ways the child was involved in home literacy events. Purcell-Gates (1995) pointed out that "when we seek to understand learners, we must seek to understand the cultural contexts within which they have developed, learned to interpret who they are in relation to others, and learned how to process, interpret or decode, their world" (p. 5). This undertaking can be approached in a number of ways—that is, by observing the students; asking questions informally to children, parents, and family members; visiting the homes of the students; interviewing parents, caregivers, siblings, or significant others; and reading research that focuses on children's home learning experiences.[3] This knowledge will allow the teacher to provide individualized instruction based on what each specific child knows and does not know about print.

---

[3]Ferdman (1990, pp. 197-198) suggested the following guiding questions in our search for understanding the student's literacy background:

a. How is literacy defined in the individual's group, and what is its significance? What behaviors are included in this definition?
b. What significance do particular texts have for the individual's cultural identity?
c. How do a particular pedagogical approach, the texts that are used, and the purpose of literacy as communicated by the school relate to the learner's motives and the sense of identity (and more subtly, what messages does a reading and writing curriculum communicate about the value of the learner's culture)?
d. What relationship does the learner perceive between the tasks assigned in school and his or her cultural identity? Must the learner change the nature of his or her self-concept in order to do what is asked?

Although children come to school at different ages and with different strengths and needs regarding literacy, they all have to become readers and writers. To attain this goal, instruction in school has to focus on two elements: the mechanics of reading and reading for meaning and fluency (Burns, Griffin, & Snow, 1999, p. 62).

The Mechanics of Reading

Children start the process of learning about literacy very early in life. Often they learn first about the functions and uses of literacy as they observe adults reading and writing for various purposes. They also have to understand the conventions that govern written language such as directionality, left to right, top to bottom, spaces between words, and punctuation. In addition, they have to learn the letters of the alphabet; acquire knowledge about the different sounds in words (phonological awareness) such as the common and different sounds in words such as "big" and "bag," or "moon," "soon," and "noon"; and understand that there is a relationship between those sounds and letters or combinations of letters (alphabetic principle) (Strickland, 1998).

There are basically two approaches to teaching the alphabetic principle. They are popularly called phonics and whole language. Strickland (1998) called them more appropriately the "systematic, intensive, code-driven phonics" and "holistic, embedded, meaning-driven approaches." Advocates of the former focus "on phonics that is highly sequenced, skills or code-driven, and initiated early in the child's schooling. Children begin by learning about the parts of the words and build toward whole words. Correct identification and automaticity of response is stressed" (p. 48). Advocates of the latter approach provide phonics lessons in the context of meaningful reading and writing while stressing the child's construction of meaning. Performance-based assessment is the preferred way to monitor student's progress (Snow, Burns, & Griffin, 1998, p. 199).

Strickland (1998) pointed out that whole language, integrated language arts, and literature-based curricula are often considered synonymous. However, although they all share "emphasis on writing and its relation to reading, greater use of trade books, increased attention to the integration of the language arts and greater reliance on informal classroom assessment, implementation and adherence to various philosophies varies widely from teacher to teacher" (p. 49). She also points out that the differences between phonics and holistic approaches are often not clear cut because teachers who adhere to the phonics philosophy used strategies typically considered holistic and vice versa. Some schools and districts decide what concepts to teach, when and how to teach them, as well as what materials will be used. However, the success of the program will depend largely on the teacher's ability to understand the students' needs and to adapt the program accordingly. In addition, regardless of the approach used, teachers are responsible for the classroom organization in terms of space and time and have to be able to use the following strategies considered effective in developing literacy in the early years.

Providing a literacy-rich environment in the classroom that promotes language development in all its forms—listening, speaking, reading, and writing—is essential. Children develop language in an atmosphere of success, one that is largely child centered, used for meaningful purposes, and presented as a whole system (Strickland & Taylor, 1989, cited in Greenberg, 1998a).

Providing a classroom environment that encourages the use of literacy at all times, not only during circle time or the language arts block time, but during play time as well is also necessary. This means designing the classroom with play centers such as a post office, a veterinarian office, an office, and adequate props that promote literacy (Morrow, 1989; Morrow & Rand, 1991; Newman & Roskos, 1990, 1992).

Classrooms need to be equipped with literacy materials such as pencils, paper, books, crayons, and other literacy artifacts not only in the library or the writing area, but also in the kitchen area, the block area, and the sciences area. Given the fact that the presence of literacy materials seems to trigger literacy activities, the availability of the materials will encourage the exploration of reading and writing (Rodríguez, 1999).

The classroom needs to be equipped with a variety of fiction and nonfiction books for children that address at least the different languages and cultures of the students within that classroom as well as their interests. The teacher may need to have a classroom lending library and start a bookstore in the school, depending on the quantity and quality of books owned by the students in the classroom and the books provided by the school.[4] Generally, families living in the inner city do not own many books for children.

Adults in the classroom should be role models for the students. They should read and write in front of the students and tell them how much they enjoy literacy. This may be a way of promoting interest and the joy of reading.

Teachers should read aloud daily to the whole class, in small groups, and if it is possible, one-on-one. There is abundant research showing that interactive storybook reading promotes children's knowledge about print, develops vocabulary and children's sense of story as well as children's interest in books and learning to read (Hiebert & Raphael, 1998; Klesius & Griffith, 1996; Morrow, 1993; Strickland &

---

[4]For ideas about how to manage a classroom lending library and a bookstore in your school, see Enz and Searfoss (1996) and Winik (1998).

Taylor, 1989; Snow, Burns, & Griffin, 1998).[5] This is especially important when the students do not have the experience of being read to at home.

In the longitudinal study reviewed here, it was found that children organized their own literacy activities and were living in an environment in which many events were happening at the same time. These young children were encouraged to focus on more than one event at the same time. Thus, it may be that these children need to explore more than one event at a time in school. Group work and having more autonomy in organizing their space and time may help these young children develop literacy skills.

Teachers need to use all means available to mediate literacy including television, computers, and the Internet. As Newman (1991) pointed out, "if children's ability to acquire literacy is said to be based on their prior knowledge, their conceptual understanding of language, and their uses of a variety of strategies, then there might be many paths to that goal, some of which may actually lie outside the printed page" (p. 195). Television, computers, and the Internet are here to stay and should be considered resources that both enhance literacy and are enhanced by advanced literacy knowledge. Following the same line of thought, Flood and Lapp (1995) suggested that television can be used to develop communication skills, interest in stories, and background information as well as to enhance second language instruction. Children's literacy learning should be assessed often in order to modify instruction and switch to more appropriate teaching practices if needed (Greenberg, 1998b; Torgesen, 1998).

Reading with Comprehension and Fluency

Students learning to read are expected to be able to read increasingly more difficult texts with understanding, talk about them, and relate the ideas encountered in books to their own lives and to other texts. This challenging task involves having a good vocabulary, good command of the linguistic structures of the text, and the ability to reflect on the ideas presented in a text. This can be fostered by involving the students in a variety of experiences, for meaningful and culturally sound purposes, across the curriculum, in order to develop the vocabulary and understanding of the world that they find in books (NAEYC, 1998).[6]

---

[5]There is a wealth of literature on different approaches to reading aloud to children in school and at home and how to teach parents to read aloud. See among others Ada (1988), Cochran-Smith (1986), Dickinson (1994), and Morrow (1995).

[6]The following articles and books provide lists of activities for children based on age: Burns et al. (1999), Greenberg (1998a, 1998b), and NAEYC (1998). The NAEYC presents a continuum of children's development in early reading

Fluency is attained when children are encouraged to use reading and writing in multiple contexts with teachers and peers. Teachers have to provide children with time in which they can read and write independently and with peers for a variety of meaningful purposes with different degrees of sophistication according to their age and experience with print (Greenberg, 1998b; Hiebert & Raphael, 1998; Morrow, 1993).[7]

Parental and Community Involvement

We know that parents play an important role in their child's literacy development. Thus, it is essential to recruit the parents' support in the school's effort to develop successful readers and writers. The following are some research based activities used in successful reading programs.

Teachers can encourage not only parents but also other people involved with the child such as caregivers, siblings, extended family, or neighbors to include their children in literacy activities. They can provide them examples of how young children may participate in their everyday language and literacy activities. (See suggestions offered in Enz & Searfoss, 1996; Greenberg, 1998a, pp. 75-76; Rodríguez, 1999.)

Teachers can share with parents what they do in the classroom regarding literacy, explain the activities and their goals, and brainstorm with them ways in which teachers and parents can work together to support home and school efforts (Enz, 1995).

Teachers can discuss with parents how to involve the community in the classroom, and invite parents, community members, and older students to come to the classroom, read their favorite story, and share how they use reading and writing in their jobs (Enz & Searfoss, 1996).

Teachers can discuss with parents the literacy materials available at home for their children and talk about ways to get other materials that they may need in their community, as well as how to share books with children in the classroom.

Teachers can ask their colleagues what they do to involve their parents in their children's literacy development.

They can get information about family literacy programs from the community and encourage parents in their classroom to get involved.

---

and writing from preschool to third grade; Burns et al. includes accomplishments and activities for children from birth to third grade.

[7]Snow, Burns, and Griffin (1998) present a review of promising strategies in developing comprehension skills and fluency.

CONCLUSION

Literacy is a social enterprise; it was originated by human beings in need of communication and is probably best learned in meaningful and authentic contexts. Today in highly technological societies, print permeates television, computer devices, and most human endeavors. Therefore, most children come to school with some kinds of experiences with print, although not always the type of experiences that the school expects and values.

Successfully teaching all children to read and write regardless of previous literacy experiences involves building on each child's home literacy traditions and experiences and providing high-quality instruction that capitalizes not only on the traditional materials used to teach literacy but also on all technologies available today, such as television, computers, and the Internet. In addition, schools, parents, and community must come together to achieve this goal rather than seeking to assign blame to teachers, parents, or the community. As the Learning First Alliance (1998) states, "if early reading were as high a priority in our society as, say, space exploration was in the 1960s, there is little question that early reading failure could be virtually eliminated" (p. 63).

APPENDIX A

Suggested Activities for Teachers/Activities that Facilitate Emerging Literacy

The activities listed below include some exemplar activities for pre- and inservice teachers and others for teacher educators in their work with teacher candidates.

Keep a journal for a week/day of the functions and uses of literacy in your life and the environmental print that you take for granted.

Interview a mother from each of the ethnic groups present in your classroom about ways literacy is used at home and whether children are involved and how.

Interview your students in order to know their perceptions of what print is all about, functions and uses of literacy at home, and ideas of how to use literacy in their daily lives in school.

Ask the students to do an ethnographic study to find out how print is used in their communities. Ethnographies will engage children in student-directed groups that use language in all forms (listening, speaking, reading, and writing) in order to collect and analyze data and reflect on issues that affect them as students, sons or daughters, and members of the larger community.

Design activities in the classroom that capitalize on what you have learned about children's home literacy experiences.

Write about what you expect your students to know about print when you start the new school year in September. If a child does not have that knowledge, do you assume that he/she does not know anything about literacy?

Interview your students about their favorite games and TV programs. Give examples of ways to use their favorite games and TV programs to develop literacy.

Use homework to make your students think about what they watch on TV or learn on the Internet.

Ask your students to write a literacy autobiography and reflect on their experiences learning to read and write.

REFERENCES

Ada, A. F. (1988.) The Pajaro Valley experience: Working with Spanish-speaking parents to develop children's reading and writing skills through the use of children's literature. In T. Skutnabb-Kangas & J. Cummins (Eds.), *Minority education: From shame to struggle* (pp. 223-238). Philadelphia: Multilingual Matters.

Adams, M. (1990.) *Beginning to read: Thinking and learning about print.* Cambridge, MA: The MIT Press.

Anderson, A., & Stokes, S. (1984). Social and institutional influences on the development and practice of literacy. In H. Goelman, A. Oberg, & F. Smith (Eds.), *Awakening to literacy* (pp. 24-37). Portsmouth, NH: Heinemann Educational Books.

Berk, L. E., & Winsler, A. (1995). *Scaffolding children's learning: Vygotsky and early childhood education.* Washington, DC: National Association for the Education of Young Children.

Bredekamp, S., & Copple, C. (1997). *Developmentally appropriate practice in early childhood programs.* Washington, DC: National Association for the Education of Young Children.

Burns, S., Griffin, P., & Snow, C. (Eds.). (1999). *Starting out right. A guide to promoting children's reading success.* Washington, DC: National Academy Press.

Clay, M. (1979). *Reading: The patterning of complex behavior* (2nd ed.). Auckland, New Zealand: Heinemann Educational.

Cochran-Smith, M. (1984). *The making of a reader.* Norwood, NJ: Ablex.

Cochran-Smith, M. (1986). Reading to children: A model for understanding texts. In B. Schieffelin & P. Gilmore (Eds.), *The acquisition of literacy: Ethnographic perspectives* (pp. 35-54). Norwood, NJ: Ablex.

Cook-Gumperz, J. (Ed.). (1986). *The social construction of literacy*. New York: Cambridge University Press.

Donahue, P., Voelkl, K., Campbell, J. R., & Mazzeo, J. (1999). *The NAEP 1998 reading report card for the nation and the states*. Washington, DC: U.S. Department of Education. Office of Educational Research and Improvement. National Center for Education Statistics. Publication #1999500.

Dickinson, D. K. (Ed.). (1994). *Bridges to literacy. Children, families and schools*. Cambridge, MA: Blackwell.

Durkin, D. (1966). *Children who read early*. New York: Teachers College Press.

Enz, B. (1995). Strategies for promoting parental support for emergent literacy programs. *The Reading Teacher, 49*(2), 168-170.

Enz B., & Searfoss L. W. (1996). Expanding our views of family literacy. *The Reading Teacher, 49*(7), 576-579.

Ferdman, B.M. (1990). Literacy and cultural identity. *Harvard Educational Review, 60*, 181-204.

Ferreiro, E. (1986). The interplay between information and assimilation in beginning literacy. In W. H. Teale & E. Sulzby (Eds.), *Emergent literacy: Writing and reading* (pp. 15-49). Norwood, NJ: Ablex.

Ferreiro, E., & Teberosky, A. (1982). *Literacy before schooling*. Portsmouth, NH: Heineman Educational Books.

Flood, J., & Lapp, D. (1995). Television and reading: Refocusing the debate. *The Reading Teacher, 49*(2), 160-163.

Garvey, C. (1990). *Play* (2nd ed.). Cambridge, MA: Harvard University Press.

Goelman, H., Oberg, A., & Smith, F. (1984). *Awakening to literacy*. Portsmouth, NH: Heineman Educational Books.

Greenberg, P. (1998a). Warmly and calmly teaching young children to read, write, and spell: Thoughts about the first four of twelve well-known principles. Part 2. *Young Children, 53*(5), 68-82.

Greenberg, P. (1998b). Thinking about goals for grownups and young children while we teach writing, reading and spelling (and a few thoughts about the "J" word). Part 3. *Young Children, 53*(6), 31-42.

Heath, S. B. (1982). What no bedtime story means: Narrative skills at home and school. *Language in Society, 11*, 49-74.

Heath, S. B. (1983). *Ways with words*. New York: Cambridge University Press.

Hiebert, E. H., & Raphael, T.E. (1998). *Early literacy instruction*. Fort Worth, TX: Harcourt Brace.

John-Steiner, V., Panofsky, C., & Smith, L. (Eds.). (1994). *Sociocultural approaches to language and literacy*. New York: Cambridge University Press.

Klesius, J. P., & Griffith, P. L. (1996). Interactive storybook reading for at-risk learners. *The Reading Teacher, 49*(7), 552-560.

Learning First Alliance. (1998). Every child reading. *American Educator, 22*, 52-63.

Leichter, H. (1984). Families as environments for literacy. In H. Goelman, A. Oberg, & F. Smith (Eds.), *Awakening to literacy* (pp. 38-50). Portsmouth, NH: Heineman Educational Books.

Miller, P., Nemoianu, A., & Dejong, J. (1986). Early reading at home: Its practice and meanings in a working-class community. In B. Schieffelin & P. Gilmore (Eds.), *The acquisition of literacy: Ethnographic perspectives* (pp. 3-15). Norwood, NJ: Ablex.

Moll, L. (Ed.). (1990). *Vygotsky and education: Instructional implications and application of sociohistorical psychology*. New York: Cambridge University Press.

Morrow, L. M. (1989). *Literacy development in the early years: Helping children read and write*. Englewood Cliffs, NJ: Prentice-Hall.

Morrow, M. (1993). *Literacy development in the early years*. Boston: Allyn & Bacon.

Morrow, L. M. (Ed.). (1995). *Family literacy. Connections in schools and communities*. Newark, DE: The International Reading Association.

Morrow, L., & Rand, M. (1991). Preparing the classroom environment to promote literacy during play. In J. F. Christie (Ed.), *Play and early literacy development* (pp. 141-165). Albany: State University of New York Press.

National Association for the Education of Young Children. (1998). Learning to read and write: Developmentally appropriate practices for young children. *Young Children, 53*(4), 30-46.

Newman, S. (1991). *Literacy in the television age: The myth of the TV effect*. Norwood, NJ: Ablex.

Newman, S., & Roskos, K. (1990). The influence of literacy-enriched play centers on preschoolers' conceptions of the functions of print. In S. McCormick & J. Zutell (Eds.), *Literacy theory and research. Analyses from multiple paradigms* (pp. 167-187). Chicago: National Reading Conference.

Newman, S., & Roskos, K. (1992). Literacy objects as cultural tools: Effects on children's literacy behaviors in play. *Reading Research Quarterly, 27*(3), 203-225.

Purcell-Gates, V. (1995). *Other people's words. The cycle of low literacy*. Cambridge, MA: Harvard University Press.

Purcell-Gates, V. (1996). Stories, coupons, and the *TV Guide*: Relationships between home literacy experiences and emergent literacy knowledge. *Reading Research Quarterly, 3*(4), 406-428.

Rodríguez, M. V. (1995). *Home literacy events in three Dominican families with young children*. Unpublished doctoral dissertation, Teachers College, Columbia University, New York.

Rodríguez, M. V. (1999). Home literacy experiences of three young Dominican children in New York City: Implications for teaching in urban settings. *Educators for Urban Minorities: Working Papers, 1*, 19-31.

Schieffelin, B., & Gilmore, P. (Eds.). (1986). *The acquisition of literacy: Ethnographic perspectives*. Norwood, NJ: Ablex .

Smith, F. (1976). Learning to read by reading. *Language Arts, 53*(2), 297-322.

Smith, F. (1978). *Understanding reading* (2nd ed.). New York: Holt, Rinehart & Winston.

Snow, C., Burns, S., & Griffin, P. (Eds.). (1998). *Preventing reading difficulties in young children*. Washington, DC: National Academy Press.

Snow, C., Nathan, D., & Perlmann R. (1985). Assessing children's knowledge about book reading. In L. Galda & A. Pellegrini (Eds.), *Play, language and stories: The development of children's literate behavior* (pp. 167-181). Norwood, NJ: Ablex.

Snow, C., & Tabors, P. (1993). Language skills that relate to literacy development. In B. Spodek & O. Saracho, (Eds.), *Language and literacy in early childhood education* (pp. 1-20). New York: Teachers College Press.

Strickland, D. S. (1998). *Teaching phonics today. A primer for educators*. Newark, DE: International Reading Association.

Strickland, D., & Taylor D. (1989). Family storybook reading: Implications for children, families and curriculum. In D. Strickland & L. Morrow (Eds.), *Emerging literacy: Young children* (pp. 4-16). Newark, DE: International Reading Association.

Sulzby, E., & Teale W. H. (1991). Emergent literacy. In R. Barr, M. L. Kamil, & D. Pearson (Eds.), *Handbook of reading research* (Vol. 2, pp. 727-757). New York: Longman.

Szwed, J. F. (1981). The ethnography of literacy. In M. F. Whiteman (Ed.), *Writing: The nature, development, and teaching of written communication* (pp. 13-23). Hillsdale, NJ: Erlbaum.

Taylor, D. (1983). *Family literacy: Young children learning to read and write*. Portsmouth, NH: Heineman Educational Books.

Taylor, D., & Dorsey-Gaines, C. (1988). *Growing up literate: Learning from inner-city families*. Portsmouth, NH: Heineman Educational Books.

Teale, W. H. (1981). Parents reading to their children. *Language Arts, 58*(8), 902-912.

Teale, W. H. (1986a). The beginnings of reading and writing: Written language development during the preschool and kindergarten years. In M. R. Sampson (Ed.), *The pursuit of literacy. Early reading and writing* (pp. 1-29). Dubuque, IA: Kendall Hunt.

Teale, W. H. (1986b). Home background and young children's literacy development. In W. H. Teale & E. Sulzby (Eds.), *Emergent literacy: Writing and reading* (pp. 173-206). Norwood, NJ: Ablex.

Teale, W. H. (1987). Emergent literacy: Reading and writing development in early childhood. *National Reading Conference Yearbook, 36*, 45-74.

Teale, W. H., & Sulzby, E. (1989). Emergent literacy: New perspectives. In D. Strickland & L. Morrow (Eds.), *Emerging literacy: Young children* (pp. 4-16). Newark, DE: International Reading Association.

Torgesen, J. (1998). Catch them before they fall. *American Educator, 22*(1 and 2), 32-41.

Vygotsky, L. (1978). *Mind in society. The development of higher psychological processes.* Cambridge, MA: Harvard University Press.

Winik, L.M. (1998). The little bookstore that grew to a thousand. *American Educator, 22*(1 and 2), 32-41.

Ten

Best Practices in Teaching Urban Second-Language Learners

Joye Smith

Urban centers remain the largest draw for the more than one million immigrants and their children coming to the United States every year in search of a better life (Peyton & Adger, 1998). While the overall number of school-aged children grew by 39% from 1980-1990, the number of English as a second language (ESL or L2)[1] learners grew by 83% during

[1]L2 is the abbreviation I will use for second language, L1 for the native language. I have chosen the term ESL because it is more positive than the term Limited English Proficient (LEP), which focuses on what students lack. The term English Language Development (ELD), also used in some studies, is too easily confused with the term Learning Disabled (LD) which most ESL students are not. English language learners (ELL) is used as well, but this term fails to distinguish adequately between native and nonnative speakers of English. ESL is often contrasted with English as a foreign language (EFL), taught in non-English speaking countries. The teaching of ESL and EFL students is generally known as Teaching English to Speakers of Other Languages (TESOL).

the same period ("Numbers of school-agers," 1993). ESL students hail from dozens of countries and language groups and represent a range of prior schooling, English proficiency, and socioeconomic privilege. Urban teachers, regardless of their subject of expertise, will probably encounter second-language learners sometime during their careers and need to know how to respond effectively to the challenges they present. This chapter will describe best practices in teaching urban second language learners, identifying what pre- and inservice teachers need to know and be able to do to foster these students' academic success. The chapter covers six areas: the student as a member of a culture, community, and family; the student as a second language learner; successful classroom practices; instruction of oral skills; literacy instruction; and assessment.

THE STUDENT AS A MEMBER OF A CULTURE, COMMUNITY, AND FAMILY

Culture is typically thought of as *high culture*—classical literature, art, and music—or reduced to isolated artifacts (piñatas and sombreros to represent Mexican culture). However, culture is not merely artifacts or even group behaviors. It is the standards shared by a group of people for thinking, feeling, acting, and judging the world around them (Goodenough, 1971). Shared cultural values provide the sense of belonging, security, and identity essential to socialization. They also form the basis of language and communication (Hamers & Blanc, 1989). When cultures, values, and languages mix, as when ESL learners enter the urban classroom, conflict and isolation can result. Some children, for example, may not be accustomed to a question-answer learning style. Others are used to learning from older peers and have little experience interacting with adults (McLaughlin, 1992). As a result of these cultural and experiential differences, ESL students' behavior may puzzle or even frustrate the teacher.

Rather than assign values or labels based on their own cultural lens, however, teachers can observe the students, learn from their interactional patterns, and become sensitive to these patterns in their teaching. This is not to deny the importance of students learning appropriate classroom behaviors for a U.S. setting, but instead to affirm the need to build new behaviors and values upon the old. Obviously, developing awareness and flexibility is particularly challenging for teachers when the students come from diverse cultures, but it can provide enormous academic support. One example, described by Au and Mason (1981), is from classrooms with native Hawaiian children. In the Hawaiian community, it is customary to tell narratives in small groups of speakers who take overlapping turns—that is, who talk while the other speaker is talking. When Hawaiian children go to school, they learn more and tell stories more coherently when their teachers allow them to do some familiar overlapping turn-taking, rather than rigidly adhering to the "one person talking at a time" rule.

Understanding and valuing the students' background also helps build bridges to one of the best sources of support for ESL students—the family and community. Cooperation between school and home increases emotional support for children (Comer, 1984) and improves attendance and behavior (Rich, Van Dien, & Mallox, 1979). The family can provide the teacher information about the student's prior education, personal interests, health status, immigration experience (if the student was born elsewhere), home languages, and family situation (with whom the student lives, who speaks English at home, what their housing situation is, whether they are in the U.S. permanently, etc.) (Walter, 1996). Family involvement is vital to academic success among language minority groups, regardless of parents' fluency in English.

How can teachers foster a closer relationship with the families of ESL students? Providing early morning or evening conferences, having translators and child care available during the conferences, giving parents native-language materials to use at home, and offering parent education classes can all help build strong links between home and school (Violand-Sanchez, Sutton, & Ware, 1991). Teachers can also support parents by inviting them to the classroom as guest experts on their culture, affirming the family structure and discipline practices, and encouraging first-language development. They can help parents tap into the resources provided by community organizations: translators, legal advocates, cultural information, English classes for parents, and after school and summer programs (Walter, 1996). They can recognize that though most of these parents are committed to their children's education, many are unable to participate in school in traditional ways because of long working hours, culture shock, or language barriers (Violand-Sanchez, Sutton, & Ware, 1991). Teachers should value and support the full range of ways that parents can be involved: (a) providing for children's basic needs, (b) communicating with school staff, (c) volunteering at their child's school, (d) participating in learning activities with their children at home, and (e) participating in governance and advocacy (Epstein, 1986).

THE STUDENT AS A SECOND LANGUAGE LEARNER

ESL students must do more than cope with unfamiliar cultural routines; they must also learn a new system of phonetics (and sometimes a new writing system), syntax, semantics, pragmatics, and sociocultural patterns. They need challenging material in order to succeed academically, but they also need assistance in accessing that material.

Sometimes regular ESL students are misplaced in special education classes where expectations of success are low, or they are assigned uncertified, inexperienced teachers. Alternately, they may simply be expected to keep up with monolingual English students without special assistance. For teachers who have never lived in another culture and learned another language, understanding the immense difficulty of the task these students face may give insight into why they need assistance and what kind is most helpful.

ESL students, in fact, have two difficult tasks before them: they must learn to communicate in the new language, and they must acquire academic and cognitive skills in that new language. Cummins (1981) describes Basic Interpersonal Communication Skills (BICS) as the prototypically oral language used to facilitate social relationships, and Cognitive Academic Language Proficiency (CALP) as proficiency in the academic uses of the language. BICS are used in context-embedded, cognitively easy tasks such as having a conversation, learning survival vocabulary, or playing simple games. CALP, in contrast, is used to process context-reduced and cognitively difficult tasks such as taking standardized tests, solving math word problems, or understanding written academic texts. As learners develop BICS, they may seem fluent and may even be placed in mainstream classes. However, these same learners may lack depth of conceptualization and vocabulary in CALP and need continued support if they are to succeed. Full cognitive development in the L2 may take from five to seven years (Cummins, 1979) or even ten years for students with no prior schooling in the native language (Collier, 1987).

One critical support to L2 learning is, paradoxically, strengthening the L1 and valuing it as a medium of learning (Hamers & Blanc, 1989). The explanation for this is that CALP is built upon BICS. If children have not yet developed communicative skills in English but already have a communicative repertoire and emergent literacy in the L1, then it is more efficient for them to continue to develop academic and literacy skills in the L1 while English communicative and literacy skills are catching up. Moreover, concepts and strategies learned in one language have been found to transfer into subsequently learned languages and vice-versa (Gale, McClay, Christie, & Harris, 1981; Skutnabb-Kangas & Toukomaa, 1976; Vorih & Rosier, 1978). In fact, the best predictor of second language literacy skill is first language literacy skill (Ramirez, Yuen, Ramey, Pasta, & Billings, 1991; Thomas & Collier, 1996). Collier and Thomas (1999), in a seventeen-year study of over one million ESL students, concluded that the optimal program serving their needs develops full L1 and L2 academic proficiency. Greene's (1998) meta-analysis confirmed that ESL students taught simultaneously in their L1 performed significantly better on standardized tests than those taught in English only.

How exactly do students progress in the L2? Researchers have found that L2 learners go through a series of intermediate stages, referred to as the *interlanguage* (Selinker, 1972). At each stage, learners are operating from a particular set of language rules based on their imperfect knowledge of the language at that moment in time. The rules are internally consistent, but some are incorrect. Similar to other types of learning, growth in the L2 occurs as new structures are learned, overgeneralized, fine-tuned, and then incorporated into some final version. When the final version of the rules falls short of L2 native speaker competence, students are said to be *fossilized* (Selinker, 1972), a process believed to occur when the learner is sufficiently fluent to communicate but does not sound like a native speaker (Schumann, 1978). Giving students positive affective feedback (I like you as a person) and negative cognitive feedback (but I don't understand what you mean) can help them break out of fossilization by forcing them to refine syntactic accuracy (Vigil & Oller, 1976).

What distinguishes second language learning from other types of learning is its extraordinary complexity. Growth in the L2 is related, in as yet poorly understood ways, to learner-external factors (L2 input, output, and interaction; the relative markedness[2] of L1 and L2 grammatical forms; the social context of learning; and social perceptions of the L1 and L2 communities) and learner-internal factors (L1 transfer interacting with L2 development, communication strategies, knowledge of linguistic universals, motivation, and age[3]) (Ellis, 1994).

CLASSROOM STRATEGIES FOR ESL STUDENTS

The teacher of ESL students must take particular care in making instruction understandable and must foster high levels of both language and content learning. Five key classroom strategies have been identified: (1) comprehensible language input and scaffolding, (2) instruction about form embedded in meaningful language, (3) cooperative learning, (4) sheltered content instruction, and (5) thematic units. Because these strategies also constitute good teaching for all students, they can be easily implemented in a mixed ESL/native speaker classroom.

In contrast to the grammar syllabus of medieval language instruction or the drills of the 1950s and 1960s, drawn from behaviorism, the Natural Approach (Krashen, 1982; Krashen & Terrell, 1983)

---

[2]The more marked a feature is linguistically, the more unusual and the less basic it is. "He broke my heart" is more marked than "He broke a cup" (Ellis, 1994, p. 713).

[3]There is debate as to whether second languages can be fully learned after age 12 (see Ellis, 1994, for a discussion).

describes second language acquisition as occurring when learners understand language input in natural communication settings. This comprehensible input, according to Krashen's hypothesis, must be somewhat beyond students' current competence and is made comprehensible through prior knowledge, realia (real world objects), context, gestures, visuals, and scaffolding, a notion derived from Vygotsky's (1978) zone of proximal development (ZPD). The ZPD is the symbolic distance between what children can do on their own and what they can do with assistance from an adult or more proficient peer. Scaffolding for ESL students could be simple and concrete, such as routines, repetitions, a stable physical environment, and rules of behavior, or it could be more sophisticated such as an interactive writing journal, an instructional conversation, or literature study circles (Peregoy & Boyle, 1997; Tharp & Gallimore, 1988).

Although most researchers would agree that understandable, meaningful exposure to the L2 is vital, Krashen's theories have been criticized for inadequate explanation of comprehensible input, little attention paid to the importance of output, especially in the feedback it provides for syntactic accuracy (Swain, 1985), and an inadequate view of the role of teaching grammar. In contrast to the Natural Approach, recent research supports teachers giving immediate, focused feedback (e.g., by verbally recasting the form correctly for the student), as long as the central focus remains on communication of meaning, the feedback is given only in informal settings (not, for example, during a formal presentation), and teachers do not overdo the corrections (Doughty & Varela, 1998). In addition, teachers might make note of error patterns, particularly those that interfere with communication, which can then be revisited in mini-lessons. The lessons must do more than label native speaker intuitions: they must demonstrate how the structure functions in syntax and give abundant practice in the context of real language (Harklau, 1994).

In addition to the teacher's providing meaningful language, accompanied by some focused attention to form, students can benefit from *cooperative learning groups* with their peers (Slavin, 1995). The academic and social benefits for native speakers also apply to ESL students: cognitively complex discussions of real problems, peer scaffolding, individualization of instruction, high motivation, positive affective climate, and improvement of the quality of student talk (Long, 1990). In large urban classes, where teacher-individual student interaction may be limited, cooperative groups can provide ESL students key opportunities to negotiate language: asking for clarification, disagreeing, getting additional information, and questioning. Calderón, Hertz-Lazarowitz, and Slavin (1998) found that third grade students participating in cooperative bilingual classrooms were significantly more likely to meet exit criteria in reading and language than comparison students. Like all students, ESL students will need modeling and instruction on appropriate ways to relate to one another, give one another feedback, work together on a project, locate resource materials together, resolve conflict, and evaluate themselves. What if many or all students are from the same native language? Although teachers should plan tasks that elicit maximum use of the L2, a rigid no L1 attitude is counterproductive, because L1 use among peers to explain vocabulary and procedures may serve as a scaffold for weaker students (Peregoy & Boyle, 1997).

Sheltered English or Specially Designed Academic Instruction in English (SDAIE) (California SDE, 1994) is another strategy that provides a bridge between native language and mainstream content instruction for intermediate ESL students, provides access to mainstream curriculum for students at various levels of English but who do not have L1 content instruction, and further develops academic English proficiency. There are two steps in SDAIE: first, selection of materials appropriate to ESL students and second, making the material accessible through modified teaching techniques, gradually removing the extra support until the student can learn unassisted. Appropriate material is characterized by comprehensibility, text supports (visuals, diagram, captions), the same high quality of information as mainstream texts, and appeal to learners. An example of making content material accessible is Short's (1993) study of the language used in regular social studies classes (technical vocabulary, concepts, language functions, text structure, and syntax), which culminated in two integrated language/social studies units on American and world history for ESL students (Short, Mahrer, Elfin, Liten-Tejada, & Montone, 1994; Short, Montone, Frekot, & Elfin, 1996).

The material is then made more accessible, but no less difficult, through teaching modifications. Background knowledge, schemata, and core vocabulary can first be presented through graphic organizers to help students understand concepts and their relationship with one another (Short, 1993). The terms may also be directly defined, expanded upon, or simplified (Diaz-Rico & Weed, 1995). Text readability can be improved by adding connecting words (*first...next...last* for sequence, *because* or *as a result* for cause-effect), by paraphrasing the text, or by having student rewrite portions of it. One approach to SDAIE, Cognitive Academic Language Learning Approach (CALLA), teaches metacognitive, cognitive, and social affective learning strategies in addition to content and language (Chamot & O'Malley, 1992). In learning subtraction, for example, students learn to do the subtraction itself, learn the language to describe subtraction (e.g., "How much is left?" or "X is more than Y"), and learn a strategy enabling them to become autonomous learners (selective attention to key numerical properties).

An essential component of SDAIE is thematic instruction in which themes or topics are selected as focal points for instruction and assessment across the curriculum (Enright & McCloskey, 1985). ESL students benefit in particular because thematic units provide choices and meaningful, relevant content learning; build on prior knowledge; integrate the four skills; and provide scaffolding, collaborative inquiry, and variety (Enright & McCloskey, 1985). Peregoy and Boyle (1997) describe one elementary teacher's thematic unit, which led students to learn about corn through mathematics and science (keeping records on growing corn plants and learning corn's nutritive value), social studies (creating a map of countries where corn is grown and eaten and learning how it is prepared in different countries), language arts (studying and dramatizing corn legends and creating an illustrated corn recipe book), and art (dyeing corn kernels and creating corn necklaces). Thematic units can also be used in the upper grades, bridging one or two subject areas (cf. Pollard, 1985).

Teaching Oral Communication

Because of the importance of literacy for school success, the teaching of oral communication to nonnative speakers is often overlooked or is so simplistic as to be of little use in developing cognitive skills. However, the oral code is primordial and forms the basis for literacy acquisition (Durkin, 1989). Integrated with reading and writing, oral skills are key to fostering cognitive skills development. For example, in lesson 8 of the language/social studies unit on the American Revolution mentioned above (Short et al., 1994, pp. 53-56), students recite/perform songs of the American Revolution, discuss these songs in small groups, and listen to other groups perform. They also read the songs and analyze their point of view, purpose, and audience. In this lesson, all four language skills are used together to enhance students' understanding of the topic and their overall academic and linguistic proficiency.

Krashen observes that learners go though four stages of oral fluency: (1) pre-production, (2) early production, (3) speech emergence, and (4) intermediate fluency. Most mainstream teachers do not see ESL learners until at least intermediate fluency (though there are exceptions when a student is placed in a mainstream class before oral fluency is attained). Pre-production learners are believed to be in a silent period, during which they gain vocabulary and concepts in the new language before beginning to speak. They are probably best served by not being forced to speak and by engaging in activities targeting their level of understanding, such as acting on simple commands or working with a buddy to imitate a demonstration (Walter, 1996). Early production students can respond to yes-no questions or simple Wh-information questions; speech emergence students benefit from more complex Wh-information questions. Intermediate fluency students can answer questions about preference, hypothetical situations, or opinions (Walter, 1996). Students should be given the opportunity to ask questions, of course, as soon as they feel comfortable.

Comprehensible input for oral language can be created through (a) visuals, realia, photos; (b) gestures, body language, facial expressions; (c) speech modifications (speaking more slowly but using the same language rhythm, increasing wait time, simplifying sentences, using intonation to enhance meaning); (d) relation of words and ideas to prior experience; (e) repetition of key phrases, idioms, and concepts; (f) provision of modeling processes through pantomime; and (h) connection of the new material to what they already know (Walter, 1996). In the course of the class, teachers might watch for signs of misunderstanding or confusion and have a small blackboard on which they can write or illustrate unfamiliar words. They should also explain puns, idioms, and jokes in the L2 so that ESL students can participate fully (Harklau, 1994).

Literacy Instruction

Literacy is usually defined as the ability to read and write, but based on how literacy is used in the real world, a new meaning has been suggested: "the ability to communicate in real-world situations, which involves the abilities of individuals to read, write, speak, listen, view, and think" (Cooper, 1997, p. 7). Although this section will focus on reading and writing, teachers of ESL learners need to think of the broader definition, word in relation to world, as they teach literacy.

As with native speakers, ESL students best learn to read and write by reading and writing in meaningful contexts. Teaching reading and writing begins with an environment created through print-rich classrooms in which reading and writing are integrated across the curriculum and with oral skills for meaningful purposes; teachers model literacy and provide access to developmentally appropriate materials; and students participate actively and receive positive, specific feedback (Cambourne, 1988). Like native speakers, L2 learners need a variety of literacy events, from lists to journals to reports to essays, from guided reading and writing to independent work, from reading and writing across the content areas to English language arts and literature.

Proficient readers make meaning from at least three interdependent cueing systems: semantic cues (context, what makes sense), syntactic cues (structure and grammar), and grapho-phonic cues (sound-spelling correspondence) (Routman, 1991). To become fluent readers, learners need instruction in all three areas. If one area is emphasized to the detriment of the others, children may have difficulty decoding text, and this is particularly true of ESL children whose main source of English exposure is often the classroom.

There was a time when ESL learners were exclusively taught syntax and grapho-phonics. Research evidence most strongly suggests, however, that phonics and grammar are subordinate to meaning and should be taught using real language to which students have already been exposed.[4] Back to the basics or standards movements may increase pressure on teachers to focus on decontextualized pieces of language rather than on the language as a whole (with focused attention to form). Teachers of ESL students can become their advocates by resisting the pressure toward reductionism.

Literacy emerges for young and low-literacy second language students in much the same way as it does for first language learners, except that the former also rely on L1 knowledge as they make meaning and learn literacy conventions. Reading in the L2 is more arduous than reading in the L1 because L2 idioms, vocabulary, and schemata are less familiar. An effective literacy teacher for ESL students (whether in language arts or another content area) creates a reading and writing environment; explains key information and connects it to students' prior knowledge (cultural cues, vocabulary, idioms); and brings to students' awareness (and provides practice in) those activities that are automatic and unconscious in proficient readers and writers. For example, teachers can support ESL students writing up science lab reports by first modeling the write-up on the overhead projector. Each section of the report can be guided by a question that also appears on the overhead as the teacher models. For example, the Methods section could be guided by "How will I conduct this experiment?," the Results section by "What did I find?," and the Conclusion section by "Why are the results important?" As the students go to write up their own reports, the teacher can give them standard phrases that are repeated from report to report (e.g., The purpose of this lab was to ...) and help them recognize and use the titles of subsections to guide their writing. Finally, the teacher can give linguistic conventions for reporting numbers (e.g., ten and under should be written out, numbers over ten can be written in numeral form except when they begin a sentence) and monitor their use of irregular past tense verb forms that appear extensively in reports.

In spite of their fluency, intermediate and advanced ESL readers still need support in extending vocabulary and acquiring complex reading strategies. To that end, teachers can employ peer scaffolding, use cognitive mapping, elicit predictions, utilize literature response journals, and transform stories into plays. Carefully designed SDAIE lessons, with goals for both language acquisition and content, can also increase intermediate students' literacy skills. Teachers can scaffold

---

[4]Routman (1991) and Cooper (1997) provide detailed strategies for teaching literacy top-down and bottom-up that are applicable to ESL students, as well as a synthesis of the research.

content area materials by helping students see underlying text structure (through subtitles, connecting words, and other cohesive ties) and literary components (setting, plot, character, and conflict); distinguish between informational and aesthetic responses to text; and develop metacognitive skills. Prereading activities for native speakers are appropriate for nonnative speakers as well, provided that vocabulary, conceptual networks, and other information gathered are readily visible and available to students as they start to read. During reading, ESL students need to learn strategies for relating new material to prior knowledge, dealing with unknown vocabulary, and using titles and subtitles to understand text structure and meaning. Postreading activities that draw on all four skills and multiple media help students extend and summarize their reading experience for a future writing project or for assessment (Peregoy & Boyle, 1997). Some examples of these are to have students reread complex but pivotal passages (Saunders, O'Brien, Lennon, & McLean, 1999); engage in semantic feature analyses; use Venn diagrams, mapping, journals, research projects; and employ KWLA charts (what I *k*now, what I *w*ant to know, what I *l*earned, and how I *a*pply what I have learned).

Because it is a more complex skill than listening, speaking, or even reading, writing should be taught as a process to L2 learners: prewriting, drafting, researching, revising, proofreading, and publishing. This approach allows students to focus on one stage at a time and receive intermediate feedback and encouragement. Prewriting and drafting should give all ESL learners, even beginners, opportunities for choice, exploration, and fluency development. Scaffolds can be prewriting activities (small group discussions, brainstorming, clustering, freewriting), patterned books on which to model writing, story maps (Walter, 1996), dialogue journals, and word or concept books (Peregoy & Boyle, 1997). Proofreading for beginners is limited to easily retrievable structures such as capitals, end punctuation, word order, and simple subject-predicate sentence structure.

Intermediate and advanced students need to add sophistication and accuracy to fluency. Language Arts teachers might try some of Ziegler's (1984) creative exercises to elicit richer development and description, sentence combining and sentence models to prompt more varied syntax, story or cognitive mapping to help with organization (Peregoy & Boyle, 1997), and research projects including formal oral presentations to draw the skills together in complex ways (Walter, 1996). As with beginners, focus on form should take place during proofreading and in preparation for publishing. More advanced students can be taught simple proofreading rules for punctuation and syntax (cf. Deakins, Parry, & Viscount, 1994). In addition to judicious use of mini-lessons, the teacher can model proofreading for students on the overhead projector using, for example, an anonymous essay, showing students how to read their writing out loud and touch each word with a pen to focus on low-level detail. Students can then practice proofreading their own writing, looking at one or two elements at a time, recording what they learn in a personal three-columned grammar log: (a) What I wrote, (b) Standard English, (c) What I learned (or a new sentence). If students are carefully prepared through modeling and clear guidelines, authors' circles/writers' workshops can also provide feedback in both content and form.

ASSESSMENT

Because their English language development is not complete, ESL learners tend to be judged primarily on their weaknesses and gaps, rather than on their strengths and accomplishments. To focus on student strengths, teachers need to evaluate students' content area knowledge separately from their English language development because the two may not develop in tandem, use multiple measurements, include input from parents, and let students evaluate themselves and one another. Three kinds of assessment are commonplace: informal, ongoing classroom assessment; performance-based assessment; and formal, standardized timed assessment (Peregoy & Boyle, 1997). Of the three, informal classroom assessment and performance-based assessment are the most useful for teachers because they give direct feedback for instruction, and they give ESL students the time and extralinguistic clues they need to process language effectively.

Informal assessment, used to modify instruction or inform parents, may include listening for miscue patterns as students speak or write (Goodman, Watson, & Burke, 1987), cloze or passage-completion tasks, commercial or teacher-made informal reading inventories (Pérez & Torres-Guzmán, 1992), rubrics (including level-appropriate criteria for the skill being assessed), Group Reading Inventory (Vacca & Vacca, 1989), journals, observations of students' interactions, teacher-student writing conferences, tests, and checklists. However, teachers should be aware of the danger of misjudging students based on impressionistic data. Audio- and videotapes can help teachers see student strengths more objectively. Teachers should also involve ESL students in their own assessment. Harklau's (1994) ESL teacher had her students tape themselves so they could evaluate their own oral skills. Rubrics for oral skills can be developed by the students themselves and used in the evaluation.

Performance-based assessment, often in the form of projects or portfolios, is probably one of the best forms of classroom assessment because it is based on clear, measurable performance objectives; is closely related to curriculum; and leaves ESL students time to revise, research, and edit their work. Project-based learning (Katz, 1989; Wolk,

1994) engages students in cooperative or individual investigations through a problem-solving approach. ESL students benefit, in particular, from combining nonverbal and verbal skills to reach a real goal and applying intrinsic self-assessment during problem solving. In one set of project assignments from their unit *Conflicts in World Cultures*, Short et al. (1996) include documentary writing, narrative writing from another person's point of view, reading for historical and personal information, and creating appropriate illustrations (pp. 147-149). A portfolio is a folder that may contain works in progress (working portfolio) or the carefully selected, revised, and organized pieces that represent the student's best work in designated areas (final portfolio). Portfolios can contain entries that are both formal (essays with drafts, tests, self-assessment rubrics, audio- or videotapes) and informal (journals, reading logs, interviews, dictations). A cover letter is often added so that ESL students can reflect on their learning and build metacognitive skills (Arter & Spandel, 1991), especially important because they are often excluded from the assessment process.

Formal, large-scale, timed examinations, usually in the form of multiple choice questions or short essays, are used by governments and school boards to gather information about students and programs in relation to one another. However, teachers of ESL students should be aware of the limitations of this kind of assessment for their students. The most serious threat to their validity is the time constraints because ESL speakers—even balanced bilinguals—have slower processing times than comparable native speakers (Hamers & Blanc, 1989). Silva (1993) found that ESL students took more time referring back to the test prompt, took longer pauses as they wrote, and produced fewer lines than did native speakers. Even with this and other problems, however, if the school district or state has opted to used standardized examinations, then the teacher of ESL students should spend some time honing their test-taking skills, balancing the need for these skills with the loss of meaningful instructional time.

FINAL COMMENT

Good teaching for urban ESL students is similar to good teaching for all students. Successful teaching of urban ESL students, however, involves knowing the students and their strengths, understanding the difficulty of what they are being asked to do, and making challenging material accessible for them. With a little extra time and effort, the teacher can pave the way for ESL students to succeed academically and find their place in the new culture.

REFLECTION AND ACTION

Below is a short set of reflective, action-oriented exercises for individuals developing competence in teaching English as a Second Language:

1. Ethnography is the study of behavior in natural settings that aims to provide a cultural interpretation of what people do and how their see their own behavior (Watson-Gegeo, 1988). Although you may not have the time to perform ethnographic research, you can observe students using ethnographic approaches such as triangulation in which data from multiple sources are gathered and interpreted. After reading Watson-Gegeo's article, select one or two ESL students and gather data about their interactional patterns from your own or the teacher's observations, from parents, and from the students themselves. Gather the data, draw conclusions, and then test your conclusions with the students and their teachers.
2. Interview someone who moved to the United States and learned English here. Find out about the person's experiences, frustrations, embarrassments, and successes. If you are currently teaching, interview the parent of one of your ESL students who is still learning English (through a translator) to see what it is like for that individual. If you have had a similar experience, compare your experience with theirs.
3. Tape-record yourself teaching or, with permission, another teacher. Listen to the tape (alone or with a classmate) and transcribe a few instances where the instruction could be modified to make it more accessible to ESL students. Discuss your modifications with an experienced ESL teacher or the instructor.
4. Select a unit that was written for native speakers of English in one of the content areas or one that spans the curriculum. With a partner, rewrite the unit to make it accessible to ESL students who need to develop academic sophistication in the four skills.

REFERENCES

Arter, J. A., & Spandel, V. (1991). *Using portfolios of student work in instruction and assessment*. Portland, OR: Northwest Regional Educational Laboratory.

Au, K. H., & Mason, J. (1981). Social organizational factors in learning to read: The balance of rights hypothesis. *Reading Research Quarterly, 12*, 24-32.

Calderón, M., Hertz-Lazarowitz, R., & Slavin, R. (1998). Effects of bilingual cooperative integrated reading and composition on students making the transition from Spanish to English reading. *The Elementary School Journal, 99*(2), 153-165.

Cambourne, B. (1988). *The whole story: Natural learning and the acquisition of literacy in the classroom.* Richmond Hill, ON: Scholastic-TAB.

California State Department of Education. (1994). *Building bilingual instruction: Putting the pieces together.* Sacramento: Bilingual Education Office.

Chamot, A. U., & O'Malley, J. M. (1992). *The CALLA handbook: Implementing the cognitive academic language learning approach.* Reading, MA: Addison-Wesley.

Collier, V. P. (1987). Age and rate of acquisition of second language for academic purposes. *TESOL Quarterly, 21*, 617-641.

Collier, V. P., & Thomas, W. P. (1999). Making U.S. schools effective for English language learners, Part 1. *TESOL Matters, 9*(4), 1, 6.

Comer, J. P. (1984). Home-school relationships as they affect the academic success of children. *Education and Urban Society, 16*(3), 323-337.

Cooper, J. D. (1997). *Literacy.* Boston: Houghton Mifflin.

Cummins, J. (1979). Cognitive-academic language proficiency, linguistic interdependence, optimal age and some other matters. *Working Papers in Bilingualism, 19*, 197-205.

Cummins, J. (1981). The role of primary language development in promoting academic success in language for language minority students. In *Schooling and minority students: A theoretical framework.* Los Angeles, CA: California State Deptartment of Education, Office of Bilingual Education.

Deakins, A., Parry, K., & Viscount, R. (1994). *The Tapestry grammar.* Boston: Heinle and Heinle.

Diaz-Rico, L., & Weed, K. (1995). *The cross-cultural, language, and academic development handbook.* Needham Heights, MA: Allyn and Bacon.

Doughty, C., & Varela, E. (1998). Communicative focus on form. In C. Doughty & J. Williams (Eds.), *Focus on form in classroom second language acquisition* (pp. 114-138). Cambridge: Cambridge University Press.

Durkin, D. (1989). *Teaching them to read* (5th ed.). Boston: Allyn & Bacon.

Ellis, R. (1994). *The study of second language acquisition.* Oxford: Oxford University Press.

Enright, D. S., & McCloskey, M. L. (1985). Organizing the classroom to promote second language acquisition. *TESOL Quarterly, 19*(3), 431-453.

Epstein, J.L. (1986, June). Parent involvement: Implications for limited-English-proficient parents. In C. Simich-Dudgeon (Ed.), *Issues of parent involvement*. Proceedings of symposium held at Trinity College, Washington, DC.

Gale, K., McClay, D., Christie, M., & Harris, S. (1981). Academic achievement in the Milingimbi bilingual education program. *TESOL Quarterly, 15*, 297-314.

Goodenough, W. (1971). *Culture, language, and society*. Reading, MA: Addison-Wesley.

Goodman, Y.M., Watson, D. J., & Burke, C. L. (1987). *Reading miscue inventory: Alternative procedures*. New York: Richard C. Owen.

Greene, J. (1998). *A meta-analysis of the effectiveness of bilingual education*. Claremont, CA: Tomas Rivera Policy Institute.

Hamers, J., & Blanc, M. (1989). *Bilinguality and bilingualism*. Cambridge: Cambridge University Press.

Harklau, L. (1994). ESL versus mainstream classes: Contrasting L2 learning environments. *TESOL Quarterly, 28*, 241-272.

Katz, L. (1989). *Engaging children's minds: The project approach*. Norwood, NJ: Ablex.

Krashen, S. (1982). *Principles and practice in second language acquisition*. Oxford: Pergamon.

Krashen, S., & Terrell, T. (1983). *The natural approach: Second language acquisition in the classroom*. Oxford: Pergamon.

Long, M. (1990). Group work and communicative competence in the ESOL classroom. In R. C. Scarcella, E. S. Anderson, & S. D. Krashen (Eds.), *Developing communicative competence* (pp. 303-315). New York: Newbury.

McLaughlin, B. (1992). *Myths and misconceptions about second language learning: What every teacher needs to unlearn*. National Center for Research on Cultural Diversity and Second Language Learning. Santa Cruz: University of California.

Numbers of school-agers with spoken English difficulty increase by 83%. (1993, March). *Numbers and Needs, 2*.

Peregoy, S. F., & Boyle, O. F. (1997). *Reading, writing, and learning in ESL: A resource book for K-12 teachers*. White Plains, NY: Longman.

Pérez, B., & Torres-Guzmán, M. E. (1992). *Learning in two worlds: An integrated Spanish/English biliteracy approach*. New York: Longman.

Peyton, J. K., & Adger, C. T. (1998). Immigrant students in secondary school: Creating structures that promote achievement. *TESOL Journal, 7*(5), 4-5.

Pollard, J. (1985). *Building toothpick bridges*. Palo Alto, CA: Dale Seymour.

Ramirez, J. D., Yuen, S. D., Ramey, D. R., Pasta, D. J., & Billings, D. K. (1991). *Final report: Longitudinal study of structured immersion strategy, early-exit, and late-exit transitional bilingual education programs for language minority children*. San Mateo, CA: Aguirre International.

Rich, D., Van Dien, J., & Mallox, B. (1979). Families as educators of their children. In R. Brandt (Ed.), *Partners: Parents and schools*. Alexandria, VA: ASCD.

Routman, R. (1991). *Invitations*. Portsmouth, NH: Heinemann.

Saunders, W., O'Brien, G., Lennon, D., & McLean, J. (1999). *Successful transition into mainstream English: Effective strategies for studying literature*. Educational Practice Report 2, Center for Research on Education, Diversity, & Excellence. Santa Cruz: University of California.

Selinker, L. (1972). Interlanguage. *International Review of Applied Linguistics, 10*, 209-231.

Schumann, J. (1978). *The pidginization process: A model for second language acquisition*. Rowley, MA: Newbury.

Short, D. J. (1993). Integrating language and culture in middle school American history classes. *Educational Practice Report 8*. National Center for Research on Cultural Diversity and Second Language Learning. Santa Cruz: University of California.

Short, D. J., Mahrer, C. A., Elfin, A. M., Liten-Tejada, R. A., & Montone, C. L. (1994). *Protest and the American Revolution: An integrated language, social studies, and culture unit for middle school American history*. Washington, DC: Center for Applied Linguistics [www.cal.org].

Short, D. J., Montone, C. L., Frekot, S., & Elfin, A. M. (1996). *Conflicts in world cultures: An integrated language, social studies, and culture unit for middle school world studies*. Washington, DC: Center for Applied Linguistics [www.cal.org].

Silva, T. (1993). Toward an understanding of the distinct nature of L2 writing: The ESL research and its implications. *TESOL Quarterly, 27*(4), 657-677.

Skutnabb-Kangas, T., & Toukomaa, P. (1976). *Teaching migrant children's mother tongue and learning the language of the host country in the context of socio-cultural situation of the migrant family*. Report for UNESCO, University of Tampere, Research Reports 15.

Slavin, R. (1995). *Cooperative learning* (2d ed.). Boston: Allyn & Bacon.

Swain, M. (1985). Communicative competence: Some roles of comprehensible input and comprehensible output in its development. In S. Gass & C. Madden (Eds.), *Input in second language acquisition* (pp. 235-253). Rowley, MA: Newbury.

Tharp, R., & Gallimore, R. (1988). *Rousing minds to life: Teaching, learning, and schooling in social context*. New York: Cambridge University Press.

Thomas, W. P., & Collier, V. (1996). Language minority student achievement and program effectiveness studies support native language development. *NABE News, 18*(8), 5, 12.

Vacca, R., & Vacca, J. (1989). *Content area reading*. Glenview, IL: Scott, Foresman.

Vigil, F., & Oller, J. (1976). Rule fossilization. *Language Learning, 26*, 281-295.

Violand-Sanchez, E., Sutton, C. P., & Ware, H. W. (1991). *Fostering home-school cooperation: Involving language minority families as partners in education*. NCBE Program Information Guide Series, Number 6 (summer) [www.ncbe.gwu.edu/ncbepubs/pigs/pig19.htm].

Vorih, L., & Rosier, P. (1978). Rock Point Community School: An example of a Navajo-English bilingual elementary school program. *TESOL Quarterly, 12*, 263-269.

Vygotsky, L. (1978). *Mind in society*. Cambridge: Harvard University Press.

Walter, T. (1996). *Amazing English!* Reading, MA: Addison-Wesley.

Watson-Gegeo, K. A. (1988). Ethnography in ESL. *TESOL Quarterly, 22*, 575-592.

Wolk, S. (1994). Project-based learning. *Educational Leadership, 52*(3), 42-45.

Ziegler, A. (1984). *The writing workshop, volume 2*. New York: Teachers and Writers Collaborative.

Eleven

Teacher as Negotiator: The Evolution of a Teacher's Theory of Practice in an Urban School

Nancy Dubetz

Despite promising approaches to urban school reform, many urban schools continue to be characterized by bureaucracy and standardization of curriculum and instruction (Lytle, 1992; Weiner, 1993). Student needs that diverge from the norm established by content-centered standards and assessment practices continue to be addressed through compensatory education, for example, pull-out programs in remedial reading, remedial math, and English as a Second Language (Passow, 1990; Weiner, 1993). Research into effective urban teaching suggests that a very different approach better serves children in urban schools. Successful urban teachers view students as individuals, embrace diversity and are culturally responsive to their students, demonstrate caring and high expectations for their students, take student achievement as a personal responsibility, and have faith in their power to help children succeed (Byrd, Lunderberg, Hoffland, Couillard, & Lee, 1996; Gay, 1995; Lipman, 1996; Rose, 1995; Waxman & Huang, 1997). These characteristics are shared by successful teachers in rural and suburban schools as well; however, implementing practices that reflect these characteristics is most challenging in urban schools where teachers face the greatest diversity of student needs in depersonalizing settings (Weiner, 1993). It is particularly challenging for beginning teachers who are some of the most vulnerable members of urban schools. This chapter focuses on the experience of a first-year teacher named Helen who attempted to put into practice the characteristics of successful urban teaching in a public elementary school in New York City.

Helen's story is grounded in research that characterizes teacher thinking as context-specific, activist, adaptive, nonlinear, and holistic (Clandinin, 1985; Elbaz, 1985; Genishi, Dubetz, & Foccarino, 1995; Paris, 1993; Rios, 1995). In this chapter, the term *theory of practice* is used to describe the relationship between the theory a teacher holds about teaching and learning and her enacted practice. A theory of practice reflects teachers' negotiation of multiple sources of knowledge, for example, personal beliefs and values, pedagogical and content knowledge, knowledge of children, and the expectations of the school culture where they work. It is continually tested and modified as teachers attempt to maintain a coherence between what they believe and what they practice. When teachers' views of teaching and learning conflict with that espoused by the school culture in which they work, classroom practice is deeply affected. In the case study narrated here, the reader is invited into the world of a beginning teacher whose story illustrates the challenges of realizing a theory of practice that is holistic and child-centered in an urban school characterized by standardization and bureaucracy.

"STORYING" A TEACHER'S THEORY OF PRACTICE

Helen's story was constructed using methods adopted from research traditions in narrative inquiry and grounded theory (Clandinin & Connelly, 1990, 2000; Glaser & Straus, 1967). Narrative inquiry is rooted in the view that we think about and make sense of the world by constructing and reconstructing our experiences through narrative thinking. Studying experience is a process of walking into the midst of stories that have begun long before researchers enter the setting and continues long after they leave (Clandinin & Connelly, 2000). Narrative inquiry is contextualized investigation, that is, it is inquiry framed by time and space. As such, the product of narrative inquiry has little value as a predictor of what might occur at a different place or time. The value of narrative inquiry is in the rich descriptions that are produced. These stories invite a reader to experience another's world and use it as a frame of reference for making sense of the reader's own experience.

The data used to construct the story narrated in this chapter include Helen's lesson plans, reflection papers from her preservice courses, and a journal that Helen kept during her student teaching experience as well as three audiotaped interviews, 29 informal conversations, and 28 observations conducted during her first year of teaching in an urban school. To capture the complexity of Helen's story during her first year of teaching in an urban public school, Helen and I engaged in multiple cycles of inquiry over a nine-month period. Each cycle of inquiry began with an audiotaped interview followed by a series of observations (documented as anecdotal transcripts) and informal conversations (documented as anecdotal recollections) that I used to write an interpretive account. Interpretive accounts were letters to Helen describing patterns in the data and questions that I had about what I had observed. These patterns were narrative in nature, focusing on matters of plot (i.e., events in the classroom, tensions between Helen and other members of the school culture, etc.), setting (i.e., time and place in which the study was undertaken), characters (i.e., Helen, individual students, the principal, etc.), and themes both within and across characters' experience.

Once Helen and I had mutually agreed that no more observations would be conducted, I reviewed all sources of data and analyzed them using the constant comparative approach borrowed from grounded theory (Glaser & Strauss, 1967). I developed a preliminary set of categories of different classroom experiences from a review of the interpretive accounts. Beginning with this set of categories, I reviewed all of the raw data from conversations, observations, and interviews. As I categorized data, I made memos, which are descriptive phrases that define the parameters of a category by describing characteristics or properties of that category. For example, memos might identify Helen's goals related to a particular category or sources of her thinking regarding the category. During this process, some of the original categories were subsumed in new categories that emerged. I constructed a written draft of Helen's story using these categories as well as the interpretive accounts, and Helen reviewed it and made extensive revisions.

After the study of Helen's first year of teaching was completed, I completed a content analysis of data collected from Helen's student teaching experience. The following story narrates the transformation of Helen's theory of practice as she moved from student teacher/full-time educator in a private school to first-year teacher in an urban public school.

SUPERWOMAN IN A SCHOOL ALMOST DEVOID OF CURRICULUM

Helen is a 31-year-old European American woman who was born and raised in Connecticut with the exception of the first two years of her life which were spent on a Navajo reservation where her father had been assigned to a medical internship. Helen's mother was a high school English teacher. Before coming to teaching, Helen worked for several years in theater. She lived in the community where she completed her student teaching and her first year of teaching.

To become a certified teacher, Helen completed a preservice program at a private university in New York City. The stated goal of the program was to develop teacher leaders, and there were five themes around which the preservice curriculum was organized to achieve this goal: the relationship between autobiography and one's conception of teaching; understanding children and schools; curriculum development and models of teaching; responding to cultural diversity; and democratic, cooperative group process. The program required that students complete at least one full semester of student teaching in an urban public school.

Helen was viewed by faculty in her preservice program as an exceptionally intelligent and articulate student and a potential teacher leader. When Helen entered her preservice program, she was working as a head teacher of a combined third/fourth grade class of seven children in a small progressive, private school with a student body that was culturally and ethnically diverse. Because she was considered a full-time educator during her preservice studies, she completed her student teaching in her own classroom and did not complete the one semester of student teaching in a urban public school that was required of students in the program. Helen characterized the school as one that "was almost devoid of curriculum." Although she was concerned about receiving little direction from school administrators, she could develop curriculum in whatever ways she thought were necessary.

As a result, Helen was able to apply many of the concepts and strategies she learned from her preservice coursework to her student teaching. For example, she engaged in ongoing assessment of individual students and planned extensively based on her assessment of individual needs as well as the needs of the class as a whole. Her theory of practice in this setting reflected four beliefs:

1. Knowledge is socially constructed and therefore learning must be collaborative,
2. Children learn when their interests and experiences are valued in the classroom,
3. Children learn in an environment of caring and mutual respect, and
4. Children learn by assuming responsibility for their own learning.

Throughout her first semester of student teaching, she worked like a "superwoman" to develop experiences for her students that reflected these beliefs. They were consistently evident in her lessons and were the framework for her teaching philosophy throughout her work in the preservice program.

FIRST STEPS IN THE NEGOTIATION OF A THEORY OF PRACTICE

Upon completion of her preservice program, Helen accepted a position in the public elementary school where administrators had told her in the interview that they were looking for whole language teachers. She had spoken with the superintendent and the principal of the school and perceived that:

> They wanted people with a whole language background. They wanted people with a big writing process background. They wanted people who were integrating curriculum. They wanted these people that could bring that to the school and start implementing it in the school and in the classroom.

The public school where Helen was hired to teach fourth grade was one of two new elementary schools that had been built to accommodate the overcrowded conditions in other schools in a district that was experiencing a sharp increase in the school-age population due to an increase in the numbers of Latino immigrants residing in the community. The school opened with approximately 700 students who came from a number of other local elementary schools. Students were housed in the first three floors of the building, and the top floor was reserved for the district offices. Thus, Helen would be teaching "literally under the district office." There were three fourth grade classes in which English was the language of instruction and one Spanish/English bilingual class. Students were streamed in classes according to ability as defined by standardized test scores and special needs.

Teaching "under the district office" had important implications in a district where most curricular decisions were made at a district level. At the fourth grade level, there were district-wide curricula for math, science, reading, and social studies. These four curricula defined the content and skills in each subject that all fourth graders must learn. Each contained books, workbooks, pacing calendars, teachers' guides with lesson plans that prescribed the content and skills to be taught, and unit tests, the scores of which teachers were required to submit to the district office. Each spring fourth graders participated in high-stakes testing in language arts, math, and science. Test scores were used to evaluate school success and to formulate school report cards that the State of New York makes accessible to the public.

Helen had 27 children in her fourth grade class. All but two of Helen's students were Latino and spoke Spanish at home. The other two students were African American and Arab American. Many of Helen's students had special academic needs. Five of her students received ESL services. Eighteen students attended pull-out remedial math classes. Sixteen students began the year in the lowest quartile on standardized reading tests and attended remedial reading classes or resource room on a daily basis. Because of their diverse needs, most of Helen's students went to other teachers during reading, during which teachers each worked with a different reading level, and were also pulled out for special services throughout the day. Many students received multiple services. As a result, Helen had the least amount of contact with those of her students who had the greatest range of needs. Due to the excessive pull outs, Helen's entire class was only together for the first 20 minutes in the morning and the last 15 minutes of the day. The number of children leaving during one period of the day was so large that Helen was explicitly told not to cover significant curriculum material during that time.

In her new position, Helen immediately began planning for curricular experiences that were rooted in the child-centered theory of practice she had brought with her from her previous experience. Early in the school year, she attempted to establish a series of projects and routines that were consistent with this theory. Two examples of these were a bilingual buddies project and centers.

In the fall, Helen approached Lorraine, a new first grade bilingual teacher, with the idea of collaborating in the creation of a buddy system between her fourth graders and Lorraine's first graders. They both agreed that the experience would benefit their students socially and academically, and they began to plan for the experience.

Before the buddies met for the first time, Helen's students wrote a letter in English introducing themselves to their first grade buddies. Helen used the letters as a way to introduce her students to Writer's Workshop. In the letters, they wrote about their own experiences in a first grade classroom. They included stories of their fears and their favorite activities as first graders in a new school. At the first scheduled meeting, Helen's students shared their letters with their first grade buddies. By focusing on helping their buddies understand what they had written, the fourth graders reinforced their own communication skills. Most of Helen's students were bilingual in Spanish and English, and used both languages in their interactions with their buddies.

The success of this first meeting inspired Helen to have her students use their letters as a springboard for publishing books about themselves for their buddies. Writing books for buddies served as a motivation for the fourth graders to share their life experiences with an audience and to engage in extensive drafting, revising, and editing.

Students drew pictures and included additional photographs to accompany their writing. The fourth graders met and shared their books with their buddies, and the two teachers made plans to continue to use the buddy project to further develop the literacy skills of both groups of children and to give the older children opportunities to develop caring relationships with younger students.

Hoping to accommodate the large number of pull outs and put her theory into practice, Helen organized content instruction around centers. During a 90-minute block in the morning, when most of her children were in her room for at least 45 minutes, students rotated through writing, social studies, and science centers in groups established according to pull-out schedules. During the centers, Helen moved from group to group monitoring children's work and meeting with students one-on-one. A scene from a typical center illustrates what children experienced during this routine.

Dianne is reading the directions from the Writing Center folder. Catalina is giving out paper. Tania looks at the story she has written thus far and says, "I don't like mine. I don't know why I don't. My first draft."

Emily says to Catalina, "You don't have to copy it down again."

Emily says, "Wait. Somebody have to read it aloud," referring to the need for someone to read the directions.

Dianne reads the direction sheet. When she finishes, Emily begins speaking to Dianne in Spanish.

Patricia asks Dianne, "We have to do the first draft or the second draft?"

Romario and Manuel are talking about football and an invitation to join boy scouts.

Tania says to Dianne, "Let me read the instructions."

Patricia asks Dianne, "How do you spell first?"

Emily reprimands Romario, who has not begun to write yet, "Mira. Tu habla. Yo trabajo. [Look. You're talking. I'm working.]"

Romario defends himself saying, "Yo trabajo! [I'm working!]" and gets a piece of blank paper from the stack in the center of the desks.

Dianne reads the directions, "Open your notebook and . . ."

Tania interrupts, saying, "Excuse me. Excuse me."

Catalina shows Patricia her second draft. Patricia tells Catalina, "I'm writing about a cat."

The scene illustrates how children were engaged in conversations about their writing and how they assumed responsibility for each other's learning. Helen continued teaching content through centers until the December break even though some children, like Romario and Manuel, continued to have difficulties staying on task. Helen's explanation for their difficulty was that her students were used to having every aspect of their learning managed by a teacher and needed time and guidance to learn how to self-regulate. She based this interpretation on her observations of the way other teachers in the school talked about their teaching and the emphasis on using pacing calendars to guide instruction.

NEGOTIATING CONTRADICTORY VIEWS OF LEARNING

In January, the district began mandating preparation for the standardized tests in reading, math, and science that the children would take in April and May. The curriculum unit test scores were monitored regularly by staff developers in language arts and math, and teachers were asked to teach test-taking skills. To address the new focus on test preparation in a schedule already fragmented by pull outs, Helen had to change her routines. The buddy system dissolved into sporadic visits by individual fourth graders to the first grade bilingual classroom, the daily centers were replaced by a single lesson in a specific content area using direct teaching methods, and specific instruction in test preparation skills was introduced. To avoid compromising her beliefs about learning, Helen reorganized her routines in an attempt to maintain opportunities for students to work together in groups and explore personal interests. To help children continue to take responsibility for their learning, she applied the centers approach to a 20-minute block of time after lunch and created Job Time, when students worked in small groups on a variety of activities that included developing a math problem-of-the-day, writing a class newsletter for parents, maintaining the classroom library, caring for class pets, and checking homework. As is illustrated in the following scene from Job Time, Helen conceptualized this as an opportunity for children to be actively involved in collaborative learning:

"I've already spoken to the table leaders, and the table leaders know what you're supposed to do. If you have questions, ask your group leader. It's Job Time," says Helen. "Let's listen from beginning to end. Before you start, I'm going to give you a signal. If it's too loud, I'll flash the lights twice. It needs to be quieter so people can think. The other thing—please try to figure out problems on our own. Do not come to me. Work out the problem. Check with your group leader. We have until 1:55."

Most of the students get up and begin to move. Stephen goes over to talk to the zoo crew even though he is a member of the library crew. Juliana and Tania, who are homework monitors, come immediately to Helen's desk to begin checking homework. Romario and Manuel, who are also homework monitors, do not join them. Juliana and Tania are discussing who will do the checking.

The publishing group, Martha, Emily, Luis, and Mark, huddle over the desks discussing the parent newsletter. Emily is the group leader and is holding the first edition of The Town Cryer. She is explaining to the others that this is going home to their parents. "You have to tell in the week what's happened," she says.

By 1:42 Romario has joined Juliana and Tania to check homework. Romario checks Manuel's math work book even though Tania and Juliana tell him that they are supposed to be checking the writing folders.

Within a few weeks after establishing job time as a daily routine, Helen was asked to dedicate more time to test preparation. As a result, the daily Job Time was regularly replaced with teacher-centered, test practice activities like the following:

Students open their books to a page of a practice test booklet, which has a reading passage with four blanks and four multiple choice questions. Heather asks the students to read it and answer the questions, and approximately twenty minutes later, Helen says, "Let's go over these together. I'll take a really quiet hand."

She asks Erica to read. Erica reads aloud the question. When she finishes, Helen calls on Angel to read. Angel is not paying attention. She calls on Arturo. She tells Arturo that they can't hear over his voice. She sits at Romario's table. She asks the class what they think will fit in the blank. She calls on Horace who answers, "beautiful." Helen checks to see if he is sure of his answer. She asks what they call the meteorite in the passage. Several students say, "beautiful!" Helen confirms and moves on the next question.

Reading instruction increasingly reflected a similar didactic approach. Helen's lessons often closely followed the curriculum materials. Many of her lessons were structured around pages in a large reading chart that accompanied the reading series, and homework assignments were from the workbooks.

As the school year progressed, children were experiencing a growing emphasis on curriculum-centered activities rather than student-centered activities. As the emphasis shifted toward increased curriculum-centered instruction, Helen began to report more and more discipline problems. She started to resist what was happening and sought allies to support her view that curriculum-centered practice was ineffective. She sought allies in the children, telling them that she was bored with the test practice work but that she had been told they must do it. She sought allies in the district coordinators who were monitoring her students' progress. She told the language arts coordinator how she had the students take one of the practice tests in pairs to show how all children improved when they were allowed to work together. Helen complained to her assistant principal that she was unable to address her students' needs because of the excessive pull outs and requested a push-in model for remedial math so that her children didn't have to leave the room. The assistant principal complied, but the collaboration was unsuccessful because there was no structure in the school to help teachers plan for collaborative teaching, and the math push-in teacher seemed little interested in working with Helen.

Final attempts to focus on student-centered practice were made by organizing opportunities for children to work together in the content areas that were not as closely monitored by district staff and to utilize the first 15 minutes of the day before reading began to engage students in personal goal setting. In social studies, the one content area where children were not tested, Helen took the content of the mandated curriculum and constructed activities that reflected her goals for her students, as is illustrated in the following scene from a social studies activity in early March, which was part of a Navajo unit which the class had been working on sporadically since December.

Helen asks if anyone in the groups brought books for their groups to work with. A couple of students respond in the affirmative. She says that some big goals for today included working on their poster. She reminds them that they need to design posters that will teach the rest of the class about their Navajo topics. Then she hands out the group folders. In each group folder, there is a group planning guide filled out by each member. The three page guide includes directions for the project and spaces for the group to write ideas on the topic, members and specific roles and responsibilities of each, and a list of materials needed.

One of the groups of students includes Dianne, Luis, James, and Emily. Dianne gets a piece of large construction paper and crayons from the closet. Dianne and Luis discuss the design of the how they will create the poster in Spanish. Dianne writes the word "puppet" at the top of the poster board, then turns it over and writes "puppet" in large letters across the middle of the poster board. Emily is copying down the student members and their responsibilities from Dianne's planning sheet to her own. James asks me if "puppet" is spelled correctly, and I tell him that it is.

Emily says, "I want to help," and moves to a chair that is directly across from Dianne. Luis explains to Emily in Spanish what they plan to do. Emily begins talking in Spanish about getting a box from the supermarket. James asks who is going to bring socks. Emily says her mother is going to come. Luis raises a question about Manuel, who is in the group but not present because he is in resource room.

At 10:35, James leaves to talk to Ignacio on the other side of the room. Luis and Dianne continue working on the poster. James comes back but soon leaves again to talk to students on the other side of the room.

To continue to provide students with opportunities to monitor their own learning, Helen introduced a new routine in which children were to define goals for themselves at the beginning of each day. The goals were to be written during the first 15 minutes of the day, one of the few times that the whole class was together. However, Helen did not regularly monitor the children's efforts because she was also trying to review homework and finish the unit on the Navajo during the same 15-minute time frame. The result was not what Helen hoped for, as illustrated in the following scene:

> It is 8:40 and students are talking off coats and putting away book bags.
>
> "I want to see everyone's homework. Andrew, you have to have that signed," she says referring to his reading record. Helen asks Janice about her homework. She asks Pedro where his homework is.
>
> Then Helen says to the class, "Take out your notebooks and write down something you want to accomplish this week. If it's 'I want to get an A on this,' write as though you're already doing it. Include words that make you feel good."
>
> Emily and Catrina are chatting and pulling things from their desk. Helen moves around the room asking for the reading charts which were to be signed by parents as homework. She looks at Pedro and asks him if he's writing his goals.
>
> At 8:50, she asks students to begin lining up to go to reading. Most of the students have left without writing a goal in their notebooks.

Goal setting was eventually abandoned. Tired and frustrated from "fighting an uphill battle," Helen believed it was time to bring our study to a close. Her assessment of the curriculum reflected the tension between her views and those held by district personnel:

> The curriculum is basically teacher proof, that's what they have, a teacher-proof curriculum. There is very little room for any kind of creativity. The problem is, with a teacher-proof curriculum, it's O.K. if you get a bad teacher, but if you get a good teacher in there, there's nothing for them to do. At least in my case, I feel absolutely shackled by it.

In June, Helen resigned and took a position at an urban public school in Connecticut where she believed her theory of practice would be better supported.

IMPLICATIONS OF NEGOTIATING A THEORY OF PRACTICE

Helen's convictions led her to resist the contextual forces that challenged the integrity of her beliefs about children's learning, and her decision to leave the school at the end of the year was a moral act as well as a political one. After unsuccessful attempts at changing the teaching culture through more subtle forms of resistance, she resigned to make public to administrators, colleagues, and parents that the school had failed her and her students.

Helen displayed qualities of a successful urban teacher. She advocated for her students and embraced their diversity of language and experience, as evidenced in routines such as the buddies project. She demonstrated high expectations for her students by creating opportunities for them to assume responsibility for each other's learning. She was proactive in attempting to adapt the curriculum to children's needs even when encouraged to use pacing calendars to determine what and how much content to cover.

However, scenes from her classroom suggest a theory of practice that was in constant flux as Helen attempted to negotiate between her own beliefs about learning and those espoused in the teaching culture where she was working. The result of her negotiation process was an enacted curriculum characterized by inconsistency and contradiction, which had unintended effects on Helen and her students. The disruption in routines resulted in fragmented opportunities for students to assume responsibility for their own learning, and the inconsistency of experiences led to management problems. At the end of the year, many of Helen's students were still struggling to take responsibility for their learning despite the projects she had initiated to help them learn to self-regulate. Although Helen developed strong ties with those children with whom she had the most contact, she expressed frustration at not adequately addressing the needs of the children who left her room for multiple pull outs. She was disappointed with the mixed results on standardized tests.

Helen entered her first year in an public school believing that she would be able to construct a theory of practice consistent with what she had been able to accomplish during her student teaching. She assumed that administrators' views of what constituted student-centered practice would be similar to her own and was either unaware of or did not recognize signals that the school might not, in fact, be able to support student-centered practice. The district's use of bureaucratic approaches such as tracking and pull outs to meet the needs of individual children should have signaled to Helen the need to further investigate the setting to determine if it would support a student-centered theory of practice; however, it seems that Helen was unaware of these practices when she accepted the position.

Typically, urban school districts do not articulate a district-wide educational philosophy in the form of a written mission or educational plan for implementing the mission. By not having such a plan in place, the mission differs from school to school or, in the case of the district where Helen was hired, is only understood through a study of the complex array of district policies on testing, student placement, access to support services, and resource allocation. When a district has in place an articulated mission and a comprehensive educational plan that guides curriculum development, resource allocation, and professional development, it is much easier for prospective teachers to determine the degree of match between their philosophy and that of the school district. It is in the best interest of a district to hire teachers who are well informed about its mission because without this match, students may be subject to inconsistent learning opportunities.

In addition, Helen's story offers several important insights for teacher education. Demonstrating the ability to clearly articulate a theory of practice should be required of all graduates of urban teacher education programs. Moral and political action grow out of a clear understanding of one's beliefs. Helen had a strong belief in student-centered instruction. Without this, she might have been socialized by the teaching culture over time to support a curriculum-centered theory of practice rather than choosing to resist it. Often teacher educators, like those in Helen's preservice program, talk about using teacher preparation as a training ground for school-change agents. Interestingly, Helen was viewed as a teacher leader by her preservice faculty, but she struggled unsuccessfully to put into practice her child-centered theory in the curriculum-driven culture of the urban public school where she was hired. Helen brought to her work a well-articulated view of student-centered instruction as evidenced by the kinds of experiences she attempted to create for children; however, her lack of knowledge of the urban public school culture led her to make a bad choice of jobs and to seek allies in others who either were too vulnerable to help her affect change, for example, the children, or to look for support from individuals who did not share her convictions, for example, the language arts coordinator and the push-in math teacher. Her story suggests that it takes more than a well-articulated program philosophy to implement an effective urban teacher preparation program.

In an effective urban education program, coursework and field work must be designed to engage students in extensive study of the historical, political, social, and economic factors that promote change in urban schools and those that legitimize maintaining the status quo. Thus, those topics that are commonly addressed in teacher preparation programs, for example, child development, pedagogical methods, classroom management, must be studied through the lens of urban education. Field experiences are critical to effective teacher preparation and prospective teachers need to be exposed to urban classrooms where they can develop and apply theories of practice in a supportive environment. Appropriate field sites should reflect the characteristics of successful urban schools,[1] and although many city schools are not

---

[1]Characteristics of successful urban schools can be found in Comer (1980/1993), Fine (1994), Raywid (1996), Waxman and Huang (1997).

successful, pockets of excellence can exist in all urban school systems (Rose, 1995). If prospective teachers are going to be exposed to urban schools that are not successful, then careful guidance that engages them in analysis of the issues that work against success in these environments is a must.

In university classroom and field settings, students should be exposed to a teaching/learning climate that reflects a commitment to effective urban education. Teachers like Helen who are committed to improving the lives of urban children deserve teacher education programs that are guided by a mission, a faculty that express a clear commitment to improving urban schools, and a well-defined plan of how to help beginning teachers prepare for their roles in urban school renewal. University-based teacher education programs should recruit successful urban teachers as clinical faculty and as mentor teachers. Teacher education faculty must be willing to assume advocacy roles for their students just as they would expect their preservice students to serve as advocates for their students. If the program promotes a student-centered view of learning, then a student-centered theory of practice must be implemented. This will mean resisting the temptation to overstandardize program outcomes and structures at a time when the national educational agenda is focused on defining standards and outcomes for students and teachers. It will mean creating programs where developing close faculty-student relationships through the induction period is emphasized over graduating high numbers of teachers. These are hard choices to make, but teacher educators must advocate for such practices if we truly want to develop in our preservice students the capacity to seek or create opportunities to realize student-centered theories of practice in urban schools.

The Story Continues

After Helen left the school, she took a position in another urban public school as a fourth grade teacher, where she was eventually tenured and asked to lead a school initiative to join the Coalition of Essential Schools. Helen's story is unfinished; the story narrated in this chapter is embedded in a larger story that continues to evolve and serve as a testament of the challenges and possibilities of urban school teaching.

REFERENCES

Byrd, J., Lunderberg, M. A., Hoffland, S. C., Couillard, E. L., & Lee, M. S. (1996). Caring, cognition, and cultural pluralism: Case studies of urban teachers. *Urban Education, 31*, 432-452.

Clandinin, J. (1985). Personal practical knowledge: A study of teachers' classroom images. *Curriculum Inquiry, 15*, 361-385.

Clandinin, J., & Connelly, M. (2000). *Narrative inquiry: Experience and story in qualitative research*. San Francisco: Jossey-Bass.

Comer, J. P. (1980/1993). *School power: Implications for an intervention project*. New York: The Free Press.

Connelly, M., & Clandinin, J. (1990). Stories of experience and narrative inquiry. *Educational Researcher, 14*, 2-14.

Elbaz, F. (1991). Research on teachers' knowledge: The evolution of a discourse. *Journal of Curriculum Studies, 23*, 1-19.

Fine, M. (1994). (Ed.). *Chartering urban school reform: Reflections on public high schools in the midst of change*. New York: Teachers College Press.

Gay, G. (1995). Modeling and mentoring in urban teacher preparation. *Education and Urban Society, 28*, 103-118.

Genishi, C., Dubetz, N., & Focarino, C. (1995). Reconceptualizing theory through practice: Insights from a first-grade teacher and second language theorists. In S. Reifel (Ed.), *Advances in early education and day care* (Vol. 7, pp. 121-150). Greenwich, CT: JAI Press.

Glaser, B. G., & Strauss. A. L. (1967). *The discovery of grounded theory: Strategies for qualitative research*. New York: Aldine de Gruyter.

Lipman, P. (1996). The missing voice of culturally relevant teachers in school restructuring. *The Urban Review, 28*, 41-62.

Lytle, J. H. (1992). Prospects for reforming urban schools. *Urban Education, 27*, 109-131.

Paris, C. L. (1993). *Teacher agency and curriculum making in the classroom*. New York: Teachers College Press.

Passow, A. H. (1990). *Enriching the compensatory education curriculum for disadvantaged students* (Report No. 61). New York: ERIC Clearinghouse on Urban Education. (ERIC Document Reproduction Service No. ED 319 876)

Raywid, M. A. (1996). *Taking stock: The movement to create mini-schools, schools-within-schools, and other smaller schools* (ERIC Digest No. 112). New York: ERIC Clearinghouse on Urban Education.

Rios, F. A. (Ed.). (1996). *Teacher thinking in cultural contexts*. Albany: State University of New York Press.

Rose, M. (1995). *Possible lives: The promise of public education in America*. New York: Penguin Books.

Waxman, H. C., & Huang S. L. (1997). Classroom instruction and learning environment difference between effective and ineffective urban elementary schools for African American students. *Urban Education, 32*, 7-44.

Weiner, L. (1993). *Preparing teachers for urban schools: Lessons from thirty years of school reform*. New York: Teachers College Press.

PART III

The Future—A Journey of Ideas, Insights, and Models

Twelve

Cyber City Education: A Future of Wonder

Kay E. Vandergrift

Picture an inner-city school that is truly a community learning center, a place where children, parents, and neighbors engage in collaborative work. This school is identified not by its physical characteristics but by the nature of the activities and experiences of those who reside there. In one corner, two youngsters are participating in an online college geology class and have just asked for a live video conference so they can show the professor their rock specimens and get help in cataloging their findings. In another area, a mixed-age group of artists are at work, some on the floor with paint and paper, others at computers working with pixels to create digital images for a group project.

A team of girls is working with a teacher and an engineering mentor from a local corporation to design a remote-controlled robot, using a kit of materials donated by their corporate sponsor. They have eight weeks to design and build their robot which will compete in an international sports competition called "Robot Games."[1]

---

[1]This project is based on one organized by Canada First [http://www.canadafirst.org] in 1994 called "Robotic Games: Turning Support into Sport." Its goals are:

Another group of children and adults are discussing how they will redesign a dining area for a local restaurant, planning an aquarium motif with exotic fish and bubble-like lights hanging in uneven arrays from the ceiling. They are concentrating on strategies for tackling this project. What do they want to accomplish? Who will work on various portions of the tasks? How much will it cost? When will it be completed?

One elderly gentleman is telling stories to a small group. Scattered individuals read traditional books and magazines while one child uses the hypermedia of her e-book to hear the pronunciation and the meaning of an unknown word in *Alice in Wonderland*. Glancing at various computer screens, we see everything from complex mathematical models to mummies to *Marvel* comics. All in all, we observe active, engaged learners eager to participate and share with others.

A student teacher from the local university is videotaping all these classroom events to take back to his graduate education class to share his analysis of the translation of activity into inquiry in K-12 education.

What is happening in the school described above? What right do all those outsiders have to come into a classroom of children? Who is in charge here? How can we evaluate student learning when the students seem to be engaged in their own projects? Is this a technological revolution? Where does the money come from to make it happen? What is the vision of education behind such a learning center?

Finally, where is the teacher in this learning center? She is present, doing what good teachers have always done—and more. She stimulates interest; helps learners find, select, evaluate, and use information sources; and maintains a social and intellectual climate to encourage learning. She serves as mentor, coach, guide, cheerleader, and knowledge manager for young and old alike, but she is also a co-investigator and co-learner. At a time when urban schools need civility at least as much as civics, she assumes responsibility for communication,

---

- To stage innovative new sporting competitions to enable students to explore technology in interesting new ways.
- To increase interest in and understanding of applied math, science, and technology and to encourage students to pursue postsecondary studies and careers in these fields.
- To build communication bridges between industry, educators, students, and parents, thereby providing students with life skills in the areas of project management, teamwork, entrepreneurship, problem solving, innovation, and creativity.
- To provide lifelong learning opportunities that extend beyond the scope of traditional textbook/classroom education.
- To facilitate the education of a work force that will better meet the needs of Canadian corporations striving to maintain a leading edge in an increasingly competitive global environment.

human relations, and social skills as well as teaching reasoning, the three Rs, and sound work habits. Her primary goal is to model and encourage a love of learning and to help those she teaches acquire the capabilities to succeed as lifelong learners, as productive workers and citizens, and as personable and social beings. She is able to do all this because she also has a team of teaching assistants, technicians, and others to help her accomplish these goals.

Is this is a distant and impossible dream? It is not only possible; it already exists. After an initial investment in technology, training, and public relations, this kind of education is less expensive, and probably considerably better, than what most schools are now providing.

A learning space like this may be difficult to imagine for those administrators, teachers, parents, and students who have grown accustomed to the crumbling walls and crumbling hopes of too many urban schools. Questions of resources, access, and control come immediately to mind. What do computers, videos, robots, and e-books have to do with schools in which traditional books and pencils are scarce and electrical outlets few and inadequate? How can schools trying to protect children from lead paint and toxic mold provide online access to resources from all over the world?

NEW MEDIA AND THE SOCIAL CONSTRUCTION OF CHILDHOOD

If we are to move toward schools in which such active, engaged, collaborative, and exciting learning takes place, we must begin, as always, with our students. The media have always been a means for young people to gain a sense of identity, a sense of connection, and a sense of control in their world. My generation sought these from the printed page, subsequent generations turned to television, and today's children turn to the Internet and the World Wide Web. In fact, Don Tapscott names those born from 1977 to 1997 "the Net Generation."[2] This kind of characterization reminds us that young people not only use new digital technologies, their very identities are shaped by these media. The Internet changes who they are and how they relate to others, to information, and to the world. Older generations tried out alternative ways of being in the world by identifying with characters in the books we read or the movies we saw. We experienced the shock of recognition that some of these fictional characters, although very different from us in many ways, were also very similar in how they thought, felt, and reacted to situations. That recognition helped to legitimize one's own sense of self. It also helped young people explore possibilities for who they might become. Some sense of security in their own identity also enables young

---

[2]This concept is explored in depth in Don Tapscott, *Growing up Digital: The Rise of the Net Generation*. New York: McGraw-Hill, 1998.

people to establish connections with others, both in the media and in the real world. Feeling a kinship with fictional characters empowers young people to believe in their ability to make connections with family, friends, and new acquaintances.

However, the connections the next generation makes with others in their world are very different from those made by previous generations, different in reach and different in kind. They reach out and communicate with others with common interests anywhere in the world through the power of the Internet. The relationships they form are also different in kind. Young people at every age can be full partners in virtual communities where age is not a barrier to participation in human dialogue. The fact that increasingly the social, cultural, and intellectual contributions of all societies are being made available in digital formats and that many of the advanced communication skills previously available only to those with many years of experience are readily available tools within the technology increases the possibility of the young as equals in virtual communities.

This has changed the whole distribution of power and the nature of relationships in modern society. It is often a child, rather than parent, teacher, or scholar, who holds the power over the technology that enables virtual communities to prosper. Thus, it is often the young person who serves as leader or teacher in the electronic environment. Children who are immersed in electronic environments, who experience their own agency, taking action and seeing results, and who are able to transform information and ideas to create new meanings are truly in control. Having this kind of control over their own learning activities in the cyberworld may make it difficult for some children to accept an authoritative teacher feeding scraps of information in a traditional classroom. Individuals who have that kind of identity, connection, and control over self and society do not and should not easily sacrifice it. Such young people require a vision of education and of technology that transforms both schools and students' lives.

For previous generations, formal education was the primary means to acquire social and intellectual control. It was in the schools that young people were exposed to a broader range of information and, in the best classrooms at least, were encouraged to think, engage in dialog, and move from information to ideas to personal meanings. This began to change with earlier broadcast media as children were exposed to increasingly more information from radio and television. Of course, this information was often not fully received or understood and seldom contextualized. It was still the task of parent or teacher to help children sort out, select, interpret, and make sense of this bombardment of media sights and sounds.

Interactive digital media, on the other hand, draw young people in as participants rather than passive receivers. Information no longer comes in complete pictures but as mosaics. Receivers actively select particular pieces of information, reshape and transform them, add their own pieces, and create a new mosaic either on their own or in consultation with other young people or with experts from anywhere in the world. Students with this kind of intellectual and technological control cannot be expected to accept the tyranny of traditional textbooks and classroom limitations.

TRADITIONAL TECHNOLOGIES OF EDUCATION

It is neither technology nor financial resources that make the kind of schools described at the beginning of this chapter possible. In fact, one might say that this kind of change can come only with the will to break the hold of traditional technologies of formal education. If technology is defined as applying a systematic technique, method, or approach to solve a problem, then schools themselves are an educational technology with a pervasive value system recognizing hierarchical relationships, an interplay of individualism and group-think, competitiveness, submissiveness to the judgments of others, and a perception of human knowledge as existing in small, discrete units. This overall technology of school has been so embedded in both our consciousness and our educational institutions that we are seldom even aware of its power to shape all of our individual and collective lives. Textbooks are a slightly more obvious technology that divide all knowledge into distinct sets and subsets and often attempt to dictate how that knowledge should be acquired and tested.

Many urban or inner-city school districts pride themselves on what is described as local control of education. However, the reality is that although local school boards have some discretion over educational resources, primary control over school content is maintained by national agencies such as Educational Testing Service (ETS) and major textbook publishers and by state education agencies. Participatory decision-making at the local level does not ordinarily extend to the power *not* to use standard textbooks or *not* to have students take state-mandated tests or the SATs. The heated contests for and discussions by local school boards in New York City may well be proof of the old adage that people fight so hard because there is so little at stake. The fact that these boards exist is proof that schooling is important to parents and community members. What is needed is a new, more realistic and more integrative and useful way for parents and communities to be involved in schooling.

FROM FACTORY WORKERS TO INFORMATION WORKERS

Tests, curricular materials, classroom practices, and testing are embedded with social and moral imperatives and with political as well as pedagogical goals. These and other technologies of schooling almost always assume a single standard of competence and perpetuate the hierarchical view of teacher (boss) controlling the activities of students (workers). This was an appropriate model to train factory workers in the Industrial Age, but it is not an adequate metaphor for an information society.

What skills do workers of the information society need for success in their personal and professional lives? In the Information Age, all professionals are knowledge managers. Most of their work is self-initiated and self-paced; they raise questions, do research, collect data, consider alternatives, and then work through an informed process to a final product. Much of this work is done in collaborative teams. In order to accomplish tasks, they must have a fairly sophisticated level of understanding of and competency in the use of various technologies. In this environment, change is continuous; and it occurs more rapidly than ever before. Thus, knowledge workers of the 21st century must learn to both manage and sometimes initiate change. They must be able to determine the sources and directions of change and the effects of that change on their own institution, on the larger global infrastructure, and on society in general.

Students must also be creative thinkers. In the early years of our nation's history, Thomas Jefferson spoke of education in three main areas: memory, reason, and imagination. More recently, literary critic Northrop Frye (1964) contended that *The Educated Imagination* is the basis for all education, as necessary for future scientists and politicians as for poets, graphic artists, and teachers. After all, an inability to imagine possibilities for new discoveries, new products, and new ways of being in the world would make it difficult to begin working toward such possibilities.

Recent emphases on multiple intelligences and constructivist approaches to learning point to the importance of creative, imaginative thinking in education. All of us bring our previous knowledge, experiences, and meanings to new situations and new data and use the intersection of old and new information to create new meanings. Thus, creative, imaginative thinking is vital to learning in all disciplines and in all aspects of education and of life.

EDUCATION FOR THE INFORMATION AGE

What kind of education is appropriate for leaders of the information society and whatever worlds might follow? First, we need to rethink formal education as we would rethink any other organization or institution that is not adequately fulfilling its mission. How can we restructure the organization to meet contemporary goals and challenges? Second, we need to re-allocate resources, to exchange old technologies for new. This includes emphasizing new technological infrastructures rather than the old brick and mortar ones and replacing the dominance of the textbook with an expanded architecture of alternative technologies for learning. Third, we need to re-educate all of society, including students and educational professionals, to separate the notion of learning from that of formal education and schooling. The latter will still be important but only as one portion of an individual's lifelong learning strategy. It is important to note also that formal aspects of education need not come only at the beginning of a life or a career. Only when we, as a society, truly value education as important in all ages and stages of human life will we develop the kind of schools that will serve all in this global information society.

Educators of the future will not be bound by geography, only by the limits of the human mind and the commitment of educators to build the information and communication infrastructures to convert what the mind can image into realities for learners. The 21st century calls for the consideration of a total restructuring of education, and advances in electronic communication networks and wireless environments make new paradigms beyond institutional boundaries not only possible but absolutely essential. The educational CyberCity of the 21st century will be made up of organizational units described by Alvin Toffler (1970) in *Future Shock* as "adhocracies" or groups of learners who come together on an ad hoc basis to complete specific tasks.

Of course, this will not happen overnight. Significant changes will have to occur in the way we think about education. New combinations of philosophical, intellectual, educational, technological, and organizational thinking are essential. These new intellectual communities will create innovative designs for computer-communication networks that support collaborative learning across national and international infrastructures as well as in neighborhood learning centers.

TECHNOLOGY IN EDUCATION

The questions raised about the new digital technologies in education are similar to those raised with the advent of every other technology from the printing press to ETV to CAI. Recall that in Plato's *Dialogues*, even the written word was seen as a threat to human dialog, then, and perhaps still, the finest form of education. History demonstrates that the infusion of new technologies in schools does not necessarily improve education. Perhaps, however, it is our traditional definitions of education, schooling, and teaching that are more at fault than the technologies themselves. If we envision new modes of teaching and learning, we may see more clearly how various technologies contribute to these processes.

We also need to reconceptualize the totality of our view of education. Most educational innovations have been piecemeal efforts to improve one particular aspect of either the organization or the content of schooling. Thus, the new math or whole language or open classrooms, along with a myriad of other potentially transformative programs, faded into the educational attic after the initial excitement was dissipated in traditional expectations and evaluations. Some of these programs and projects lasted longer than others, and all left traces of their influence on the students and teachers who truly engaged with them. Some are rediscovered or recycled after a number of years with new names and new research and new insights to support them. The generation of classroom teachers now approaching retirement will recall the similarities between the language experience approach of the 1960s and 1970s and the whole language approach 20 years later.

Without a totally new vision of education, all such individual pieces of the schooling puzzle are doomed to failure because they are not part of a larger and cohesive whole. Also they are seldom clearly communicated to parents and the community, and even educators fail to recognize that we cannot evaluate new ways of teaching and learning with old assessment tools and techniques. Active, collaborative, self-motivated teachers and students engage in learning that crosses disciplinary lines and demand high standards of achievement for themselves. They determine their own criteria for performance-based work that is not adequately measured by paper and pencil standardized tests. It is ironic that the new call for standards in education, assumed to mean standardized tests, comes at a time when nonstandardized learning is truly possible and may even be gaining a foothold in our schools. Of course, we need standards, but surely we can create standards that match the possibilities and achievements of new learners and new learning technologies.

TECHNOLOGICAL SUPPORT FOR SCHOOLS

According to E-Rate and the *Digital Divide: A Preliminary Analysis From the Integrated Studies of Educational Technology*,[3] a federal report

[3]The report is based on an analysis of E-Rate administrative records covering the first two years of program operation that were linked to detailed

released in September 2000, 96% of U.S. schools were connected to the Internet by the end of 1999. Those districts with the highest poverty rates, serving 26% of public school children, received 60% of all e-rate dollars committed. In spite of these figures and two decades of computer use in schools, the impact on public education is still not clear. However, many teachers in our inner-city schools are clear that the influx of technology in schooling, as it applies to their schools and to their students, is often just one more way to increase the distance between the *haves* and the *have-nots*. Both national and local community leaders have organized weekend wiring parties and have solicited donations of hardware and software for school use. Even when these activities reach the most needy of our schools, the physical plant may not be adequate to support the technology, teachers and students may not have been adequately prepared to use the new technology, and often no budget exists for maintenance, upgrades, and training. As a result, by the time students and teachers figure out how to successfully integrate the technology into the educational program, that technology no longer works or is obsolete.

One aspect of concern is the issue of balance between technology and content. The introduction of a new technology in schools almost always results in a focus on that technology itself rather than on its usefulness to the content already deemed important. Early adapters of computers in education will recall the drive to teach programming and the operation of the computer itself rather than an analysis of the computer-as-tool to help educate students more effectively and efficiently. However, when focus is shifted from the technology to the content, it appears that significant progress in learning can be made.

TECHNOLOGICAL EDU-TAINMENT

What of all those urban schools that lack even the basic necessities and can barely dare to dream of having access to modern technologies? Perhaps we need to pay attention to the influences of technology on our students outside of the classroom. Some children living in poverty do have access to electronic and digital entertainment devices. Many of the technological products already in the hands of children in even the most economically depressed communities have the kind of power available in only large research computer labs not too many years ago. The ubiquitous Gameboy, for instance, could no doubt accommodate a variety of educational programs as well as entertainment. We might also develop

---

national data on all public and private schools and libraries in the U.S. (a combined total of nearly one million records). A copy of this report as a PDF file can be located at [http://www.ed.gov/offices/OUS/PES/ ed_reform.html#tech_chall]

a Gamegirl with programs that would interest females and help to close the digital divide of gender.

Earlier technologies such as television and videogames and more recent PDAs and Play Stations could all be powerful learning tools. There is already a blurring of the lines between entertainment and education. Perhaps parents and teachers should lobby software developers to harness the power of multiplayer, online role-playing games so that young people's enthusiasm for these games would lead to educational and cultural pursuits rather than virtual violence. Software for popular entertainment technologies is already available at an extremely advanced level. What is needed is more positive educational content with the same ability to capture and maintain interest and excitement. As the cost of digital devices for entertainment, communication, and assistance in everyday tasks decreases and access increases, it is young people who are leading the way in their use. For many students, coming into their schools and classrooms is like stepping back in time. It is no wonder they question the relevance of these institutions.

Educators need to build on the excitement and the experiences of these technologically savvy young people to bring education into the digital world of the 21st century. The first thing this requires is a change in the mindset to one that allows and encourages teachers to learn from their students. An acceptance of learning from each other is merely an acknowledgment of what already exists outside the walls of school and classrooms. Many older faculty first learned to use computers with the assistance of youngsters who were more eager and willing to experiment on their own than we were. As educators, we know that we learn by teaching, and I am certain that my first young computer tutor learned more in our lessons than I did. These kinds of experiences should tell us something about how we might integrate computers in schooling. Until we have adequate computer access throughout our schools, perhaps we should consider placing a computer on every teacher's desk rather than grouping them all in a computer room or even having one student computer station in the corner of each classroom. Most teachers would at least use that computer to search the web for information or for specific teaching and learning materials. They would probably also find that the computer serves as a magnet to students, drawing them into dialogue with, and perhaps even teaching, the teacher as they use the technology for their own purposes.

DIFFERENTIATED STAFFING

This subtle shift in student/teacher roles can be the first step in a totally new conception of staffing in education. What educational technologists call unbundling is a case in point. Most often teachers are expected to be primarily deliverers of content and spend most of their time selecting, organizing, and presenting that content to students. It is obvious, however, that teachers are not always the most efficient or effective deliverers of content. As more and better content is captured in silicon or electronic environments, differentiated staffing, long discussed in education, may become a reality.

Master teachers might orchestrate the activities of an extended educational community in which instructional developers organize and package materials while mentoring teachers guide learners in the use of those resources. Of course, there would be technical support teachers who combine educational and technical knowledge to assist the entire community of learners, including other teachers. Personal, social, and academic counseling is essential in this learning environment, and intellectual and social content are equally important. As described in earlier chapters in this book, school and college or university partnerships bring teacher educators and students of education into local schools to work with students and teachers to develop new models of teaching and learning.

This active, collaborative learning benefits all participants in the educational community. It models for students the respect for flexibility, individuality, and the kind of project- and research-based inquiry common in the world of work. Teachers too benefit as existing organizational hierarchies break down, allowing them to maximize their greatest talents rather than expecting all to be generalists. This nonhierarchical teaching team also provides incentives for good teachers who, after a year or two as teaching generalists, can plan a career path that both recognizes their strengths and provides opportunities for advancement without leaving teaching.

Subject specialists, either from the university or from industry, with in-depth expertise in the disciplines work with child development and education experts to tailor intellectual content to particular developmental levels, or even personal interests, of learners. Thus, students have access to appropriate content, beyond the limitations of a single community, school, classroom, or teacher. Embedding disciplinary content in electronic media differs from traditional textbook packaging in a number of ways. The most obvious, and probably most important, difference is that printed and bound books take a long time to produce and may be obsolete by the time they are available to students. Because textbooks are costly and not frequently replaced, that misinformation becomes a staple of schooling. Online information, on the other hand, can be immediately and continuously revised. In the best of all possible worlds, there would be a number of open source educational sites in which some of the best minds in the various disciplines would exchange ideas and exert quality control over site contents. Young people and novices in the field could explore the contents of these sites, raise questions, and participate in a scholarly community unbounded by age, gender, culture, or geography.

Even in a less than ideal world, there would be multiple sites and multiple perspectives on many of the topics of interest to learners. Teachers or librarians would be available, evaluating and selecting the best and most appropriate sites and working with students to develop their own critical skills.

PARTNERSHIPS

The notion of partnerships in education has become very popular in recent years, but a partnership means very different things to various people and institutions. The partnerships discussed by the authors in this volume are primarily those between educators in colleges or universities and those in K-12 schools. These educator-partners have a great deal in common from their own education and experiences, and they come together for a common purpose: to improve both teacher education and education in the K-12 schools in which those new teachers will work. Faculties in higher education are often accused of being out of touch with the reality of the young people and the classrooms their students will encounter upon graduating and entering the world of work. Partnerships such as Project SCOPE I and II answer that charge by bringing together committed teachers from college and K-12 classrooms, student teachers, and young students in collaborative learning ventures. As they work together to discover new opportunities for improving education, they document that process so it can be shared and serve as a model to other educational enterprises. These kinds of adaptive, self-reflective, context specific partnering have proved to be effective means of improving education in urban or inner-city schools. Unfortunately, these are still just a small bandaid on a very large social ill.

In this Information Age, technology partnerships have become very popular and very important in bringing schooling into the mainstream of technological innovations. These partnerships, too, mean many things to many people. One of the most common types of these new technology partnerships occurs between schools and hardware companies who place their computer equipment in schools that could not afford such equipment on their own. These are often generous, altruistic gifts, but they also benefit the hardware vendor by educating the next generation of technology workers on specific proprietary equipment that they are likely to favor in the future. As schools become more dependent on technology, they often have a need for network and information systems (IS) managers to manage equipment and applications and to provide ongoing support. Staff training and administrative applications (student information and assessment, purchasing, and financial data) may also be handled by technology partners.

In the best of all possible worlds, these two types of partnerships would overlap and expand to include cooperative ventures with government, parent and community groups, public libraries, local businesses, and other educational agencies. Beyond the geographical village, these partnerships would also include online cooperation with others engaging in similar pursuits around the country and around the world.

The Boston Public Schools are a case in point. In 1996, with a very wide "digital divide" between the city schools and those in wealthier suburbs, Mayor Thomas Menino challenged the entire city to close that technological gap. He called for higher standards, improved facilities, an influx of computer technologies, and extended school days. Within two years, computer labs and classrooms were equipped with a least one classroom computer for every four students plus one for each teacher. All 130 city schools were networked with high speed Internet access and linked to the Boston Public Library and to approximately 100 community centers. This was accomplished with the aid of a $1 million equipment donation from the 3Com Company and donations of time and materials from a local union of electrical workers. An after-school program called TechBoston helps young people earn professional technology certificates and then use those skills to assist the schools, public libraries, and community groups with technology training and support. Another Boston program called Technology Goes Home works with community centers to determine home computer needs, provides training, and then allows those who complete that training to take a computer home or to work. This kind of total community involvement has indeed built a technology partnership and a bridge to the 21st century.

DISTANCE EDUCATION

One of the key elements of the computer-telecommunications infusion in education that has the greatest potential impact on urban schools is distance education. As technologies improve and costs decrease, more and more colleges and universities are offering online, distance education courses. Both from an economic and a service perspective, the courses most likely to be delivered online are the large introductory courses in the disciplines. Because these are also most likely to be the advanced placement (AP) courses taken by middle and high school students, the lines between school and college will begin to fade. Greater numbers of high school students in these online courses will make this mode of delivery of content more visible in our communities and ultimately more desirable, both in schooling and for learning outside and beyond the school. Online courses expand learning communities across age and institutional boundaries as well as geographical ones. Younger children and older caregivers looking over the shoulders of AP students will begin to use the Internet to satisfy their curiosity and meet their own information needs. Soon this will be an accepted, and then an expected, means of learning, open to all.

Distance education is not new in elementary and secondary schools. The Massachusetts Corporation for Educational Telecommunications was established by that state's legislature in 1982. This has now become "The Mass Interaction: Where Technology, Government, and Learning Converge" [http://www.massinteraction.org/home.nfs]. Mass Interaction's Distance Learning Network (formerly Mass LearnPike) broadcasts extraordinary educational, professional development, and enrichment programs to enhance the learning process and now includes over 100 programs for K-12 students and their teachers in subject areas from the arts to world literature.[4]

The Star Schools Project[5] began with satellite broadcasts for rural schools in the late 1980s and developed a number of innovative, interactive distance learning projects. As the available technologies grew, these projects moved to web-based designs, including online multimedia and video presentations, searchable data bases, and threaded discussions.

Other K-12 distance education programs include those offered by universities either for local area students or for any with online or satellite access. Oregon State University, for instance, in collaboration with Corvallis School District and Hewlett-Packard, and in response to shrinking education resources, began Project *S*cience *E*ducation

---

[4]Program content is aligned with national curriculum frameworks and is developed by teachers. It focuses on the arts, health, history, social science, language arts, mathematics, science, trends in education, and world languages and includes electronic field trips. Partnerships include Harvard University, NASA, MIT, CNN, and the United States Holocaust Memorial Museum, among others. Programs support both state and national standards. Programs are delivered to viewers across the United States using the latest satellite and Internet-based technologies. They are also available over local cable channels and proprietary LANs and WANs.

[5]The most detailed overview of the Project is found at the Distance Learning Resource Network [http://www.dlrn.org/]. This is an extensive website that includes current research and news items and covers a multitude of topics from information on the Star Schools projects to K-12 courses offered at a distance. Visitors can use the searchable database to find current information on the courses and resources available from the Star Schools projects, or peruse the library to find a variety of useful information on Distance Learning topics.

PartnershipS (SEPS).[6] Recently SEPS scientists assisted in an upgrade of the molecular biology curriculum at both the 6th grade and high school levels. SEPS actively supports the Outdoor School program and is working with NASA to develop a K-12 astronomy curriculum. The University of Vermont uses interactive television and the WWW to deliver AP courses to high school students in Vermont and neighboring states, including courses in Calculus and English Literature and Composition.[7] Mindquest[8] is an innovative program from the Bloomington, Minnesota, public schools that offers the possibility for students who are at least 17 years old to make up high school credits and earn an online high school diploma. This program makes computer equipment and full Internet access available free to eligible students living in Minnesota and to others for a fee.

Another exciting innovation was built by young people themselves. The Peace It Together Community Center in Massachusetts was designed to teach teenagers to interact with their peers to prevent violence.[9] This online site includes curriculum resources, case studies, testimonials, artwork, role-playing, an interactive comic strip, a web magazine, and electronic discussion areas, as well as an Ask the Experts opportunity to get advice from violence prevention experts.

The ThinkQuest Internet Challenge is an international program for students ages 12 through 19 that encourages them to use the Internet to create information-rich Web-based educational tools and materials. Students form teams with their colleagues from around the world and are mentored by teachers or other adult coaches. In the running for scholarships and awards totaling more than $1 million, student participants learn collaboration, leadership, and critical thinking

---

[6]For all K-12 teachers, SEPS offers a series called "Hot Topics in Science." OSU and HP scientists are showcased as they explain their research and talk about science in the news. Recent topics have included life on Mars, global warming, cloning, and nuclear energy [http://www.bcc.orst.edu/seps/whatis.html].

[7]This includes not only the courses but an intense preparation for the AP examinations [http://dmdl.uvm.edu/dln/dln_ap.html].

[8]Mindquest [http://www.mindquest.org/] offers:

- Customized courses developed for online education,
- Interactive teaching and learning with strong teacher support,
- Portfolio-based learning and assessment,
- Opportunities to complete high school from home through the Internet.

[9]At this site opportunities are provided to meet other teenagers, educators, parents, youth service providers, and other community members who are working to decrease violence in their communities, home, and schools and to learn how to implement a model violence prevention program in community or school [http://www.mcet.edu/peace/index.html].

skills that help raise their level of education and technological expertise.[10] From its beginning in 1996, ThinkQuest[11] has grown to include 10,000 students and teachers from 75 countries. Given the current international excitement over the children's book character Harry Potter, the development of a multilingual site on Harry and Hogwarts was inevitable. Students in Germany completed this design and between flying owls with envelopes, house selection, and the golden snitch of Quidditch, the visitor to the site easily could become a regular.[12]

Students from John F. Kennedy High School in New York City received ThinkQuest support for their project "Why Is the Mona Lisa Smiling?" several years ago and now have expanded that work to a new project designed to predict how art will influence human life in the next 100 years. This new project, entitled "Arti FAQS 2100," completed with the help of teacher Steve Feld, was a first-place winner in the NYC Beyond 2000 Millennium Contest.[13]

Online mentoring takes place naturally in many virtual communities, but there are also websites that specifically provide that kind of help for learners. Number2.com[14] offers young people who can not afford expensive SAT or GRE classes or tutorials free guidance and practice. They also offer a coaching system that encourages students to identify a coach who will be informed about and monitor their growth in competency and performance on interactive tests. The personal touch of a human mentor has proved to be very successful.

---

[10]Taken from the ThinkQuest Internet Challenge web page at [http://www.thinkquest.org/tqic/].

[11]There are several projects listed in the award categories that are intriguing to students, teachers, and the general population [http://www.thinkquest.org./tqic/finalists_2k.html].

[12]The website is found at [http://library.thinquest.org/C006090/].

[13]Using Renaissance achievements as a platform, students pose key inquiry questions that will prompt their vision of art in our lives within the next 100 years. Through probing past inspiration and methods, students can use available data to make reasonable predictions for the future. It is located at [http://library.thinkquest.org/13681/data/nyc/timess/html].

[14]Number2.com was created by University professors and graduate students with years of experience in the area of test preparation. Professor Vincent Crespi began the site over four years ago as a way of providing students with exposure to the material tested by the SAT and GRE. Two years ago, Eric Loken took time off from his graduate program at Harvard University to teach free SAT prep courses to low-income kids in the Boston area. *Time* magazine and *U.S. News and World Report* list this site as one of the top websites for college-bound students [http://Number2.com/].

CONCLUSION

In this chapter, I have tried to look to the future of education and have seen it as a future inextricably bound with the future of technology. The process of looking forward by looking back, perhaps using McLuhan and Fiore's (1967) rear-view mirror, has also reminded me that formal education has always been both a technology itself and an institution framed by other technologies. Too often we have allowed a technological ideology, rather than an ideology of education, to shape and govern schooling. We have allowed the tools to determine the tasks. We have placed information above education and used new technological tools to more efficiently achieve antiquated goals. Real learning is not just a consumption of facts or data, and the old "read, regurgitate, and forget" model of schooling is not improved by faster distribution or more current data. The dawn of a new century is an appropriate time to shine a new and brighter light on the basic beliefs that underpin education in this country.

Today's interactive technologies are no longer just tools. They not only change the ways we do our work; they change who we are, individually and collectively. They present possibilities for changing the self of each person who engages with them. The power, the relationships, and the interactions with others and with machines change the very nature of a person's identity, connection, and control in contemporary society.

The popularity of robo-pets with increasingly more sophisticated technologies and programming is representative of new relationships between human beings and inanimate objects. The warm, furry bodies and wet kisses of live pets are missing, but Sony promises ERS-210,[15] the successor to AIBO,[16] their original robo-dog, is capable of "intimate interaction with people." Sony is serious enough about this development to set up a separate organization just to handle their robo-business. Bill Joy's provocative article in *Wired*[17] focuses on the future of

---

[15]Although priced at $1,500 in the U.S., the robo-pet was quickly sold out and may be indicative of what we will see in future years. ERS-210 has a camera in its nose and can better express anger and joy [http://www/msnbc.com/news/475751.asp].

[16]The first robo-pet, AIBO, had a computer built in with state-of-the-art technology and a rather steep price. In a number of reported engagements with AIBO, the robo-pet appears to mimic and to be versatile in responding within an environment [http://www.sel.sony.com/SEL/consumer/sonystyle/archives/0200/aibo.html].

[17]In "Why the Future Doesn't Need Us?" Bill Joy suggests that we may have to stop our current technological directions and seriously consider the implications of our current path. *Wired*, April 2000 [http://www/wired/com/wired/archive/8.04/joy/html].

nanotechnology, genetic engineering, and robotics, raising the question of whether successively more intelligent and more powerful machines will make human beings obsolete.

For those of us who spend a disproportionate amount of our lives with the technologies that dominate both work and entertainment, it sometimes slips our minds that real life is the original, and still the best, multimedia educational experience. Young people may learn a great deal about trees from the finest scientific and teaching minds available through computer programs or online education, but this is no substitute for looking at, touching, and hearing the wind rustle through the leaves of a particular tree that has some significance in one's own life. Watching the leaves change color and fall, crunching through them, and jumping in a pile of them results in a social and aesthetic knowing that is as important as knowing the scientific explanations of how and why those leaves change color and texture. Playing around a tree, sitting under it to dream, perhaps building a treehouse in its branches implants the essence and the importance of trees in human life. Equally important is the contact with informed and caring human beings who can share, model, and contextualize that joyful learning experience. All of us are so saturated with illusions of life on computer screens and in videos and motion pictures that we often ignore evidence from our own eyes, and it is increasingly difficult for some to know for themselves what life really looks like.

Education is indeed a lifelong sense-making process. Individuals, as learners, are in the continual process of connecting their own knowing to established communities of knowledge to make new, personally significant meanings. The availability of vast quantities of knowledge and the accessibility to those who create and shape that knowledge via the Internet and other digital media relieves schools from the necessity of packaging and processing content in traditional ways. Empowered Internet-generation students also express new expectations and demands. Formal educational organizations must face these challenges with a critical pedagogy that resists unexamined assumptions.

Education for the CyberCities of the 21st century must balance multiple alternatives, respecting differing voices, content, contexts, delivery systems, and teaching and learning styles. Participants in community learning centers must be valued for their creativity and imagination as well as for their knowledge, for it is only with these qualities that learners can progress from data to knowledge to wisdom. As Alfred North Whitehead (1929) said many years ago "Culture is activity of thought, and receptiveness to beauty and humane feeling. Scraps of information have nothing to do with it" (p. 13).

REFERENCES

Frye, N. (1964). *The educated imagination*. Bloomington: Indiana University Press.

McLuhan, M., & Fiore, Q. (1967). *The medium is the message*. New York: Random House.

Toffler, A. (1970). *Future shock*. New York: Random House.

Whitehead, A. N. (1929). *The aims of education and other essays*. New York: New American Library.

Thirteen

Oppression and Resultant Violence in the Inner City: Causes, Effects on Students, and Responsibilities of Educators

Ann C. Diver-Stamnes

Writing about violence in the inner city and its effects on the children and adolescents who live there involves a very real conundrum: how does a writer clearly articulate the realities of the lives of this population of young people without demonizing them or perpetuating stereotypes about them? That is the central challenge of this chapter. The objectives for the chapter include elucidating the socioeconomic realities and living conditions in the inner cities of the United States, exploring the reasons for inner-city violence, defining the effects of such violence on children and adolescents, and providing preservice and inservice teachers unfamiliar with the inner city with a framework for self-examination and for working in inner-city schools in which their students' life experiences will—by definition—differ dramatically from those of students from middle- and upper-class family backgrounds.

Prior to beginning a discussion of the inner city, it would be beneficial to note who makes up the teaching population in this country. The majority of public school teachers are European American middle-class women (Darling-Hammond & Sclan, 1996). In short, many of the teachers who enter inner-city schools have little or no experience in inner cities and as such may view their students and the communities in which their students live through their own cultural lenses, which are inaccurate and skewed when applied to inner-city culture. For example, whereas European American middle-class individuals may be very conversant within their own cultural milieu, they may be completely uninformed in regard to the "code of the streets" (Anderson, 1994, p. 81). The central theme to the code of the streets is respect, which is conveyed and communicated in ways that may be beyond the ken of people who do not reside in an inner-city community—for example, eye contact, dress, jewelry, and so forth (Anderson, 1994). As a high school teacher in the Watts community of Los Angeles in the 1980s, I observed a classic example of the lack of intercultural competence of a teacher new to the community who was unaware of the code. Two students were involved in an altercation, and the teacher intervened, saying in some exasperation to one student, "He was just looking at you, for heaven's sake!" She did not understand that the other student had made prolonged eye contact with a particular facial expression that required the other student to retaliate in order to maintain his social standing and respect. Seen through her cultural lens, the student's response was extreme; seen through the students' cultural lens, the response was reasonable.

Thus, the question becomes, how can classroom teachers become conversant in the cultural realities of their students, even when those realities may differ significantly from their own? Further, how can they learn to suspend judgment so as to appreciate and understand the contextual realities of their students' lives without placing them in juxtaposition to their own values and norms? This is a difficult endeavor that becomes emotionally charged when we observe the level to which violence in the inner city impinges on the lives of the children and adolescents who enter our classrooms each day.

DEFINING VIOLENCE

The word *violence* carries different meanings for different people. For example, one study of 100 individuals in a very high-crime neighborhood in New York City revealed varied and complex definitions of violence from the personal level (a man who had abused his wife and children) to community violence (an individual who pointed out that the high level of gunfire on the streets had resulted in it becoming the norm and, as such, no longer seeming to be violent) to structural inequalities ("economic violence") (Fullilove, Héon, Jimenez, Parsons, Green, & Fullilove, 1998, p. 925). Thus, although it may be true that people think of physical violence when hearing the term *inner-city violence*, inner-city residents see violence to be a much more complex issue that ranges from the personal to the societal levels.

Certainly, the physical aspect of violence creates a charged and difficult atmosphere "characterized by the seeing, hearing, and experiencing of many different forms of violence, including police harassment or indifference, drug-related violence, crowd violence, and family violence. Gunshots [are] often heard in the streets" (Fullilove et al., 1998, p. 925). For young people in the inner city, gun-related victimization dramatically exceeds that experienced by students on the national level (Sheley, McGee, & Wright, 1992). The violence in the community often results in restrictions of movement for the residents who fear being on the streets, in the blooming of anomie, and in a lack of a sense of united community (Fullilove et al., 1998). Family life in the inner city contains realities beyond the experience of those who do not live in the community:

> The witnessing of murders; anxieties about having one's money or other valuables stolen; the fear of leaving the house even to go to the corner store; the need to keep bats and knives around the house for protection; feeling that one must almost board up one's doors at night to keep thieves away; the resignation that one's own life might be as short as that of friends and family members who have fallen victim to crime, drugs, or poverty; and the desire to move away to a more peaceful place—all these thoughts—indeed, concerns for basic safety—occupied the minds of the 8- to 13-year-old youngsters with whom I spoke. How much energy and attention could these inner-city youth have left for spelling, mathematics, and social studies? I wonder. (Towns, 1996, p. 387)

My students in Watts shared similar issues with me, and I struggled with and was grieved by the notion that they had to miss school in order to stay home to guard the house or apartment when a parent or guardian had to be away from home or that they watched helplessly from a window at night while a group of individuals broke into the family's car and, with complete impunity, stole everything that they could dismantle or that a gentle male student was attacked and beaten with a hammer while awaiting a bus.

However, violence is not simply physical, aimed at humans, animals, or inanimate objects. Violence occurs at the societal level as well, in the tacit acceptance of the existence in this country of children in poverty who go hungry, who lack adequate medical care including immunizations, and who live in abysmally impoverished conditions (Diver-Stamnes, 1995). Much of the violence experienced by individuals in the inner city has its roots outside of the community. ". . . [T]he cumulative effects of poverty, racism, and other forms of social injustice are not only potential causes of violence but forms of violence in and of themselves" (Fullilove, et al., 1998, p. 927). The oppression that allows the existence of some individuals who are well-off and others who live in poverty is indeed a form of violence, one that is difficult to contemplate for those who have lived lives of relative ease. As noted by Freire, "With the establishment of a relationship of oppression, violence has *already* begun. Never in history has violence been initiated by the oppressed. . . . There would be no oppressed had there been no prior situation of violence to establish their subjugation" (Freire, 1970, p. 41).

Thus, it is clear that we cannot discuss violence in the inner city on a simplistic level, confining its definition to a single realm. Instead, it exists in multiple dimensions, from the individual to the community to the society. Each of these dimensions has an effect on the lives and life options of children and adolescents in inner cities across the United States.

CAUSES OF VIOLENCE

As with so many issues pertaining to the inner cities of the United States, attempting to undertake a causal analysis becomes a complex task precisely because no single cause exists, but rather a multiplicity of causes that are interwoven and mutually interdependent. Even before asking why violence exists in the inner city, one must ask why inner cities themselves exist. What has created the conditions in which hopelessness and despair so often reign?

The changing economy has had a tremendous impact on the lives of working class and poor people in the United States. "The economy has churned out tens of millions of new jobs in the last two decades. In that same period, joblessness among inner-city blacks has reached catastrophic proportions" (Wilson, 1996b, p. 27). For people whose life options are limited, who are unable to finish high school, who will not attend college, blue-collar jobs once provided the means to make a living wage and support a family. The industrial economy jobs of turning raw materials into finished product, for example, working in tire plants or steel mills, did not require advanced education and still provided workers with the means to sustain themselves and their families (Diver-Stamnes, 1995).

However, in the postindustrial economy, companies have downsized in order to become more competitive in the world market, and industrial jobs have been moved overseas where labor costs are much lower (Giroux, 1996; Wilson, 1996a). The jobs that are available and that create upward social mobility are those that require highly specialized knowledge—for example, computer technology, finance, and marketing—for which many inner-city residents—living in hypersegregated inner-city communities, having attended often inadequate inner-city schools, and as a result suffering from "academic poverty" (Diver-Stamnes, 1995, p. 9)—are unprepared. The jobs that are available to inner-city residents are those that provide low status, low pay, and few if any benefits—for example, in the food or clothing industries. My students in Watts joked about working for "the colonel or the clown," a reference to working for fast-food restaurants such as Kentucky Fried Chicken or McDonalds, which poignantly illustrated the lack of life and work options that were available to them. Thus, the changing economy and resultant dearth of jobs in the inner city have caused a huge chasm between the haves and the have nots, ultimately resulting in an increasingly hypersegregated inner city where young people are not being exposed to the skills they need to take part in the postindustrial economy and where opportunities for work that would provide a living wage are scarce.

An underground economy exists in the inner city in the form of the drug economy. For those who are not able to find jobs, drug sales provide a source of income for some inner-city residents. As such, involvement in illegal drugs is enticing in an environment in which few opportunities exist. The presence of drugs and drug sales of course dramatically changes the community in which they are being sold. Many inner-city residents point to drugs as being the causal factor in their communities' decline.

> In high violence segments of the community, the reign of terror of the drug lords . . . altered movement in the streets and interactions among neighbors. . . . Respondents were depressed by the deteriorating neighborhood, public spaces occupied by drug dealers, stores cluttered by day but shuttered with metal gates at night, and graffiti covering walls and street signs. Drugs were universally held to blame for the deterioration of the neighborhood. The wars between drug dealers became increasingly dangerous in the 1980s, when guns began to be an integral part of the battle for territory and power. (Fullilove et al., 1998, pp. 925-926)

Communities that once were viable, healthy, and diverse have in essence folded in upon themselves, creating spaces in which people learn to avoid contact with others, focus on keeping their children off the street in order to ensure their safety, and sense that they must compete for the few resources available. Out of such circumstances, gangs are able to grow and flourish. They have their roots in the myriad problems that beset inner cities: few resources to support schools and families, few jobs, lack of ability for older community members to work and thus to fulfill the role as agents of control and socialization for the young, destabilized neighborhoods, and the resultant hopelessness that leads to drug activity, which in turn brings violence and instability into the community (Fagan, 1999).

EFFECTS OF VIOLENCE

Simply on an intuitive level, one would have to suspect that exposure to violence, especially unremitting community violence, must have an effect on children. Research on the number of children witnessing and experiencing violence in the inner city reveals the unmistakable evidence that they have a high rate of exposure. Inner-city youth experience a greater degree of violence, both as witnesses and as victims, than do older, more affluent youth (Gladstein, Slater Rusonis, & Heald, 1992). Richters and Martinez reported a high rate of exposure to violence among even very young children living in a low-income neighborhood that was moderately violent, resulting in children displaying such symptoms as anxiety and depression (Richters & Martinez, 1993a; Martinez & Richters, 1993). In a study of 96 students in Miami/Dade County who were from low-income inner-city neighborhoods, 86.5% of the participants had witnessed a mugging, 63.5% had witnessed a nonfatal stabbing, 60.4% had seen a nonfatal shooting, 66.6% had seen dead bodies, 19.8% had witnessed a suicide, 41.6% had witnessed a murder, and 37.5% had been a victim of mugging (Berman, Kurtines, Silverman, & Serafini, 1996). As the authors of the study concluded, ". . . the probability of exposure to violence, either as witness or victim, is dramatically high among inner-city youth" (Berman et al., 1996, p. 334).

Of the 246 participants in another study, 42% had witnessed someone being shot or knifed, 22% had witnessed someone being killed, 9% had seen more than one person killed, and 50% had concerns about being attacked in the street (Schubiner, Scott, & Tzelepis, 1993). "This level of community violence is likely to impact the quality of life of all inner-city adolescents, affecting their decisions about the clothes they wear, the routes they travel, school activities, and their choice of friends" (Schubiner et al., 1993, p. 217). Gorman-Smith and Tolan (1998) noted that 80% of the 245 male participants in their study reported having had exposure to violence in their lifetimes, with 65% reporting such exposure during the last year. Individuals who experience a greater degree of exposure to violence were found to be older rather than younger, male rather than female, African American rather than European American, violent offenders rather than nonoffenders, and those residing in high-crime as opposed to low-crime areas (Selner-O'Hagan, Kindlon, Buka, Raudenbush, & Earls, 1998).

The high rate of children and adolescents experiencing and witnessing violence in the inner city is not without its social, emotional, psychological, and academic repercussions. Exposure to violence either in the home or the community was found to be associated with and predictive of Posttraumatic Stress Disorder (PTSD), with 29% of participants in one study exhibiting clinical symptoms of PTSD (Berton

& Stabb, 1996). PTSD symptoms include sleep difficulties, eating problems, social and emotional problems, fearfulness, flashbacks to the stressor incidents, and so forth, and children who are continually exposed to violence may exhibit "persistent patterns of psychological maladaptation" (Marans & Cohen, 1993, p. 282). Indeed, exposure to violence functions as a strong predictive factor of PTSD (Fitzpatrick & Boldizar, 1993). PTSD seems to function as a mediating variable in that first individuals are exposed to violence, then exhibit PTSD symptomatology, which then can lead to serious and negative mental health issues (Mazza & Reynolds, 1999). Increases in aggression and depression are also related to exposure to violence in the community (Gorman-Smith & Tolan, 1998; Martinez & Richters, 1993). Exposure to violence is strongly associated with externalizing behaviors—that is, antisocial behaviors and willingness to use physical aggression, and internalizing symptoms—that is, depression, anxiety, and somatization (Schwab-Stone, Chen, Greenberger, Silver, Lichtman, & Voyce, 1999).

Thus, we know that inner-city children and adolescents are exposed to high levels of violence at a crucial time of development in their lives. We know that this exposure places them at risk for depression, antisocial behaviors, sleep and eating problems, aggressive behavior, anxiety, and serious mental health problems, to name a few. As Tolleson points out:

> The steady onslaught of violence throughout early life requires that the developing child make extraordinary adaptations at all levels of his psychological functioning in order to preserve his sense of well-being. The lethal violence experienced by the inner-city child is, from early on, characterized by its chronicity, its proximity, its human causation, and by the fact that it preexists him. His relationship to violence, therefore, does not necessarily produce eruptions within an already stable adaptation (like war veterans, for instance), but rather organizes his development from the beginning. . . . Indeed, his developmental task is unique upon the American social landscape, namely, to accommodate himself to a world in which the possibility of his own violent death is considered a normative feature of existence. (Tolleson, 1997, p. 416)

This is the often brutal life experience inner-city children and adolescents bring with them as they enter the classroom. "If this situation of continual violence were occurring inside the four walls of a youth's home, rather than in the community-at-large, the State's Department of Public Welfare would be involved" (Bigelow, 1993, p. 548). It seems quite obvious that, even at a very early age, their life experiences differ quite dramatically from those of their peers growing up in middle-class or wealthy communities, who have some sense that their environment is safe, stable, and predictable and who are able to focus on issues of development rather than survival of self and of those they love. Clearly, these life experiences impinge upon not only their development and their psychological and emotional well-being, but upon their academic functioning as well.

PEOPLE'S PERCEPTIONS OF INNER-CITY RESIDENTS

As mentioned earlier, the majority of teachers in the United States are European American and middle class. Their experiences in and knowledge of the inner cities of this country are minimal, and their understanding of the inner city is often informed by the popular media, including newspapers and magazines, films and music. At the university at which I now teach, some of my teacher credential candidates unfailingly ask me each year if the movie *Dangerous Minds*, an unrealistic portrayal of inner-city teaching that perpetuates negative stereotypes about young ethnic minority adolescents, is an accurate depiction of teaching in the inner city, if it mirrors what I experienced as an inner-city high school teacher. With some notable exceptions, my students' perceptions of inner-city life and culture often tend to be polarized: they have either a romanticized or a demonized view of the inner city and of teaching in the inner city, both notable for their lack of accuracy.

Popular media portray inner-city residents in ways that both demonize them and perpetuate negative stereotypes. Giroux notes that stories focusing on African Americans in mainstream media are "reprehensible" in that "they not only reproduce racist stereotypes about blacks by portraying them as criminals and welfare cheats, but they remove whites from any responsibility or complicity for the violence and poverty that has become so endemic to American life" (Giroux, 1996, p. 66). Indeed, the negative image of African Americans is embedded deeply in the national psyche, having its roots planted 400 years ago when the first Africans were enslaved, and continuing in the present day devaluing of African Americans (Sellers-Diamond, 1994).

People in poverty, particularly ethnic minorities, are often portrayed as "other," as "different," and it is precisely this otherness, this difference that seems to absolve the majority of people in the United States from feeling a sense of horror, an awakening of compassion at the plight of the poor. How else can we explain the fact that we allow children in poverty to go hungry every day in this country of tremendous wealth (Diver-Stamnes, 1995)? In this society, we tend to turn a blind eye to the plight of the poor because they represent a population of devalued people whose lives are somewhat incomprehensible to us. We see the popular culture movies—for example, *Boyz N the Hood, Menace II Society*, and *Clockers*—only to have reinforced the perception that African Americans, in particular those who are male and poor, are alien and are by nature violent.

These perceptions are so deeply embedded in our cultural perceptions that they even have been the basis for government policy and have been presented as rational and reasonable. For example, in 1992, Dr. Frederick Goodwin, then Director of the Alcohol Drug Abuse and Mental Health Administration, announced a set of policies in regard to the reduction of violence that came to be known as the Violence Initiative. Its premise was that violence in the inner city is biologically based, can be detected at very early ages, and can be controlled through a variety of methods including the use of drugs (Breggin & Breggin, 1998; Sellers-Diamond, 1994). Inner-city children were, in essence, viewed as having a high likelihood of becoming violent because of "an inherent vulnerability, an unalterable state of being" (Sellers-Diamond, 1994, p. 436). In his introduction of the Violence Initiative, he compared male monkeys, whose behaviors he characterized as being hyperaggressive and hypersexual, with inner-city residents (Breggin & Breggin, 1998; Seller-Diamond, 1994). Although the Violence Initiative was ultimately canceled, it is important to note that this focus on individual causation of violence as opposed to systemic inequities, poverty, hunger, and joblessness, was widely discussed as a viable approach to the reduction of violence in the inner cities of the United States. As Sellers-Diamond (1994, p. 437) notes, "It seems a startling proposition that when children have barely learned to walk and speak, their dangerous propensities for deviant behavior could be marked, and that perceptions of them in the eyes of society should be solidified."

Unless individuals seriously attempt to learn about the realities of the lives of people who live in inner-city communities, they run the risk of assimilating the omnipresent negative messages about them. It is these perceptions that can be most damaging when they are held by individuals who want to teach in inner-city schools. Teachers who enter inner-city schools with such perceptions of the children they will teach can do unimagined harm to their students. Ryan notes ". . . teachers in ghetto schools are, in fact, imbued with these kinds of expectations and attitudes. They expect that the children will do poorly and, ultimately, their expectations are borne out" (Ryan, 1971, p. 57). In the inner-city high school at which I taught, I found an expectation of failure: each semester, teachers received classroom rosters with bloated enrollments that assigned far too many students to a particular class (Diver-Stamnes, 1995). During my first semester at the school, I questioned this in some alarm in that I did not have enough desks to hold all the students I had on my class list. I was told not to worry because the majority of the students would stop coming to school after the first week or two, and then the class size would be manageable. School personnel in essence planned for the failure of these students and indeed counted on it. Having previously taught in both rural and suburban high schools, I found such egregious practices to be foreign and unethical, a further form of systemic violence that guaranteed the academic failure of a population of young people who had already been poorly served by the educational system. The difficulty arose in confronting such practices which stemmed from the culture of the school and were based upon widely held beliefs and perceptions about the capabilities and worth of inner-city adolescents.

It seems axiomatic that poverty, ethnicity, and family will have an effect on children's and adolescents' academic performance. The question is why? Is it because they have an effect on the children and adolescents and their ability to learn or because they have an effect on the teachers' perceptions of their students' abilities and as a consequence on their expectations for those students? Ryan asserts that, ". . . the primary effect of poverty, race, and family background is not on children, but on the teacher, who is led to *expect* poorer performance from black and poor children" and that "the expectations of the teacher are a major determinant of the children's performances" (Ryan, 1971, p. 53).

Each year, I tell my students who are credential candidates that we as educators have the potential to do great good in the lives of our students, and we also have the potential to do great harm. Teaching inner-city students without first examining the systemic violence that has created the conditions in which their students' live, the realities of their students' lives which include a high level of community violence, their own biases and stereotypes, and their own reasons for wanting to teach this population of young people is an example of the potential to do great harm. Such examination of self and society is crucial. As Freire notes, "Those who authentically commit themselves to the people must re-examine themselves constantly" (Freire, 1970, p. 47).

ROLES AND RESPONSIBILITIES OF INNER-CITY EDUCATORS

Prior to accepting positions in inner-city schools, preservice educators need to become inquisitive and open-minded students in their analysis and assessment of life in the inner city. They need an in-depth knowledge of the causes of poverty in this country and the inequities from which violence arises. They need a clear understanding of their own biases, a willingness to accept and move beyond them, and a commitment to become advocates for social change. They need to embrace learning about their students' lives and to be willing to respect and honor the realities of their lives.

Teaching is an inherently political act. Teaching in the inner city is a profound political act that necessitates a commitment to standing with people in poverty in this society, people who are by definition oppressed. "Conversion to the people requires a profound rebirth. Those who undergo it must take on a new form of existence; they can no longer remain as they were. Only through comradeship with the oppressed can the converts understand their characteristic ways of living and behaving, which in diverse moments reflect the structure of domination" (Freire, 1970, p. 47).

A certain vigilance is necessary to be an effective and compassionate educator in an inner-city school. Because of the pervasive nature of negative stereotypes of inner-city residents, in particular adolescents, and because of the often negative perceptions held about inner-city children and adolescents in the very schools they attend, it is all too easy to become jaded and cynical, to allow expectations to deflate. For example, an inner-city mother who was concerned over her daughter's reading level was told not to worry about it by the girl's teacher who said that the child was "doing very well, for this neighborhood" (Ryan, 1971, p. 30). Such pernicious views corrode parents', guardians', and children's beliefs in their own worth and convey the highly classist impression that children in poverty should somehow be satisfied with an inferior education because it is all they are due and perhaps all they are capable of assimilating.

Teachers and administrators in inner-city schools must be involved in "observing keenly, listening carefully, and interpreting critically to bring forth insights that will make a difference in the education of these children" (Towns, 1996, p. 388). Awareness of the ways in which violence in the community impacts their lives is crucial. Examples of insensitivity abound. When I taught high school in the Watts community, a young man was killed one evening at a public telephone on the street. The police response was very slow in this incident, and the body was still sprawled on the pavement when children and adolescents walked to their elementary, middle, and high schools the next morning (Diver-Stamnes, 1995). When the first class began at the high school, some teachers started to teach their regular lesson despite the fact that they had students in the class who were quite obviously in grave distress at having just walked past a dead body on the way to school.

Towns provides another example of such insensitivity:

> The adults at the school went about their daily tasks, pretending to teach, but apparently oblivious to what was going on in the surrounding community and in the lives of the students from that community. For example, when third-grader Michael was suspended for "failing to show respect to his elders," his teacher told me that she thought he was acting up because his favorite uncle had been arrested. This awareness, however, did not prevent him from being suspended, nor did it alter that teacher's expectation for Michael to turn in his homework on time. In another case, a sixth-grade teacher failed to excuse an obviously exhausted Robert from a classroom discussion on prefixes and suffixes, even after he informed her that he had not been able to sleep the night before because his mother's brother had been killed on the street, and she had been up all night crying. (Towns, 1996, p. 377)

Such obliviousness on the part of some educators to the painful realities of the lives of their students constitutes yet another form of violence in which the students receive the tacit message from school that the traumas they experience have no importance, and that they are expected to function and learn regardless of loss, grief, shock, or pain. I am always amazed not by how many inner-city students we lose in the process of "educating" them, but by how many stay despite being devalued and placed in a context that is often completely disconnected from their real lives.

EMPATHIC RESPONSE AND ACTION: EDUCATORS AS ADVOCATES

What are some possible and proactive ways to assist inner-city children and adolescents to deal more effectively with the high level of violence in their lives as well as become academically successful? What can inner-city educators specifically do to impact the lives of the students with whom they work? Is there anything educators can do to provide support for them? I repeatedly caution my credential candidates not to underestimate the influence of a single classroom teacher, even in the midst of a school culture that may be neither affirming nor respectful of students.

Certainly, on the macro level, strategies that "affect the overall health (i.e., economic, educational, medical, and social) of inner-city communities have the potential to solve this complex problem" (Schubiner et al., 1993, p. 218). The societal inequities that fostered the creation of inner cities in this country must be addressed and ameliorated. It is so much easier to blame the poor for their own circumstances rather than attempting to do a causal analysis (Diver-Stamnes, 1995). Blaming the poor means that they can be written off, that the violence in their communities is their own fault and as such does not merit the ameliorating efforts of those who do not live in inner cities. However, such a position is dangerously short-sighted. Violence does not spring from the poor, as Dr. Goodwin hypothesized, because they are somehow genetically programmed to be violent. It is the social conditions in which they live that often give rise to the violence, "the lack of jobs that pay a living wage, the stigma of race, the fallout from rampant drug use and trafficking, and the resulting alienation and lack of hope for the future" (Anderson, 1994, p. 81). Indeed, in order for the United States to reduce youth violence, "serious consideration needs to be given to the societally-inflicted violence of raising three to 10 times more youth in poverty than other western nations" (Males, 1996, p. 109).

The kind of societal introspection that needs to occur is not popular in the United States where the focus is on the individual and where it is commonly believed that people should be able to get ahead through their own effort and hard work. Such a perception does not take into consideration the differences in life realities and opportunities between those born into comfortable circumstances and those born into abject poverty. In short,

> . . . it is likely that the violence perpetrated by urban children will prevail until its *causes* have been substantively addressed, until the need for it has been reduced. Violent children, after all, are mirrors of the surround, manifestations of all that is both corruptibly vile in society's neglect of its poor urban children and splendidly resilient in the children themselves. (Tolleson, 1997, p. 429)

As a former inner-city high school teacher, I firmly believe that inner-city teachers must be agents of social change, unceasingly vocal advocates for children and adolescents who live their lives in poverty and find their life options and future opportunities defined by that poverty. Inner-city teachers must function at the micro level, creating a safe community and high quality learning environment in their classrooms, and at the macro level, advocating and agitating for the necessary changes in our society that place children at the heart of social policy so that all children have enough to eat, adequate medical care, safe neighborhoods, and excellent schools. These are not the sole birthright of the rich; they should be the birthright of all children, and inner-city educators are in unique position from which to give voice to those who are so often voiceless and who indeed have the least power in our country: inner-city children and adolescents who live in poverty.

Beyond these needed sweeping social changes, family structure that is connected and emotionally supportive may help to buffer the effects of exposure to violence for the young in the areas of anxiety and depression (Gorman-Smith & Tolan, 1998). Working with families may provide a crucial link in supporting inner-city children through helping "families learn to manage and cope with these stressors so they are then able to provide the consistency, structure, and support children need" (Gorman-Smith & Tolan, 1998, p. 114). Some success has been noted as well through community-based policing in which police officers are trained to recognize vulnerable and at-risk individuals, for example, children who have been traumatized by a violent event, and to intervene and refer for mental health and other services (Marans & Cohen, 1993).

Successful inner-city students exhibit certain resiliency factors that may help to facilitate academic success for inner-city youth: imagining their own destiny, developing of a strong internal attitude and focus on goals, being adept at functioning within the school culture, engaging in regular renewal, and being involved in caring relationships (Wong, 1997). These behaviors include students visualizing themselves being successful, talking to themselves in ways that are self-affirming, maintaining a focus on their goals that is not shaken by negatives in their environment, understanding how to be successful in school, taking time for self-renewing activities, and being involved in relationships with at least one supportive adult.

Educators certainly have a role in assisting students in their development of these resiliency factors, and we must not only teach the traditional curricula taught in most schools but must also expand our role so that we assist students in learning skills they need to be successful in school and life in general. Both academic success and failure can be meaningful learning experiences if we know how to process them. However, these are skills that are not intuitive and must be taught. Educators can assist students in understanding how to be involved in efficacious behaviors in the events of academic success and failure. Students may simply give up in the case of failure, choosing not to assess the causes of the failure and often internalizing negative self-concept information as a result (Stamnes, 1987). They may also engage in "personal sabotage" in the event of a success in which the individuals do not give themselves credit for that success but rather attribute it to factors outside their personal control (Stamnes, 1987, p. 26).

Awareness of the ways in which the realities of inner-city students' lives can and do impinge upon their learning is a crucial element in effective teaching in inner-city schools. Perhaps one of the most difficult aspects of teaching in the inner-city is the realization that the children and adolescents are all too aware of the differences between their lives and those of their more fortunate peers. The television shows and movies they watch paint pictures of family and community life dramatically different from theirs, and they are well able to assimilate the painful messages about their worth and value implicit in those differences. In teaching in an inner-city high school, I noted the importance of honestly discussing with my students the inequities in our society that had created the conditions in which they lived. I perceived it to be my job to assist them in gathering knowledge and refining reasoning skills so that they could analyze and assess their society. Such discussions often grew heated as the students became increasingly aware of the differences between the lives of middle- and upper-class teenagers and the lives they themselves were living, the anger a natural by-product of awareness and understanding. I felt it important to face that anger, to create a place where it could exist and be processed, even as some of my colleagues cautioned me against doing so. However, I found that through the use of such an emancipatory curriculum, my students became articulate, passionate, committed, and socially conscious activists who found their own voice, which was a powerful transformation.

For example, I took my students to a conference during my first year at the school, and they were intimidated and shy. They followed me, rather than striking out on their own to attend workshops. When we gathered in the hallway to discuss what had happened to change them from being self-confident students at school to bashful and uncomfortable participants at the conference, they told me in hushed voices that "everyone here is white." One African American student told me that when he had walked down the hallway without me, an adult with the organization that was putting on the conference had begun to follow and observe him, making him "feel like a thief."

I had to acknowledge that I had in a very real sense failed them in that I had not adequately prepared them for this new experience. Over the course of the next year, we not only explored issues of social justice, poverty, community violence, economic violence, and perceptions of ethnic minority youth, we also focused on attaining dominant-culture social skills such as the use of eye contact, firm hand shakes, and nonverbal and paraverbal cues so that the students were truly multicultural and comfortable in a wide variety of environments: at school, at home, on the streets, in a job interview, and even in conversations with university faculty and state politicians. The students learned to become bidialectical as well; that is, they learned to speak the English of the job market as an alternate dialect to that which they spoke with family or friends, both of which, we agreed, were valid when used within the appropriate context. Students were in essence becoming prepared for life beyond the hypersegregated context of the school they attended and the community in which they lived.

When we later attended conferences, the students put on workshops for both adults and other students in which they literally shone. At experimental workshops we conducted on race/ethnicity and social class (Diver-Stamnes, 1994), they were passionately articulate, intelligent, and compassionate, demonstrating the ability to intellectually challenge participants to think about societal inequities and the ways in which they translate in people's lives. I watched them shatter people's stereotypes of inner-city youth and noted with great satisfaction the cognitive disequilibrium experienced by adults and students alike as they interacted with them. They were brutally honest about the poverty and violence in their community, much to the discomfort of many participants, and yet were able to build coalitions with the other participants who suddenly had a compelling human face to place on inner-city youth, on people living in poverty. These same students became deeply involved in altruistic endeavors as well, including making lunches each week for homeless people on Skid Row in Los Angeles, collecting money for Meals on Wheels—a program that delivers food to elderly people—and writing letters on behalf of political prisoners through Amnesty International. Thus, they became politically and socially active change agents themselves.

This kind of exploration of social issues and multiculturalism is impossible to begin unless the relationship between the teacher and students is one based upon respect, honesty, and true caring. Teachers need to be willing to become the caring adult in the lives of their students. The classroom itself can be an oasis in the midst of a violent community or a chaotic school. Teachers and students can create such an oasis through the creation of a community that emphasizes mutual interdependence, acceptance, support, and commitment. This type of classroom differs from the traditional teacher-centered classroom. Rules are created by the entire classroom community, students and teacher together, rather than being created and imposed in a top-down fashion by the teacher. In addition, sanctions are discussed and agreed upon by the classroom community. Social skills, such as those described earlier, are explicitly taught and discussed. For example, I taught my students how to comfort someone who is grieving so that when students experienced the violent death of a friend or family member, the other students did not look to me as the teacher to always fix the problem, but rather provided emotional support and comfort and gently helped the individuals talk and process their grief. This kind of empowering community becomes self-monitoring and obviates the need for the teacher to take on the constant role of behavior monitor. Of course, difficulties such as behavior or management problems do arise. The difference, however, is that these difficulties are not the sole responsibility of the teacher; they are instead the responsibility of the classroom community, the subject for a community meeting where everyone participates in talking about the issues, generating suggestions for solutions, and agreeing upon the final course of action. This is in stark contrast to the kind of draconian management policies of so many inner-city schools that offer yet another negative message to children and adolescents: we know you cannot control yourselves so we will create policies to control you and set sanctions that we will impose upon you if you break any of our rules. Thus, children and adolescents in the inner city often go from a community in which they have no control over the occurrence of violence to a school in which they have no control over the rules and sanctions by which their lives will be governed.

Not only is it important to acknowledge the day-to-day hardships inner-city children and adolescents experience, as well as the chronicity of the traumas in their lives, it is also essential to note that without assistance in dealing with these traumas, unassisted students may begin to channel their reactions and emotions into nonproductive, self-sabotaging, and failure-producing behaviors in school.

> There is no doubt the violence to which inner-city children are exposed affects their school performance, but so does the violation of trust they experience from teachers and school administrators who attempt to ignore what is going on in the communities these children call home. More closely, however, my observations reveal that students whose patterns of socialization have not provided them with mechanisms to

> redirect the pain, anger, and frustration that community violence spawns may display it themselves—in the forms of in-school violence, discipline problems, and/or passive resistance to instruction, all of which lead to failure in schools. (Towns, 1996, p. 387)

Caring inner-city educators attempt to direct their students toward academic success, and this means that by definition they interact with their students in ways that go beyond the traditional curricula. I have heard teachers state that they did not enter this profession to do social work, that they do not want to deal with social ills in children's lives, but rather they want to teach their subjects, to teach math or science, language arts or music. I counter this perception by stating that we do not teach subjects. We do not teach math, science, reading, writing, art, or music; we teach kids, and as such, we must meet them where they are in order to have any hope of positively and respectfully impacting their lives. Equitable education by definition means that we give to each student according to his or her needs, not that we give to each equally. In an inner-city classroom, this translates into doing what some teachers do indeed perceive to be social work: assisting students in coping with the violent deaths of family and friends, helping families receive the social services to which they are entitled, finding drug abuse counseling for a student or family member, or finding shelter for a homeless family. If we are unwilling to authentically share in the complex lives of inner-city students, we will have to resign ourselves to the fact that ultimately we will be unable to reach many of them. As Freire eloquently stated,

> Educators must ask themselves for whom and on whose behalf they are working. The more conscious and committed they are, the more they understand that their role as educators requires them to take risks, including a willingness to risk their own jobs. Educators who do their work uncritically, just to preserve their jobs, have not yet grasped the political nature of education. (Freire, 1985, p. 180)

Thus, it is through a truly critical pedagogy that inner-city educators will be able to positively and profoundly impact the lives of their students, lives that are marked early by poverty and its resultant unremitting violence.

REFERENCES

Anderson, E. (1994, May). The code of the streets. *The Atlantic Monthly*, 81-92.

Berman, S.L., Kurtines, W.M., Silverman, W.K., & Serafini, L.T. (1996, July). The impact of exposure to crime and violence on urban youth. *American Journal of Orthopsychiatry, 66*(3), 329-336.

Berton, M.W., & Stabb, S.D. (1996, Summer). Exposure to violence and post-traumatic stress disorder in urban adolescents. *Adolescence, 31*, 489-498.

Bigelow, A.M. (1993). In the ghetto: The state's duty to protect inner-city children from violence. *Notre Dame Journal of Law, Ethics and Public Policy, 7*, 533-567.

Breggin, P.R., & Breggin, G.R. (1998). *The war against children of color*. Monroe, ME: Common Courage Press.

Darling-Hammond, L., & Sclan, E.M. (1996). Who teaches and why: Dilemmas of building a profession for twenty-first century schools. In J. Sikula (Ed.), *Handbook of research on teacher education* (2nd ed., pp. 67-101). New York: Macmillian Library Reference.

Diver-Stamnes, A.C. (1994). Simulating society: An experimental approach to exploring race/class relations. *Resources in Education*. (ERIC/CASS)

Diver-Stamnes, A.C. (1995). *Lives in the balance: Youth, poverty, and education in Watts*. Albany: SUNY Press.

Fagan, J. (1999). Youth gangs, drugs, and socioeconomic isolation. In D. J. Flannery & C.R. Hugg (Eds.), *Youth violence: Prevention, intervention, and social violence* (pp. 145-170). Washington, DC: American Psychiatric Press.

Fitzpatrick, K.M., & Boldizar, J.P. (1993). The prevalence and consequences of exposure to violence among African-American youth. *Journal of the American Academy of Child and Adolescent Psychiatry, 32*, 424-430.

Freire, P. (1970). *Pedagogy of the oppressed*. New York: Continuum.

Freire, P. (1985). *The politics of education: Culture, power, and liberation*. South Hadley, MA: Bergin & Garvey.

Fullilove, M.D., Héon, V., Jimenez, W., Parsons, C., Green, L.L., & Fullilove, R.E. (1998, June). Injury and anomie: Effects of violence on an inner-city community. *American Journal of Public Health, 88*(6), 924-927.

Giroux, H.A. (1996). *Fugitive cultures: Race, violence, and youth*. New York: Routledge.

Gladstein, J., Slater Rusonis, E.J., & Heald, F.P. (1992, June 1). A comparison of inner-city and upper-middle class youths' exposure to violence. *Society for Adolescent Medicine, 13*, 275-280.

Gorman-Smith, D., & Tolan, P. (1998). The role of exposure to community violence and development problems among inner-city youth. *Development and Psychopathology, 10*, 101-116.

Males, M.A. (1996). *The scapegoat generation: America's war on adolescents*. Monroe, ME: Common Courage Press.

Marans, S., & Cohen, D.J. (1993). Children and inner-city violence: Strategies for intervention. In L. A. Leavitt & N.A. Fox (Eds.), *The psychological effects of war and violence on children* (pp. 281-301). Hillsdale, NJ: Erlbaum.

Martinez, P., & Richters, J.E. (1993). The NIMH community violence project: II. Children's distress symptoms associated with violent exposure. *Psychiatry, 56*, 22-35.

Mazza, J.J., & Reynolds, W.M. (1999). Exposure to violence in young inner-city adolescents: Relationships with suicidal ideation, depression, and PTSD symptomatology. *Journal of Abnormal Child Psychology, 27*(3), 203-213.

Richters, J.E., & Martinez, P. (1993a). The NIMH community violence project: I. Children as victims of and witnesses to violence. *Psychiatry, 56*, 7-21.

Richters, J.E., & Martinez, P. (1993b). Violent communities, family choices, and children's chances: An algorithm for improving the odds. *Development and Psychopathology, 5*, 609-627.

Ryan, W. (1971). *Blaming the victim*. New York: Vintage Books.

Schubiner, H., Scott, R., & Tzelepis, A. (1993). Exposure to violence among inner-city youth. *Journal of Adolescent Health, 14*, 214-219.

Schwab-Stone, M., Chen, C., Greenberger, E., Silver, D., Lichtman, J., & Voyce, C. (1999, April). No safe haven II: The effects of violence exposure on urban youth. *Journal of the American Academy of Child and Adolescent Psychiatry, 38*(4), 359-367.

Sellers-Diamond, A.A. (1994, Spring). Disposable children in black faces: The Violence Initiative as inner-city containment policy. *UMKC Law Review, 62*(3), 423-469.

Selner-O'Hagen, M.B., Kindlon, D.J., Buka, S.L., Raudenbush, S.W., & Earls, F.J. (1998). Assessing exposure to violence in urban youth. *Journal of Child Psychology and Psychiatry, 39*(2), 215-224.

Sheley, J.F., McGee, Z.T., & Wright, J.D. (1992, June). Gun-related violence in and around inner-city schools. *American Journal of Diseases of Children, 146*(6), 677-682.

Stamnes, A.C. (1987). Development and application of a model of self-efficacy: Implications for understanding academic success and failure (Doctoral dissertation, University of California at Santa Barbara). *Dissertation Abstracts International, 48*, 11A.

Tolleson, J. (1997, June). Death and transformation: The reparative power of violence in the lives of young black inner-city gang members. *Smith College Studies in Social Work, 67*(3), 415-431.

Towns, D.P. (1996). "Rewind the world!": An ethnographic study of inner-city Africa American children's perceptions of violence. *Journal of Negro Education, 65*(3), 375-398.

Wilson, W.J. (1996a). *When work disappears: The world of the new urban poor*. New York: Knopf.

Wilson, W.J. (1996b, August 18). Work. *New York Times Magazine*, pp. 26-31, 40, 48, 52, 54.

Wong, M. (1997, March). How risky is "at-risk"? Building the cords of resiliency. *American Secondary Education, 25*, 1-7.

About the Contributors

James V. Bruni is Dean of Education at Lehman College of the City University of New York. He is a nationally recognized mathematics educator, served on the executive committee of the Urban Systemic Initiative-Bronx, served as the Co-PI for the National Science Foundation New York City Mathematics Project, and is currently a Co-PI for the New York Collaborative for Excellence in Teacher Preparation.

Anne Campos is Associate Director of the Institute for Literacy Studies at Lehman College, The City University of New York. She is a K-12 policy specialist and has served in various capacities in the public and higher education sectors. Prior to joining the Institute, she served the Deans of the Faculty of Arts and Science and the School of Education at New York University in the areas of grants management, policy studies, and program development. She was a K- 12 education program analyst in the Executive Offices of the Governor of Illinois. Ms. Campos received an M.A. in public policy studies from the University of Chicago and a B.A. in history from Kenyon College.

Linda A. Catelli is a Professor of Education in the Elementary Education Department at Dowling College. She specializes in school-university partnerships, education reform, and the analysis of teaching. She holds emeritus status at Queens College of the City University of New York (CUNY). She received her B.A. from Hunter College/CUNY, and her M.A. and Ed.D. from Teachers College, Columbia University. Earlier in her career, she was a teacher of physical education in the New York City schools, a teacher at the Bank St. Elementary Lab School, and the Agnes Russell Lab School at Teachers College, Columbia University, where she also served as an instructor in the Department of Curriculum and Teaching. She has taught courses in education at New York University, William Paterson University, Lehman College/CUNY, Brooklyn College/CUNY, and The City College/CUNY. In the 1970s, she served as acting principal of the Agnes Russell Lab School and then went on to a faculty position at Queens College/CUNY where she founded and directed a school-university partnership program with teachers representing schools in the New York City area. In 1990, she was one of 56 professors from around the nation selected and honored by the American Association for Higher Education as a pioneer in school-college collaboration. In 1991, she received the City University of New York Faculty Achievement Award for creative achievement and pioneering work in school-college partnerships, and in 1996 she was selected by a committee of referees from the University of London to serve on an international panel of experts to represent the U.S. perspective and to carve out new and innovative forms of teacher education and school improvement. She has spoken and written articles, chapters, and research papers on a wide range of topics in education. Her work with school practitioners has been directed at instituting change and holistic reform in K-12 education and teacher education with a vision of a K-18 education system in the 21st century.

Sarah E. Church holds an Ed.M. in Human Development and Psychology from Harvard Graduate School of Education and is currently working on an Ed.D. in Instructional Leadership at St. John's University. She was the former Director of Academic Programs, School of Education, Dowling College. Prior to that position, she was the Program Coordinator of the Community Tutoring Project at Brooklyn College in New York City on programs such as the Bedford Stuyvesant "I Have a Dream" project, Joshiah Macy program at Clara Barton High School, and programs in multilingual and bilingual high schools in Brooklyn. Her research on teacher preparation field-placement programs provided a foundation for Dowling College's site-based collaborative model for student-teaching programs. As a member of the New York State Regents Visiting Committee on Low-Performing Schools, she observed numerous urban schools that were low performing and recently made suggestions for providing high caliber education for youngsters in the schools she visited. Currently, she is an Adjunct Assistant Professor at the Queens College School of Education and Research Fellow at St. John's University, Queens, New York.

Ann C. Diver-Stamnes is a Professor of Education and chair of the Department of Education at Humboldt State University, which is part of the California State University system and is in Arcata, California, where she has taught for the past eleven years. She received her B.A. in English grammar and composition from Johnston College of the University of Redlands, and her M.A. and Ph.D. in Educational Psychology from University of California at Santa Barbara. She has taught in rural, suburban, and inner-city high schools. She has published three books, two on moral development and reasoning with co-author R. Murray Thomas, and one entitled *Lives in the Balance: Youth. Poverty. and Education in Watts* that examines the lives of inner-city adolescents at a high school in the Watts community in Los Angeles. She has also published in the areas of ethnic minority students' perceptions of the culture of their university, adolescent development, ethnicity and human development, peer counseling programs, child abuse, and race/class relations among high school students. She was Humboldt State University's Outstanding Professor for the year 2000, and she was selected as the Teacher Educator of the Year (2000) by the Credential Counselors and Analysts of California.

Ray Durney is the Director of the New York City Mathematics Project at the Institute for Literacy Studies at Lehman College of the City University of New York. He coordinates all professional development activities related to the improvement of mathematics instruction in schools (K- 12), particularly as they apply to recent reform efforts in mathematics education. For six years prior to this position, he was the chair of the mathematics department at a large inner-city high school. His teaching experiences include 22 years in middle schools and high schools.

Nancy Dubetz is an Assistant Professor in the Department of Early Childhood and Childhood Education at Lehman College/CUNY, where her primary responsibilities are to teach courses in the undergraduate teacher preparation programs and to work with colleagues in the redesign of the urban elementary and bilingual preservice programs. Her research interests include teacher thinking in urban settings, TESOL, and teacher education. She received a doctorate in education from Teachers College, Columbia University, an M.A. in TESOL and foreign language education from Ohio State University, and a B.A. in Spanish and English from Kent State University. She has been a teacher in middle and high schools in the United States and abroad. She works closely with elementary and middle schools in New York City to design effective bilingual and TESOL programs for children.

Stephen J. Farenga is an Associate Professor at Dowling College, where he is responsible for teaching undergraduate and graduate courses in science education and educational research. Prior to his work at Dowling College, he taught science for sixteen years in urban and suburban schools in New York. He holds a B.S. in Education and Psychology from St. John's University, an M.S. in Education from Long Island University, and an Ed.D. from Teachers College, Columbia University. Currently, he is co-editor of "After the Bell" for the journal *Science Scope,* coordinator of clinical education at a private learning center in New York, and a consultant for local school districts on Long Island. He has served on national and state committees promoting integrated science education, and as an adjunct professor he has taught courses in research, special education, and curriculum for gifted students at Teachers College, Columbia University. He has published in the areas of science teaching, teacher preparation and technology, and gender equity.

Beverly Joyce is an Associate Professor at Dowling College, specializing in the areas of research, measurement, evaluation, statistics, and technology. She received a B.S. in Psychology from Boston State College and an M.Ed. and Ph.D. in educational research, measurement and evaluation from Boston College. As an adjunct professor at Boston College, Teachers College, Columbia University, and Lesley College, she has taught courses in mathematics, education, and psychology. She has worked as an educational-psychological evaluator for children at risk at Tufts-New England Medical Center in Boston, as director of research at a market research company in New England, and as a clinical instructor at a private learning center in New York preparing middle school students with skills for academic success in high school. Her research and publications are in the areas of science education, gender equity, teacher preparation, and technology. Currently, she is co-editor of the section "After the Bell" in *Science Scope,* a middle school science journal.

Daniel Ness is an Assistant Professor of mathematics education in the Department of Elementary Education at Dowling College. His areas of expertise include the development of mathematical thinking from birth to adolescence, mathematics and culture, and young children's mathematical thinking in the everyday context. He assumed editorship of the newsletter for the International Study Group on Ethnomathematics (ISGEM) in 1999.

Phyllis Opochinsky has been a teacher in the New York City High Schools for 30 years. She was instrumental in the design and initiation of the Walton/Lehman Pre-teaching Academy (1984-present) and was the coordinator of the academy for the first fifteen years. She was the first recipient of the Reliance Award for New York City High School Teacher of the Year, which recognized her teaching ability and contribution to the development and continued success of the Pre-teaching Academy. She will serve on the New York City Pre-teaching Institute.

Kathryn Padovano is presently the Dean of the School of Education at Manhattanville College, Purchase, New York. She was previously the Dean of the School of Education (1991-1999) and Professor of Education (1999-2001) at Dowling College on Long Island. She was also President-Elect of the New York State Association of Teacher Educators. She received her B.A. in Elementary Education from Felician College, her M.F.A. from Montclair State University, a second M.A. in Educational Administration from New York University, and a Ph.D. in Administration and Policy Studies in Education from the University of California, Los Angeles. Earlier in her career, she was an Art Teacher at the elementary level, Adjunct Professor at Bank Street College and Adelphi University, Director of Institutional Research and Planning at Long Island University, and Curator of Education and Community Services for the Queens Museum in New York City, where she created numerous urban education and community programs as well as a temporary shelter program for children and parents. As the 1996 ZONTA Woman Educator of the Year, she worked diligently to advance the status of women in the profession. Recently, she has created a multitude of partnership programs with school districts and business corporations on Long Island and New York City. As a member of the New York State Visiting Committee on Schools Under Review and Registration, she has made recommendations to the Board of Regents for the restructuring of low-performing schools in urban and suburban areas of New York and served on the New York Regents Task Force Teaching Committee. She has written, published, and spoken on a variety of educational issues, and as Dean of Education she has a particular concern with teacher education and the preparation of teachers for work with all children.

M. Victoria Rodríguez is an Assistant Professor in the Department of Early Childhood and Childhood Education at Lehman College of the City University of New York. She received her B.A. in Special Education from the University of Barcelona (Spain), her M.A. in elementary bilingual education from City College of the City University of New York, and her doctorate in education with a specialization in early childhood special education from Teachers College, Columbia University. She has worked for 20 years as a preschool, elementary, and special education teacher in urban settings in Madrid and Barcelona (Spain) and in New York City. Her areas of interest include early learning experiences of culturally and linguistically diverse students, emergent literacy among linguistically diverse students with and without disabilities, and the role of professional development schools and schools of education in the preparation of teachers in urban settings.

Anne L. Rothstein, a faculty member at Lehman since 1965 (when it was Hunter College in The Bronx), has been Director of the Lehman Center for School/College Collaboratives since its inception in 1988 and has raised over $80M in funding for school/college programs since 1985. She is a Professor of early childhood and childhood education at Lehman College of the City University of New York and serves the Provost and Senior Vice President as an Associate for Sponsored Program Development. Her collaboration with Walton High School began in 1984, when, as Associate Dean of Professional Studies, she worked collaboratively with Walton High School and the Bronx Superintendent's Office to conceptualize, plan, and initiate the Walton/Lehman Pre-Teaching Academy. In addition to developing a series of projects designed to assist students in high school and college to prepare for careers in teaching, she conceptualized and began to implement a K-Ph.D. Corridor to Mathematics, Science, and Technology (MST) in 1984 through programs serving urban students at all levels, assisting them to develop the abilities, knowledge and skills needed to enter MST professions. Funding has been received from sources such as NASA, Howard Hughes Medical Institute, Fund for Improvement of Post-secondary Education, Drop-out Demonstration Assistance Program, and Fund for Innovation in Education. She serves on the Advisory Committee for Recruiting New Teachers. She is also assisting RNT to design and publish a national evaluation model for precollegiate teaching programs. She has been a featured speaker and consultant to schools and school districts seeking to plan and implement replications of the Walton/Lehman Pre-teaching Academy. Her interest in assisting teachers to improve teaching and learning through application of research results led her to edit and publish a national journal with associated monographs that applied research to teaching. She is co-chair of the New York City Board of Education Advisory Commission on Education and Youth Services established by the Occupational Education Advisory Council and is a member of the steering committee for the project to develop pre-teaching high schools in each New York City borough.

Roberta Senzer, former Director of Student Teacher Placement and Certification, is now Project Director of a multi-million dollar New York

State Goals 2000 Literacy Collaborative Grant. A partnership between Eastern Suffolk Board of Cooperative Educational Services, Lesley University, Ohio State University and New York University, this project facilitates long-term professional development and systemic support for teachers in 32 public school districts. She holds a B.A. in Biology from Hunter College, an M.S. in Reading from Hofstra University, and she is currently a doctoral candidate at Teachers College, Columbia University, in the Department of Organizational Development and Leadership. Her dissertation study deals with transforming schools into professional learning communities. She has been a classroom teacher and literacy specialist in urban settings for the New York City Public Schools and suburban districts on Long Island, as well as a central office administrator, curriculum writer, and teacher trainer. Currently, a member of the New York State Staff Development Leadership Council, she works closely with the New York State Education Department to set policy for implementation of effective practices for professional development. She is a frequent presenter at workshops and professional conferences related to advancing student achievement through teacher professional development. Working with the Regents Visiting Committee on low-performing schools, she visited Schools Under Regents Review (SURR schools) to review existing policies and practices and to make recommendations to the New York Board of Regents and the State Education Department designed to improve teaching and learning in low-performing schools.

Joye Smith is an Assistant Professor of Education at Lehman College of the City University of New York. Her research interests include alternative assessment, teacher education, and the specific needs of urban second-language learners. She recently received a grant to study the effectiveness of three programs in meeting the needs of long-term limited English proficient high school students in urban settings. She holds an M.A. in Teaching English to Speakers of Other Languages and an Ed.D. in Applied Linguistics from Teachers College, Columbia University. Currently, she directs the M.S.Ed., TESOL, and foreign language education programs at Lehman College. She teaches courses in teaching second language acquisition, the teaching of grammar, and educational research; sponsors master's theses; and supervises student teachers in the New York City School System.

Dorothy Stracher is Professor of Education at Dowling College, where she teaches courses in education for the learning disabled, reading and writing, and children's literature. She has written and spoken nationally and internationally on the subject of dyslexia and currently directs a program for learning disabled college students at Dowling College. She has served as a consultant in School District 7 in the Bronx, as coordinator and specialist of reading and writing programs at St. John's University, East Williston and Center Moriches School Districts, and as an adjunct professor in the departments of reading at Adelphi and Hofstra Universities. In her earlier years, she was a teacher of English and reading in the New York City school system and the Great Neck school system on Long Island. She received her B.A. from Brooklyn College of the City University of New York, an M.A. from Teachers College, Columbia University, and a Ph.D. from Hofstra University. Her research interests and publications are in the areas of education for the learning disabled, reading, writing, and children's thinking skills.

Bernadyn Kim Suh is an Associate Professor at Dowling College, where she supervises student teachers and teaches courses in social studies and language arts. Starting her career as a fifth-grade teacher in Hawaii, she then secured teaching positions in New York City public schools at the elementary level. As an assistant professor at Hofstra and St. John's Universities, she taught courses in methods of teaching, language arts, and social studies. She has a B.A. from the University of Hawaii in Elementary Education, an M.A. and an Ed.D. in curriculum and teaching from Teachers College, Columbia University. She has served on dissertation committees at St. John' s University, and her research interests are in the areas of the gifted and talented, children's literature, and student learning styles with a particular focus on Korean students.

Linda Roemer Whetzel, curriculum developer and writer, has been a teacher at Walton High School for 33 years and a mentor teacher in the Pre-teaching Academy since its inception. Co-author and editor of the Walton/Lehman Pre-teaching Manual, she has developed innovative curricula for a wide variety of courses and has created a number of interdisciplinary programs at the high school. In this project, she will design the scope and sequence of courses for the 9th and 10th grades, develop courses of study and select textbooks for Learning/Teaching 1, 2, 3, and 4, write sample lesson plans, and elicit student and teacher feedback on the curricula as each course is taught. In addition, she will develop and write a Coordinator's Handbook and a Cooperating Teacher's Handbook, update the Pre-teaching Manual, and edit the scholarly journal that will be published via website. She will also assist in developing a literacy curriculum for the Saturday and Summer Academy.

Author Index

Subject Index